ELIJAH OF THE ALPS

Elijah of the Alps

The Life of William Farel, the Swiss Reformer

William M. Blackburn

Solid Ground Christian Books
Birmingham, Alabama USA

Solid Ground Christian Books
6749 Remington Circle
Pelham AL 35124
205-443-0311
mike.sgcb@gmail.com
www.solid-ground-books.com

ELIJAH OF THE ALPS
The Life of William Farel, the Swiss Reformer

by William M. Blackburn (1828-1898)

First published in 1865

First Solid Ground Edition: March 2013

Cover design by Borgo Design

ISBN- 978-159925-338-1

PREFACE.

THIS volume treats of no common man and no ordinary times. A recent writer says: "The story of the times in which the Swiss Reformation was wrought, is surrounded with a sublimity, romantic grandeur and interest that attach to no part of the great German movement under Luther." Part of this story is told in Dr. Merle D'Aubigne's "History of the Reformation of the Sixteenth Century;" it will be more fully related when, with the good hand of God upon him, he completes the "History of the Reformation in Europe in the time of Calvin." Here and there, through these Histories, are glimpses and pictures of a man whose life was second to that of no other reformer in brave adventure and heroic deeds. In it was gathered most of the romantic daring and endurance of the Swiss Reform. This man was William Farel. Michelet calls him "the Bayard of the battles of God." He was the forerunner of John Calvin, who called him the "father of the church at Geneva." Enemies honoured him with the title of the

"Valais Luther," even before he had entered upon the noblest part of his career. We cannot refrain from calling him the Elijah of the Alps.

So important and instructive were his labours and character, so intense his devotion to God, and so sublime his earnestness of purpose, of preaching and of prayer, that immediately after his death, his intimate friends took steps to secure a record of his life. Since then it has been written several times by Europeans, but such works are either not translated, or they are not readily obtained in this country. To supply their want is the design of the present effort. The author cannot complain, as Calvin once did, of "a forest of materials," for he is not writing in an Old European Library where the original documents are stored, and yet there is at hand much material which he has not used. If it be thought that the author has done little more than copy and re-arrange the pictures found in D'Aubigne's Histories, he will be content. The other works consulted are chiefly these; The "Swiss Reformer, or a Life of William Farel, from the German of Melchior Kirchhofer" (abridged:) "Life of John Calvin, by T. H. Dyer;" "Life and Times of Calvin, by Paul Henry, D. D.;" "Wilhelm Farel und Peter Viret, von Dr. C. Schmidt." "Letters of John Calvin, compiled by Dr. Jules Bonnet." These four volumes of Letters are a monument to the enterprise of the Presbyterian Board of Publication, which has the praise of first publishing the entire collection in an English translation.

In opening these admirable "Letters" we at once perceive the fragrance of Farel's name along with that of Viret. Toward these men Calvin poured forth his brotherly love, acknowledging himself lonely and almost helpless without their presence. Among all the persons to whom these "Letters" were addressed, he saw none so often, he wrote to none so frequently, and to Farel most of all. Although his "upright brother" of Neufchatel dropped in so many times to see him, yet, of these six hundred and eighty-three letters, about one eighth are written to Farel. Often they seem to have been written just for love, or relief to Calvin's own mind. Calvin tells him his faults, when he finds any, and although, "that indefatigable soldier of Christ, my guide and counsellor," is so independent an host in himself, and so likely to be provoked if any fellow-rider should seize the rein of his impetuous spirit, yet he is willing to be restrained when he sees that the checking hand is that of Calvin or Viret. Boanerges is still the apostle of love. His friendship and character can bear the severe test of long familiarity. It is very touching to find the strong theologian of Geneva dreading the prospect that Farel, the aged father, might die first of the two, and even praying that the venerable missionary might have the longer lease on life. He thought Farel had the fortitude to endure the separation. But the old man, who had seen the beginning of the great reformer's ministry at Geneva, saw with distress the end of it, and nobly wished to die in his stead. And when the dying Calvin pointed with failing hand to "the archives of the correspondence that, during a quarter of a century, he had kept up with the most illustrious personages of Europe," did he not think of William Farel as his "sound-hearted brother and matchless friend," who had morally forced him to labour in Geneva? To "the good man Master William" he wrote the last letter of this collection and, perhaps, of his life, giving him one more adieu before he went to God.

The man, who thus was loved, was surely worthy of those epithets of endearment which Calvin lavished upon no other friend. The great theologian and the great missionary of the sixteenth century were thus heart and hand together, and after death their names should not be separated. If, in our day, the advocate of the richest and grandest theology is called a "Calvinist," there is an equal propriety in calling the ardent missionary of our day, a Farellian. When the Calvinistic churches are Farel-like in their labours, bright will be the dawn of the hastening millennium.

To understand the Reformation in France and Switzerland, one needs to know William Farel: and to know him there must be some attention paid to his times and contemporaries. His biography is a history. In this work he does not stand forth alone, for along with him are presented some of his partners in labours, in perils and in sufferings. If, in this volume, the reader shall find any refreshment for his faith, or stimulus to his zeal, or renewed reason for confidence in the final victory of the gospel over all perverseness of religion, the author's present effort will not be in vain. W. M. B.

Trenton, N. J.

CONTENTS.

CHAPTER I.
PAGE
THE HOLY CROSS—Village of the Farels—A bold boy—Visit to the Holy Cross—Superstitious devotion... 15

CHAPTER II.
NOT BATTLES BUT BOOKS—William objects to making chevalier Bayard his model—Taste for study—Goes to Paris—The University—Sorbonne—Budœus—Lefevre—A Reformer before the Reformation—Stations of the cross—The Bible opposed to the Romish church—Lives of the Saints—William enters a convent.............. 23

CHAPTER III.
A STRANGE VOICE IN PARIS—"God will renew the World"—Faith and Works—Students form two parties—Lefevre's eloquence—Farel's belief—Prayers to Saints—Truth conquers—The dial—Farel needs a Church—Lefevre in advance of Luther. 40

CHAPTER IV.
A CIRCLE OF FRIENDS—Farel known by his company—Allmain refutes papal infallibility—Louis XII. rejoices—Bishop of Meaux—The two Roussels—Francis I.—Margaret of Valois—Louisa the Wicked—The new Faith of Margaret—Duprat "the most vicious of bipeds"—Beda the Persecutor—A Victim wanted—Lefevre saved from a Scaffold—Berquin talks against the Sorbonne doctors—Noise about Luther—German Students spreading the Gospel in Paris—Beda in a Rage.......... 55

CONTENTS.

CHAPTER V.

MEAUX THE CRADLE OF FRENCH REFORM—Bishop Briçonnet invites Lefevre—Calls the Priests to Account—Farel grows bold in Paris—Beda's police on the watch—Farel, the Roussels and Mazurin flee to Meaux—New Testament in French—Erasmus—Harvesters carry abroad the Gospel—Rome's Threats—Briçonnet's fall—Lefevre in Danger—Farel departs—Leclerc believes—Placards—Persecution—Agrippa at Metz—Chatelain—Toussaint—Leclerc unwise—Breaking Idols in pieces—The first French Martyr in Modern Times...................................... 68

CHAPTER VI.

FAREL A WANDERER—Home again—Brothers converted—Chevalier Anemond—A Knight in Reform—Peter Sebville preaches—Farel hunted—Goes to Basle—Hospitality of Œcolampadius—Farel cheers up his Host—Refugees—French Church at Basle—Erasmus versus Farel—The Five great Words—Farel holds a Debate—Senate outwits the University—Farel strong enough to destroy the Sorbonne—Needs more of the Dove—Farel visits Zwingle—Must leave Basle—Leaves his zealous spirit upon his Host.. 85

CHAPTER VII.

A NEW FIELD—Montbeliard open—Farel boldly goes to Basle—Ordained in private—Goes to Montbeliard—Priests call him a Heretic—A Friar selling Relics—A Tract and Bible Society—Anemond pushing on the printing—Lefevre's Testament—Farel's pen—The Work at Lyons—The French army under Francis—The Spiritual army under Margaret—Preachers in Dauphiny—Sebville arrested—Meetings in Secret—Sebville to preach the Lent sermons in Lyons—Spiritual forces Scattered—Farel throws an Image into the River—Must flee from France. 99

CHAPTER VIII.

MOURNING AND MADNESS—Anemond dying—Farel refused a refuge at Basle—A Wail in France—The King a captive—Blame laid on the Reformers—Louisa at Work—Terrors and Tortures—Meaux attacked—Mazurier falls—Briçonnet returns to Rome—Sorbonne wins—Beda hunts Lefevre—Berquin's good Work—Translates Luther's Tracts—In Prison—Heroic Faith—Beda attacks Erasmus—Margaret goes to Spain to rescue her brother—Clement Marot—Peter Toussaint—Trials of Faith—Chevalier Esch—A new Martyr—More Exiles—Esch braves the Storm—Toussaint in Prison.. 110

CONTENTS.

CHAPTER IX.

PAGE

FAREL'S TURNING POINT—Lefevre at Strasburg—Farel Preaching there—A Brotherhood—Count Sigismund—Pellican—A Shout of Joy—Francis returned—Margaret Intercedes for the Reformers—Exiles invited back to France—Farel Excepted—Lefevre and Roussel with Margaret—Who would be the Reformer of France—Berquin?—Plan to Invite Farel—How it Failed.. 125

CHAPTER X.

THE ALPINE SCHOOL-MASTER—A hard Journey—Master Ursinus—Village School—A Flock gathered—Farel declares himself—Preaching opposed—Priests of Lausanne—A cool Chaplain—A Pen-skirmish—A brawling Monk—Farel silences a Friar—Wakes up the idle Priests—Fearless in Duty—Arguing with Clubs—Gospel takes Root in four Parishes—Vote for the Reform—Trouble with Ballista. 144

CHAPTER XI.

THE ROMANCE OF PREACHING—Farel at Morat—Neufchatel attracts the Eye—A Boat Ride—Standing on a Stone to Preach—Sermons in the Streets—Cry of Heresy—Farel's extreme Sufferings—The "French Luther"—A Mass stopped—Placards in Neufchatel—Sermons in Hospital Chapel—In Cathedral—A Memorial Day—Reform victorious—A "little miracle"—A Monument to the Gospel...................... 162

CHAPTER XII.

MY LORDS OF BERNE—Williamette in her Tower—Dreads Farel—Will shut him out of Valangin—Farel takes a Pulpit from a Priest—Noise of Bells—Beaten for the Gospel—In Prison—Neufchatel Vespers—Farel beaten at St. Blaise—Anthony Marcourt—Sack of Valangin—Christopher Fabri—Farel lying Wounded at Morat—Viret the good Burgess of Orbe—Peter Viret—A Friar selling Pardons—A puzzling Customer—Farel appears and Preaches to the Crowd—Friar Juliani will preach down the Reform—The Women's Plot—Juliani put in Prison in Hollard's place—Romain the school-master—Farel at Orbe—"A glorious Noise"—Women's League against Farel—The Bailiff orders an Audience for Farel—Viret's first Sermon—Lord and Lady Arnex Converted—Lord's Supper celebrated first at Orbe.. 183

CHAPTER XIII.

THE HUGUENOTS APPEAR—Farel among the Monks—The Women of Grandson—Christmas Eve at Orbe—Waldensian Visitors—Bonivard—Berthelier—Duke of

CONTENTS.

Savoy wants Geneva—Gouty John made Bishop—Young Hugues—Patriots' League—The Name Huguenot—Berthelier and his Weasel—A Martyr to Liberty. 205

CHAPTER XIV.

LAYMEN IN THE FIELD—Lefevre's Version in Geneva—Mystery—Plays—The good Ab Hofen—New Bishop steals a Girl—Bishop flees—Plan for Preaching—Farel's eye on Geneva—Toussaint refuses to go Thither—Hugues dies—The Prisoner of Chillon—Olivetan goes to Geneva—Gospel talks—Genevan Placards.................. 226

CHAPTER XV.

THE PREACHERS AT THE INN—Farel and Saunier in Geneva—A Sermon at the Tour Perce—A literary Nun has something for her Journal—A Stir in Geneva—Farel near Death—Fearless in Peril—Expelled... 246

CHAPTER XVI.

FROMENT'S LITTLE SERMONS—Froment Teaches in Geneva—Olivetan Translates the Bible—Froment's Talks draw the People—A prejudiced Hearer—Claudine Levet reads the Testament—Sells her Jewels for the Poor—A Sermon on the Square—Froment silenced—Working at the Loom—Secret Disciples—The Lord's Supper in a Garden... 256

CHAPTER XVII.

FAREL IN HIS ELEMENT—Christians banished from Geneva—A bad Bishop brought back from Exile—Berne defends Farel—Wonders expected of Friar Furbity—Farel masters the Friar—A bell rung providentially—Farel Preaches—The Lord's Supper—Plots frustrated—A Pulpit taken—The Cathedral gained—The Senate summons Farel—He gives the Nuns a chance to hear him—Flight of the Nuns of St. Claire—Citizens take Oath to support the Reform.................................. 270

CHAPTER XVIII.

CALVIN UNITED WITH FAREL—The Placards of Paris—Calvin Exiled from France—Story of the invisible Preacher—Visits Viret in Geneva—Farel forces Him to Remain—Calvin's first Sermon—Enthusiasm for Him—A Creed and Catechism—Courault in Geneva—Troubles—The Reformers banished—Refuge at Basle......... 281

CONTENTS.

CHAPTER XIX.

PEACE TO THE STORMS—Farel settled at Neufchatel—Fabri's labours—Images traded for Oxen—Caroli the Troubler—Changes with the Wind—Farel's tenderness—Farel's difficulties as a Pastor—Calvin invited back to Geneva—Farel urged to join Him—Farel visits Metz—Priests raise a Storm—The Plague—Farel visits the Sick—Preaches at Gorge—Farel wounded—Caroli prepares for a Masterstroke.. 301

CHAPTER XX.

FAREL'S NEIGHBOURLY VISITS—Goes to Geneva—Result of a New Suit—Geneva calls for Farel—Berne objects—Neufchatel keeps Him—Farel pleads for Calvin—Sickness of Farel—Farel attends Servetus to the Stake—Genevese offer Farel a Feast—The Refugees.. 319

CHAPTER XXI.

OLD LIFE WITH NEW LOVE—Farel still making new Conquests—Marries at Sixty-nine—All France on the Point of becoming Protestant—Farel visits Dauphiny—Scrap from an old Journal—A Christian Duchess.. 336

CHAPTER XXII.

THE CALL TO GLORY—Farel visits the dying Calvin—One more Missionary Journey—Death of Father Farel—Fabri his Successor—A Letter of Love—Farel's power of Prayer.. 348

WILLIAM FAREL.

CHAPTER I.

THE HOLY CROSS.

(1489–1500.)

AMONG the Alps of Dauphiny is a mountain called the Bayard, near which the traveller passes on the road from Grenoble to Gap. At the foot of the Bayard, about a stone's throw from the high-way, may be seen the old village of the Farels, called by the people of the district, Fareau. It is a mere group of houses, half hidden by the trees, and it shows only the relics of what it was three centuries ago. On a broad terrace, above the hamlet, a cottage now stands on the spot where once stood an elegant mansion. In those days of war and marauding, it was, doubtless, fortified. In that ancient chateau dwelt a family, which had some claims to nobility, and yet their name is rescued from silence by the child who was born at Fareau in 1489, and named William de Farel. Rank, fortune and a heroic spirit might have made him more celebrated than his three brothers, Daniel, Walter and Claudius, even had he not become a reformer. Of them and of his one sister we have an occasional glimpse in these pages. We know not but that he was the youngest son. If so the last became the first.

The Farels may have had some knowledge of the Waldenses and their doctrines, but they had reason enough to know that it was a perilous thing to renounce the traditions of the Romish church, and accept the simple truths of the gospel. Certain Waldensian teachers had dared to cross over from Piedmont into Dauphiny, and tell men the glad tidings of a Saviour, as their Lord had done among the hills of Judea. Their doctrines were taking root upon the western slopes of the Cottian Alps. Some of the people believed and longed for the Bible. Many, who had been, all their lives, deceived by the priests, became bold in faith, and stood up bravely against the superstitions of the Romish Church. The new converts to the truth were likely to speak more openly than their teachers, for good news must be told to everybody who will hear. The goat-herd could tell his neighbours how he had talked with the missionary at the hedge, the traveller how he had walked with him on the high-way, the chamois hunter how he had met on the mountain-path a man who told him of the true cross and of the good shepherd, and the young man, returning home from the town, could tell how he had heard a man, on the corner of the street, declare "This is a faithful saying, and worthy of all acceptation, that Christ Jesus came into the world to save sinners." Too good news to be kept, it began to find its way to many an ear, into many a heart, and many a home, and it may have reached the village, and the very door of the Farels.

But the Romish priests and bishops took the alarm. They claimed the field, and if good seed was sown therein, they were the fowls of the air ready to gather it up. They were the thorns growing up to choke it. They saw that if the kind and harmless Waldenses gained ground, the priests must lose the people. If Jesus Christ should win the hearts of men by his free gospel, the pope would be forsaken, and popery renounced. They talked, they threatened, they laid their plans, and persecution arose.

"These Waldenses and their followers must be destroyed," said the priests.

"Will the pope send an army to crush them?" asked the bishops, and Innocent VIII., one of the most guilty of mortals, was pleased with the question.

"To arms!" responded the pontiff, "To arms! and trample these heretics under foot as venomous serpents."

The trumpet rang, the drum was beaten, and an army of more than eighteen thousand men, entered the valleys of Dauphiny, and drove these poor disciples of Christ into the mountains, where they took refuge in caverns and in clefts of the rocks, as birds take shelter from the gathering storm. The misnamed Innocent died, and the vicious Borgia continued the cruel work. This bad pope seemed to be more fearful of these unarmed Christians, than of the legions of the French King, Charles VIII., who was threatening to sweep Italy with war, and the persecution of a few quiet disciples seemed to please him more than the gift of the New World lately made to him by Columbus. Not a valley, nor a wood, nor a rock, was left unexplored by the persecutors. The door of the Farels was not open to these hunted Christians, yet, while they were hiding from their merciless foes, a child of that house was lying in his cradle, or in boyish rashness clambering up the rocks of the Bayard, who would one day set the Swiss Alps aflame with that fire which the Saviour kindled on earth. He should be greater than any of the nameless ones who had cast the good seed in the valleys of his native land, and been driven away before it grew to the full harvest, and should gain for himself the title of "the Valais Luther."

The soldiers, who were ready to bind the Lord's hidden ones in their retreats, or burn them in the villages, had no cause to persecute the Farels, nor had the priests any reason to suspect them of the least departure from the Romish faith and customs. The father and the mother believed everything taught by their church, and brought up their children in its rites and devotions. William, whose nature it was to do nothing by halves, threw his whole soul into the follies of popery. He could cross himself, go to the confessional, respond at the mass, adore the wafer, count his beads, pray to the Virgin Mary, eat no meat on Friday, and tell the Saints' days in a manner that must have delighted the parish priest. It was said of him as he grew up, that "he was more popish than the pope himself."

William was a bold boy, fond of daring exploits. Like the young David, at home among the wild hills of Bethlehem, he scarcely knew fear, and would not allow defeat where success was possible. He had the moral courage always to tell the truth. What he feared was a lie. If any one could swim the Buzon when it was high with the torrent from the melting snows, or venture to the pass of the Glaize when the storm threw fearful risk in the path, he was likely to boast of such a daring feat. Men said that nature made him for a brave knight, or a cavalier, but the truth is, God made him for a bold, fearless, unflinching reformer. His temper needed to be curbed, his rashness to be subdued, and his lively imagination to be tamed. His parents had often to check his impetuous nature. If, however, he was bent upon having his own will, it was probably enough to tell him that if he had his own way, he should be kept at home the next saint's day, or he should not be taken to see "the holy cross," one of the seven wonders of Dauphiny.

"I can see crosses any day;" we fancy the lad saying, "there is one at almost every corner where two roads come together. Are they not all holy? I always bow to them and say the 'Ave Maria.'"

"None is so holy as the one at Sainte Croix," his parents would answer. "The cross in that place is made of the very wood on which Christ was crucified."

"What is it there for?"

"It was put there by some of the saints or angels, so that good people can make pilgrimages to it, and get an indulgence for a month or two."

"Then I am going to the holy cross when I am old enough. Why don't you take me now?"

'You are not good enough yet, my son."

"But if it will make me better, I ought to see it."

The wish to visit the holy cross grew stronger in the mind of the child, and his father's talk about it took the form of a promise. It was before him as an expected visit to Jerusalem was before the mind of a young Hebrew. When William was about eight years old, his parents resolved to take him on the pilgrimage. They went about nine miles to the town of Gap, and then twelve miles southward, to Tallard, and then walked up the hill, that rises above the roaring stream of the Durance, on which stood the cross.

When they reached the foot of the highly venerated cross, they fell down before it in adoration. They gazed intently on the sacred wood, believing that it once bore the sacred body of the dying Saviour. They looked at the copper on it, which the priest said was taken from the basin in which Christ washed the feet of his disciples. The wondering pilgrims then turned their eager eyes to a little crucifix fastened to the larger cross.

"Why is the little cross there?" they asked by their silent gaze.

"When the devils send us hail and thunder," said the priest, "this crucifix moves about so violently, that it seems to get loose from the cross, as if desirous of running at the devil, and it continues throwing out sparks of fire against the storm: if it were not for this, nothing would be left on earth."

The credulous pilgrims, with their hair almost standing on end, were deeply moved by the account of these prodigies. No doubt, the father had often argued that the cross was only the sign of the crucified Lord, and that he did not worship the sign, but the Saviour whom it represented. Even if the pilgrims intended to adore the Christ, they were not assisted in their devotions by the lying priest. They were not in a mood for even the better sort of Romish devotion.

"No one," continued the priest, "sees or knows aught of these things except myself and this man."

"What man?" thought the pilgrims, for they had been so engaged with the cross, and so startled by the prodigious stories, that they had not seen him. On turning their heads, they saw one of the strangest of mortals. William never forgot his appearance, for in old age he said that, "it was frightful to look at him. White scales covered his eyes, whether they were there in reality, or Satan only made them appear so." Those who did not credit these marvels called him "the priest's wizard." The sight of him was enough to provoke, in the minds of the visitors, a doubt of what the priest had declared.

"Is it not all true?" the priest asked of the wizard, as if no one would dare to doubt the man with the scaly eyes.

"True, all true," said the wizard, "and there's no blessing to those who do not believe it."

A new folly was introduced. If the bewildered pilgrims had not heard enough, they were now to see enough to cause them to suspect the morals of the priest. That they were not filled with disgust, only proves how they were steeped to the eyes in Romish superstitions. William remembered the scene to his last days, and in his book on "The true use of the cross," he thus wrote of it, so that men might know how deep the Romish priests were sunk in folly and crime. "There came up a young woman, intent on other devotion than that of the cross, carrying her infant wrapped in a cloth. Then the priest went up, took hold of the woman and child, and led them into the chapel. I may safely assert, that never did dancer take a woman and lead her out more gallantly than these two did. But such was our blindness, that neither their looks nor their gestures, appeared otherwise than good and holy."

Immoral priests and blinded people! Such were the two elements in almost the entire Romish church of those days. There were some exceptions, but they were found among those who shook off the fetters of popery, and were labouring to reform the church. William Farel was to see some of the worst delusions and vices of Romanism, in order to prepare him for exposing them to the people whom he would point to the true cross of Jesus Christ. The family returned home, and this is the last we hear of their pilgrimages to Sainte Croix.

Crosses similar to the one thus visited are often seen in Romish countries. On a mountain-side in Switzerland a tourist once stopped in the road, before a cross set up in a little "oratory," or place for prayer, which looked somewhat like the small shelter for a watchman on the railroad. It was built of stone, with the front open, and appeared quite ancient. An image of the so-called Virgin Mary was very conspicuous. A small crucifix was fastened to the larger cross, and although the rain was falling, it did not spin around nor throw out sparks of fire, as the priest declared of "the holy cross." Upon a board was an inscription, which is thus translated:

"Forty days' indulgence will be given to any one who will recite before this oratory one Pater Noster, one Ave Maria, and an act of contrition."

There was Romanism.

While standing there the attention of the traveller was arrested by the music of a little rill of the purest water, gliding down the mountain, and directly crossing the path. There it was, free, full, clear as crystal, and right in the way of the pilgrim, a type of the waters of the river of life flowing unceasingly from the throne of God. There was a symbol of Protestantism, which ever sets forth the free grace of God in salvation.

CHAPTER II.

NOT BATTLES, BUT BOOKS.

(1500—1512.)

YOUNG FAREL was sincere, although superstitious. He believed in Romish miracles, and wished to see whatever pretended to be one. But he was not willing that ignorance should be the mother of his devotion. He thirsted for knowledge. And if the Bible had not been a forbidden book, he must have found the truth at an early age. He knew of no such book as the word of God. He asked permission to study.

"Study what?" we imagine his father saying.

"Whatever is taught in the best schools. I want to be something in the world."

"Be a soldier then. Put on the armour that hangs in the hall, take the rosary* for your heart, and the sword in your hand, and enter the service of Gaston de Foix, or fight for the pope; he needs brave warriors now. Let the sword-hilt be your cross, and you may become a valorous knight before you are gray."

* The rosary of Dominic was a necklace of beads intended to insure the repetition of the "Lord's prayer" fifteen times a day, and that of "Hail Mary" one hundred and fifty times, the beads being passed through the fingers as the task was accomplished. This invention was thought such an honour that the Dominicans were sometimes called the Order of the Rosary.

"I would rather be a scholar. Let me read of Cæsar before I try to be like Cæsar. Let knowledge be my armour and the pen be my sword. I want not battles, but books."

"Folly, my son! War leads to greatness. Whose name is now on every breeze that comes across the Alps? That of our neighbour, the Chevalier Bayard, the brave knight without fear and without reproach. All Dauphiny is talking of him, since his victory in the battle of the Taro. Like him be fearless and stainless, and you will come to the honours of knighthood."

"Such are not the honours I wish."

"Not an honour for one to say with the Chevalier Bayard, 'My soul is God's and my life is my country's!' Not an honour to guard a bridge against a legion of foes! and when he rebukes profane swearing, and is told it is only a little fault, hear him say, 'Sir, that cannot be a trifling fault which is a great sin of the age.' And when a family, in whose house he lodges, offers him a large sum of money for protecting it from the pillage of soldiers, he refuses it, because he defends it for goodness' sake, and not for gold. Be noble then, and brave as Bayard. This is your best road to glory."

Thus the father opposed the taste for study which his son manifested, but the young man persisted in having a chance to indulge it. Nobler conflicts and victories were before him, than those of the famous Chevalier, and God had his good hand upon him. He was to be clad with "the whole armour of God," and wield "the sword of the Spirit." Long and earnestly did he plead with his father, who felt it to be a great blow to all his hopes of seeing the young noble enter upon a military career, but at last the old gentleman gave way, and began to inquire for a competent teacher.

The learned school-master was not then abroad in the land. If priests were the instructors, the education of the mind was likely to be at the expense of the morals. Young Farel would have gained little from the schools of Dauphiny, had there not been in him the strong spirit of self-help. In the text-books the wheat and the tares grew together, and the teachers could scarcely point out the difference between them, nor show the students what to gather into the garner, and what to burn in the fire. But he applied himself to his books as zealously as ever Bayard pushed on into the battle. The difficulties only fired him with ardour to overcome them, and having acquired the most of what his native province could afford, he turned his eyes to the brighter lights of the capital city.

The University of Paris had long been renowned in the Christian world. It was described as "the mother of all learning, the true lamp of the church, which never knew eclipse, that clear and polished mirror of the faith, dimmed by no cloud, and spotted by no touch." Thus it appeared to the devout Romanist, and thus to the young aspiring Dauphinese. To the Protestant eye of Milman, before whose clear vision marched the centuries of Latin Christianity, it rose stately in its superiority, and powerful in its independence. He says,—"If Bologna might boast her civil lawyers, Salerno her physicians, Paris might vie with these great schools in their peculiar studies, and in herself concentrated the fame of all, especially of the highest—theology. The University of Paris had its inviolable privileges, its own endowments, government, laws, magistrates, jurisdiction; it was a state within a state, a city within a city, a church within a church. It refused to admit within its walls the sergeants of the Mayor of Paris, and the apparitors of the Bishop of Paris; it opened its gates sullenly and reluctantly to the king's officers."

If it excelled in theology, how low must have been the standard of theological attainments! The principal department of theology was called the Sorbonne. The "true lamp of the church" must have been too dim for an eclipse to be possible, when its doctors "looked upon the study of Greek and Hebrew as the most deadly heresy." They had declared to the parliament that "Religion is ruined, if you permit the study of Greek and Hebrew." They must have agreed with the monks, who asserted that "all heresies arose from those two languages, and particularly from the Greek." And, why this hatred to these two languages? Because, in them the Bible was written. If they were studied, the Bible would be read, and the errors of their church exposed. One of them was bold to say,—"The New Testament is a book full of serpents and thorns. Greek is a new and recently invented language, and we must be upon our guard against it. As for Hebrew, my dear brethren, it is certain that all who learn it immediately become Jews!"

But, in spite of the Sorbonne, there was in Paris a revival of learning, and the man who led the advance was a proof of the saying, "The last shall be first." Who had supposed that the young William Budœus, "giving the rein to his passions, fond of the chase, and living only for his hawks, his horses and his hounds," would ever cherish in himself, and awaken in others, a thirst for a purer literature? Yet, there was a rein upon him, held in the unseen hand of God. "On a sudden, at the age of twenty-three, he stopped short, sold his hunting-train, and applied himself to study with the zeal he had formerly displayed in scouring the fields and forests with his dogs." It was his honour to be the chief cause of the revival under Francis the First. So devoted was he to his studies, that he seemed to have little memory for anything else. Even on the very day of his marriage he forgot what was expected of him. The hour for the wedding came, but he did not appear. A messenger was sent to tell him that the affair could not proceed unless he was present, and he was found absorbed in writing his Commentaries. But he consented to drop his pen and be married to one who could sympathize with him in his pursuits, and aid his memory. His wife was of great assistance to him in his studies, and used to find out and mark the various passages suitable to his purpose. In a rare book, in the British museum, is another anecdote about his literary devotion. One day the servants came running to him, in a great fright, crying out,—

"Sir, sir, the house is on fire!"

"Why do you not tell your mistress of it?" replied Budœus, coolly. "You know I never trouble myself about the house."

This man, no doubt, did much to call attention to Erasmus, who, toiling up from obscure orphanage, had given all his time to learning, spent his money, when he could get any, upon Greek authors; entered a convent, but soon left it in disgust; come to Paris and studied at the University, and was soon to bring out his edition of the Greek Testament. Budœus may have aided the influence of John Reuchlin, who had passed through the same university, and was preparing to do for the Old Testament what Erasmus was doing for the New. The art of printing came just in time for the publication of the Bible, a proof that God was managing the forces of truth for a great reformation. Whatever the Sorbonne might think, religion was not to be ruined by the study of the sacred languages. It was to be revived and raised from the dead by the voice of Christ, borne to the hearts of men by the word of God.

William Farel, leaving home for the capital city, was going forth upon a wide, wild sea of opinions; but he was to be guided to the true landing place, not by the university, as a public lighthouse, with its brightening lamp of literature, but by the private torch of a man, walking, in meditative mood, along the shore. This man was seeking for the pearl of great price, and, because of the deep moral darkness, he held his trembling light so carefully, that it could not fail to catch the watchful eye of the young student from the mountains of Dauphiny.

Among the learned men of the university, was one of very small stature, mean appearance, humble origin, and poor advantages in early life. His name was James Lefevre, and he was born about 1445, at Etaples, a village of Picardy, the country of Calvin. His early education would have been rude and scanty, had he not depended upon his genius rather than upon his masters. He struggled up into knowledge, like one clambering a mountain to see the sun gilding the peaks of an Alpine range, and hence his nobleness of soul drew admiration from his friends, who cherished hopes of his greatness. He travelled abroad, even into Asia and Africa, became a doctor of divinity, and in 1493 a professor of the University of Paris, where Erasmus put him in the first rank of scholars. His intellect, learning, and eloquence had a wonderful attraction for all who heard him.

He soon saw work enough to be done, and earnestly assumed the task. He must reform the evil practices of the Romish church, for he loved the church of his birth too well to see it in error. He must attack "the barbarism then prevailing in the University," and join in reviving the study of languages and learned antiquity. The classics must not crowd out the Bible. Philosophy must give way to religion. Therefore he began at the only point where a reformation can properly begin. He went to the heart of the Bible, so that it might go to the heart of man.

No man was more captivating in his artless, earnest, and familiar ways of teaching. Serious in the pulpit, he was genial with his students. "He loves me exceedingly," wrote one of them to his friend Zwingle. "Full of candour and kindness, he often sings, prays, disputes, and laughs at the follies of the world with me." Thus he drew a great number of disciples, from almost every country, to sit at his feet. They saw that he passed quite as much time in the churches as in his study, and were likely to imitate his devotion. Because the church was in error, he did not abandon it, for if the ship was in a storm and the officers drunk, there was all the better reason for every sailor to be at the post of duty and of danger. He regarded himself as a child in the church, rather than a doctor over it, and because willing to search, he was certain to find the truth which would save.

Lefevre was a reformer before the reformation. He protested against error before there was any system of Protestantism. Five years must yet pass before Luther would nail his theses to the door of the old church in Wittemberg. Luther had but just found the chained Bible in the convent of Erfurth, and had not heard the good Staupitz say, "If thou wouldst be really converted, follow not these mortifications and penances. Love him who first loved you. God is not against thee, but thou art averse to God. Remember that Christ came hither for the pardon of sins. Cast thyself into the arms of the Redeemer. Trust in him, in the righteousness of his life, in the expiatory sacrifice of his death." Could Lefevre have heard such words, he would have found much sooner the treasure which he sought on the shores of truth.

In the year 1510, Luther was on his way to Rome, to witness its abominations, and William Farel was on the way to Paris to study in the University, and to find in Lefevre a friend among strangers, a guide to the truth, and a father in Christ, for by the private light of this man, the young provincial was to make sure his landing upon the Eternal Rock of salvation.

On the walls of most Romish Churches are hung pictures of different scenes in the sufferings and death of our Lord. The worshippers begin at the first, and pass around to the last, kneeling before each one, and repeating the words of their penance or prayers. These kneeling-places are called stations on the way of the cross. To make the circuit is a pilgrimage.

William Farel had not come to Paris to stroll through the streets, nor to lock himself up in his room and pore night and day over his books. He was a close student, but he did not neglect his religious devotions. He took time for a regular attendance at church, and made it a matter of conscience to visit the stations along the way of the cross. What a privilege to the young villager to kneel before better pictures than he had seen at home, and confess to a more accomplished priest.

One day, when on his pious pilgrimage, he saw an aged man going the rounds, all absorbed in his devotions. He prostrated himself at the stations and lingered, repeating his prayers. He seemed the model of fervour and contrition; as the tears fell, the lips quivered, and the voice rose full and clear in the responses of the public service. There was much in his manner to charm the young stranger, and he could not forget the earnestness of the good old man, saying of him years afterward, "Never had I seen a chanter of the mass sing it with greater reverence." This little, unpretending, aged man, of the tearful eye and kind face was the eloquent popular and beloved Lefevre. To become acquainted with him was now the student's most ardent wish, and without it he could not be happy.

How they met, we know not, but Farel "could not restrain his joy when he found himself kindly received by this celebrated man." It seemed as if he had gained his object in coming to the capital. "From that time his greatest pleasure was to converse with the doctor of Etaples, to listen to him, to hear his admirable lessons, and to kneel with him devoutly before the same shrines. Often might the aged Lefevre and his young disciple be seen adorning an image of the Virgin with flowers; and alone, far from all Paris, far from its scholars and its doctors, they murmured in concert the fervent prayers they offered up to Mary." The teacher, warring against certain errors, still held to some of the most absurd; and the student, who had refused to take the sword, still clung to the rosary.

Farel was sincere. He thought that he was right. He was not hoping for a rich benefice, nor preparing to fleece some flock over which he might be placed, nor dreaming of the vicious life then led by so many of the priests. A soul like his was above loving popery for money, or for power, or for indulgence in sin. In his view the pope sat on a throne of God, and ruled in the place of Christ. To obey and worship him as Christ was a part of salvation. If any one said aught that was ill of the "holy pontiff," he would "gnash his teeth like a furious wolf," and was ready to call down the lightnings of heaven "to overwhelm the guilty wretch with utter ruin and confusion."

"What do you believe?" we presume to be asked of him by some student who has caught up certain sarcastic remarks of Erasmus about the follies of Romanism. "Do you really believe that a wafer is converted into the very body of Christ?"

"I believe," said Farel, "in the cross, in pilgrimages, images, vows and relics. What the priest holds in his hands, puts into the box, and then shuts it up, eats, and gives others to eat, is my only true God, and to me there is no other, either in heaven or upon earth."

Still he was not satisfied. His spirit hungered, his soul found no rest. Everything was going from bad to worse. The study of the profane authors brought him not one crumb of the bread from heaven; in the rites of the church there was not one drop of the water of life to quench his thirst. Lefevre scarcely dared tell him the little truth that he was leaning upon, for he was not quite sure of it himself, and no lame man likes to give away his staff. The student went restless and wretched to several doctors of the age, but they only sent him away more wretched than before. He told them that he wanted to be a real Christian, and they gave him Aristotle as a guide! He read books, bowed to images, adored relics, invoked the saints, kept the fasts and festivals, carried his reverence for Mary to a superstitious extreme, and yet all proved worse than in vain. It was sending him to the brambles, under a delusion that from them he would gather grapes.

In his severe mental sufferings he learned one piece of good news. It was that the "holy father, the pope," was willing to allow the Old and New Testaments to be called the Holy Bible. Thanks to his holiness for this concession! If he had gone farther and said, with one of the English martyrs, "No writings are holy but the Bible," it would have settled an important question in the anxious minds of hundreds, who like young Farel, knew not which to believe, Christ or the pope. That question was, which shall we follow, the word of God, or the word of the church? Farel thought that since the pope acknowledged the great good book to be the Holy Bible, he might read it for himself. Surely the pope and the apostles must agree in their teachings! But as he read the sacred page, he was amazed at seeing how they disagreed, and how different everything in Romanism was from the pure Christianity of the New Testament. Where was the mass taught in the Bible? Where prayer to the saints? Where the adoration of relics? Where the worship of the Virgin Mary? Where confession to priests? Where the paying of money for a pardon? Where purgatory? Where salvation by an endless round of mere works? Certainly not in the Bible. It taught repentance instead of penances, faith in the Crucified rather than the adoration of the cross, prayer to Jesus and not to the saints, and love to God rather than the fear of the pope. In its light he could see that any one might pray to God in the name of Christ; every one might come to Jesus and find rest; and no one need to buy his pardon of a priest, nor an indulgence of the "holy father." He could see that penitents would be safer at Jesus' feet, and pilgrims better off at home. The thought must have risen in his mind that if priests could convert a wafer into the Deity, they could make anything a God,* and if the elevation of the host be a crucifixion, then Jesus must be always suffering for our sins.

The young Bible-reader went far enough to see that the word of God did not agree with the word of the Church.† He scarcely dared to go farther. He had severe pangs of mind, and strug-

* An Englishman had said, "If every consecrated host be the Lord's body, there are 20,000 gods in England."

† This was one of the first things to be seen before there could be a reformation. Among the many predecessors of Luther, who perceived this, was John, of Wesalia, an aged doctor of divinity, who was tried for heresy, at Mentz, in 1479. He held that "nothing was to be believed not found in the Scriptures," and was charged with saying,—"I despise the pope and his councils. I love Christ; and may his word dwell in us abundantly."

gled to know which to accept. His first effort was the very reverse of what young Luther was now doing, when making the Church give way to the teachings of the chained Bible. The monk of Erfurth thought, in his best hours, that Christ must stand, and the pope must fall, God must be believed, though the Church went to ruin. The Dauphinese student scarcely ventured to think, but first attempted to make the Bible give way to the teachings of popery. If he read any passages of Scripture that opposed the Romish practices, he hung his head, cast his eyes upon his breast, as if trying to get a kind look from his conscience. He blushed, as if ashamed to deny his Lord, and yet dared not believe the word of God. Fearing to keep face to face with the gospel writers, he turned his eyes from the holy book, saying, in deep mental anguish,—"Alas! I do not well understand these things. I must give a different meaning to the Scriptures from that which they seem to have. I must keep to the interpretation of the Church, and, indeed, of the pope."

Thus he must warp and wrest the sacred words, in order to make them agree with his prejudices; and it was hard and painful work. One day a doctor of the Church happened to come in, and he found him reading the Bible. Instead of "a word in season to him that was weary," a sharp rebuke fell from the tongue of the learned. "No man," said he, "ought to read the Holy Scriptures before he has learnt philosophy and taken his degree in arts." It was filling the student's head with lead. It was giving a stone to him who asked for the bread of life. Farel believed him, although no such literary preparation was required of the disciples when, as fishermen, they entered the school of Christ, nor of any of the common people, who heard him gladly. His rule was one which holds good in all ages, and among all people,—"Search the Scriptures." The Bible-reader was in the depths of mental darkness, and, long after, he gave thanks for the great and wonderful work of God, in raising him from such an abyss. He looked back, and said,— "I was the most wretched of men, shutting my eyes, lest I should see."

It seems that he began to be afraid of the Bible, lest it should destroy his faith in the Church, and his love for its rites. As he left it unopened, his Romish fervour returned. He threw his whole soul into his mistaken devotions. He gained, among the people, a reputation for zeal. The keener-sighted Romanists cultivated him, as the shrewd priests in Zurich had sought to enlist young Zwingle in their interests, lest he should think too much, see too many gross evils, and have his mind turned toward a reform. They had learned from the boldness of Huss, Savonarola, Jerome of Prague, and the various "reformers before the Reformation," that such men must be managed in time, if they were prevented from making a noise in the world, and striking such blows at the papacy that its wounds could never be healed. It was wiser to use gentle arts, and persuade them into active service when young, than to allow them to mature their powers by reading and thinking, and then burn them in old age for "heresy."

"You grow thin by study—your mind is oppressed," they would say; "you need exercise; you should do something that will engage your heart in good works, and thus relieve your over-burdened intellect."

"My pilgrimages give my heart exercise," we hear Farel replying. "I try to do all the good works that will save the soul."

"True, they may save the soul; but you must not wear out

your body. The Church wants a long life from you. Visit the poor. Give them charities. Urge them to the stations, the confessional, and the mass."

"Ah! I am not worthy thus to imitate Christ."

"But we have work for you to do. There are poor students here, who need help, and there are rich men to aid them. We can trust you. Let us put the money in your hands, that you may dispense it among the needy."

Farel assented, and many devout rich persons in Paris intrusted him with various sums, to be given to the poorer students. The work was faithfully performed by one who had the nicest scruples of conscience in all matters of honesty and charity.

"Cheer up your mind by reading the lives of the saints," we hear the eagle-eyed watchers saying to the still sad student.

"Were not the apostles the best of saints?" he replies. "Their teachings give me trouble."

"They are too exalted for you. You are not prepared to understand them. Take first those nearer to our own age."

"The fathers of the Church, then,—but they would not agree with the Church of our day."

"Leave them until you have your degree of arts. Read not of those who wrote their doctrines, but of those who were poor, who made long pilgrimages, who fasted in deserts, who mortified themselves in caves, who had visions, who wrought miracles, and who left for us the merit of their good works and penances."

"Show me the books. Their works may give me more light than the words of those who taught what we must not now believe."

The books were furnished, and Farel read them until his imagination was inflamed by the legends of the saints. In his heart he admired the invented stories of their zeal, their coarse fare and rough burry garments, their bare-foot pilgrimages, their self-tortures, the visits paid them by angels and by the Virgin Mary, and their entire freedom from mortal sin. The most disgusting tales of their voluntary filthiness were beautiful romances of a willing humiliation. He mistook their low and idle lives for that of a high and almost heavenly existence, and began to think of living like them.

In the deep shades of a forest near Paris, was a monastery of Carthusian monks, useless on earth, but making the world serve them better than was suspected abroad, in its reverence for their supposed piety. Farel was attracted toward them. Perhaps he had heard of their brethren in the old convent of Chartreux (Cartusium,) not far from his native place. There was something romantic in its history. Bruno of Cologne had become disgusted with the evils in the church in that old city, rather than with the world, and he sought to get out of both as nearly as possible. He coveted solitude. In the wild valley of the Chartreux, not far from Grenoble, he settled himself, about the year 1084, with twelve companions. They built a monastery for their worship, but did not live in it lest they should be too much together. They built separate cells by the side of it, and each one spent his time by himself in silence, study and labour enough to keep him alive. Their order increased in numbers and influence, and several branches were established in Europe, like the one in the woods near Paris. Their rules were most severe, if we may judge from those laid down for the monastery of Camaldula, built on one of the bleakest of the Apennines. Two words expressed them, solitude and silence. All else was but an exception to the rules. They met at worship, they ate silently together on certain festivals, and they met at times to inflict each other by speech-
4

less discipline. One daily meal of bread, or vegetables, and water, was often given up, so that they might enjoy the merit of a severer fast. Money they might not touch, and no comforts were allowed in their cells. Their silence was broken only when they prayed or chanted, and when they indulged in a little talk at eventide. The recluse among them took an awful vow of perpetual silence and seclusion. His voice might be heard in lonely prayer, and three days in the year he could attend the mass of Easter week, but he must speak to no human being, save the priest, whom he called by the sound of his bell to hear his confession. Such monks might easily lose their senses, and thus imagine that they were rid of their sins.

These severe rules had a charm for young Farel, now carried away by reading the lives of the saints. He went to the forest, and was admitted to the group of gloomy cells. He looked on the inmates with reverence, and shared, for a little time, in their austerities. The benefit he received is strongly set forth in his own words, penned at a later day. "I was wholly employed, day and night, in serving the devil, after the fashion of that man of sin, the pope. I had my Pantheon in my heart, and such a troop of mediators, saviours, and gods, that I might well have passed for a papal register."

The darkness in his soul could not well grow deeper. He was sunk quite as low in Romanism as Luther when, but lately, he was on his knees creeping up Pilate's stair-case in order to gain the pope's indulgence. But Luther seemed to hear a sound in his ears, as if an angel spoke to him, as he there remembered the words, "The just shall live by faith." He started up, ashamed of his folly, and fled with all haste from the scene. It was the power of a well-read and remembered Bible. But Farel was alarmed by no such memory of a great truth which opposed Romanism. How or when he left the Carthusians we know not, but his stay was not long. Perhaps he was attracted to Lefevre, at whose voice the morning-star was soon to arise, and chase the heavy gloom from his heart.

CHAPTER III.

A STRANGE VOICE IN PARIS.

(1512–1520.)

"MY dear William," said Lefevre one day when returning from the mass, as he grasped the hand of his young friend, "God will renew the world, and you will see it."

"Often have you said this to me, but I do not yet fully understand your words."

"Ah, one cannot tell what light is until it fills his eye, nor what life is until he feels it in his soul. God will soon give us both; new light by his holy truth, new life by his Holy Spirit. The word of God will take the place of the word of the church. We must give up the 'Lives of the Saints,' and read the words of the apostles."

"But are you not going on to publish those lives? I have been delighted with the two monthly numbers now issued."

"No, no: I began with zeal the laborious task of collecting and arranging them in the order of their names in the calendar. But I am weary of them. They disgust me. They are foolish legends at best, and many of them are the false tales of monks, who could write a life to order without any knowledge of the facts."

"You astound me, father Lefevre."

"I wish to, if there be no other way to keep you from having anything more to do with these legends. They are puerile superstitions, and are no better than brimstone fit to kindle the fire of idolatry. They cause us to idolize the saints, and to treat our Lord with neglect. They are too paltry fables to keep us from the sublime word of God."

"How came you to know this so suddenly?"

"By one of those beams of light, which come from heaven through the Holy Scriptures all at once, I was struck with the impiety of addressing prayers to the saints. Go, dear William, to the Bible."

Lefevre had taken a long and sure step. The Reformation began in France at the moment when he laid aside the wondrous tales of the monks, and put his hand on the word of God, fully resolved to interpret all other things by it. Not the Breviary, but the Bible should henceforth be his authority. He studied the epistles of Paul, and light beamed on his mind; life was breathed into his heart. By the press, and from the pulpit, he began to teach men, and "open unto them the Scriptures." That favourite idea, "God will renew the world," so often expressed to Farel, appears in his Commentary* on Paul's Epistles. "God, in his great mercy, will soon revive the expiring spark in the hearts of men, so that faith and love, and a purer worship will return."

Strange doctrines were then first heard publicly in Paris—strange, because they had been lost for centuries, and yet stranger, inasmuch as they were boldly declared in the very bosom of the Sorbonne. The roof of the university had reason

* "The first edition, if I mistake not, is that of 1512. The learned Simon says that 'James Lefevre deserves to be ranked among the most skilful commentators of the age.' We should give him higher praise than this."—*D'Aubigne.*

to cry out in astonishment, as it reëchoed the words of Lefevre. "It is God alone," he declared, "who, by his grace, through faith, justifies unto everlasting life. There is a righteousness of works, there is a righteousness of grace; the one cometh from man, the other from God; one is earthly, and passeth away, the other is heavenly, and eternal; one is the shadow and the sign, the other the light and the truth: one makes sin known to us, that we may escape death, the other reveals grace, that we may obtain life."

"What, then!" asked his hearers, as they listened to this teaching, so opposed to that of four centuries. "Has any one man ever been justified without works?"

"One! they are innumerable," replied the zealous preacher, whose young disciples were aroused and eager for the truth. "How many people of disorderly lives, who have ardently prayed for the grace of baptism, possessing faith in Christ alone, and who, if they died the moment after, have entered into the life of the blessed, and that without works!"

"If, therefore, we are not justified by works," said his listeners, "it is vain that we perform them."

"Certainly not! They are not in vain. If I hold a mirror to the sun, its image is reflected; the more I polish and clear it, the brighter is the reflection; but, if we allow it to become tarnished, the splendour of the sun is dimmed. It is the same with justification* in those who lead an impure life."

Thus taught the Paris doctor,—not altogether free from error, but so near the greatest truth which man can know, that the light was brilliant. And, while all wondered, many believed. From this time, there were two parties in the university, two

---

* Had he said *sanctification* in those who fall into inconsistencies, he would have been more nearly correct.

people in the city, and there began to be two great divisions in Christendom,—those who put works above faith, and those who put faith before works,—one people exalting the Church of Rome as the infallible teacher, and the sole dispenser of eternal life on earth; the other trusting to the word of God as the only unerring guide, and adoring Christ as the only Saviour of men.

Farel listened, as for life, to this teaching of justification by faith, and he saw, at once, in which great division to take his place. The doctrine that Jesus was the only Saviour, and one such Saviour was enough, had a weighty charm for his heart, and a glorious power over his soul. "Every objection fell, every struggle ceased. No sooner had Lefevre put forward this doctrine, than Farel embraced it with all the ardour of his nature. He had undergone labour and conflicts enough to be aware that he could not save himself." He forgot his admired saints; he lost all sympathy with the monks of the forest; he gave up all human merit; he believed in Jesus. To himself he seemed strange; it was the old Saul of Tarsus trying to make out who was the new Paul; the old Simon astonished at the new Peter. In later years he wrote,—"Lefevre extricated me from the false opinion of human merits, and taught me that everything came from grace, which I believed as soon as it was spoken." Thus, with trembling step, he took his place in the ranks of the men of faith.

The men of works were not slow to fall into line, and prepare for the contest. There were professors in the colleges and doctors of the Sorbonne ready to display their generalship; there were students ready to volunteer in defending human merit. Many, whose works were bad and disgraceful, urged, all the more zealously, their dependence in *good* works. They knew little of the great question, for they had passed through no struggles of soul for life, and, instead of caring for the Bible, they had been "engaged in learning their parts in comedies, in masquerading, and in mountebank farces," so much so that parliament had summoned their teachers and forbidden "those indulgent masters to permit such dramas to be represented in their houses." In these plays the great were ridiculed, the princes caricatured, and the king attacked. The government felt obliged to interfere.

But the hand of parliament could only provoke the disorderly students. The voice of the preacher gave them a new and powerful diversion. From comedies their thoughts were turned to debates about faith and works. "Great was the uproar on the benches of the University," and every student must take sides with Lefevre or with the Sorbonne. With the latter gathered not only the young men of careless minds and evil deeds, but also many whose lives were the least at fault. The more upright class took credit to themselves for their moralities, and not willing to let the doctrine of faith condemn their "good works," they urged that James, their apostle, was opposed to Paul, the apostle of Lefevre. The gospel doctor was quicker than Luther to see how these two apostles perfectly agreed together, one looking at faith as the starting point, and the other at works as the evidence of salvation.

"Doth not St. James in his first chapter declare that every good and perfect gift cometh down from above?" asked Lefevre with the gentle persuasion of a Paul, eager to carry his hearers with him by arguments. "Now who will deny that justification is the good and perfect gift? . . . . If we see a man moving, the respiration that we perceive is to us a sign of life. Thus works are necessary, but only as signs of a living faith, which is followed by justification. Do eye-salves or lotions give light to the eye? No! it is the influence of the sun. Well these lotions and these eye-salves are our works. The ray that the sun darts from above is justification itself."

Faith is the link that binds us to Christ, and yet it is more than a link, it is a life. Lefevre did not dwell on this living link alone; he went farther and exhibited Jesus in whom he believed. Like Luther he could almost paint the true cross in his eloquence, and still he felt that no tongue could do justice to the vicarious death of Christ. It was unspeakable. "Ineffable exchange," he declared, "the innocent One is condemned and the criminal acquitted: the Blessing is cursed, and he who was cursed is blessed; the Life dies, and the dead live: the Glory is covered with shame, and he who was deep in shame is covered with glory."

Then rising still higher toward that sovereign love which sent such a divine Redeemer to sinful men, and dwelling on the privilege of being loved before they loved God, and being chosen before they chose Jesus, he exhorted his hearers to live as if their lives were hid with Christ. "Oh! if men could but understand this privilege, how chastely, purely and holily would they live, and they would look upon all the glory of this world as disgrace, in comparison with that inner glory which is hidden from the eyes of the flesh."

Was this too lofty a strain of eloquence for some of his hearers on whose corrupt minds a gross darkness lay? He would give them a word in season, for the arrow of truth must prepare them for the balm of Gilead. He must not prophesy smooth things. Even the clergy of his day must be rebuked for their revels, and the sins of the times he touched with unsparing fidelity. With an indignation against sin, tempered by love for the sinner, he exclaimed, "How scandalous it is to see a bishop asking persons to drink with him, gambling, rattling the dice, spending his time with hawks and dogs, and in hunting, hallooing after rooks and deer, and frequenting the worst of houses and haunts! . . . . Oh men deserving a severer punishment than Sardanapalus himself!"

Did not Farel remember the "holy cross," and wish the priest of Sainte Croix could hear such reproofs? The tales there told to him when a child now appeared as the baldest lies. He saw too the evidence of a general deception in the use of "holy relics." The "holy cross" near Tallard was said to be made of the very wood of the one on which Christ was crucified. In Paris he had been adoring another cross of which the same story was told. Yet the wood was of a different kind! For others still there were the same lying pretensions, and he now wondered how he had ever been so stupid as to believe that the real cross of Calvary had been preserved. He repented, with deep sorrow, of his blindness, credulity and superstitious reverence.

"When the corruptions of the Romish church" wrote Farel in after years, "are unveiled to the soul that has been drawn aside by them, its sense of their enormity is so overwhelming, that only the clear exhibition of the welcome doctrine of salvation by Christ can prevent a man from utter despair or losing his senses."

But it was only day-light with the young Dauphinese; not yet was it clear sunshine. Some clouds must be broken and scattered before his noon would come. He had closed the Bible, and he must open it again and from the very fountains drink the crystal waters of eternal life. He must hear, not only the voice of Lefevre, but the voice of Jehovah.

Thus Lefevre preached; thus Farel believed. But, at length,

the admiration of the saints returned upon him like a Satanic spell. To pray to them seemed easier than to pray to Christ. They had no merit to give him; they must not be trusted in for salvation; Jesus only was the Saviour on whom his faith must be fixed. He saw all that; but, yet, might not the saints help bear his prayers to God? Christ, alone, must be trusted; but, was Christ alone to be invoked? He was troubled, and he carried his question to Lefevre.

"My dear son," said the spiritual father, "we cannot be sure that the saints hear any words we speak. We know they cannot hear different persons, in different places, at the same time. We are sure that Jesus, the Father, and the Holy Ghost, do hear us, and to this holy Trinity only we are at liberty to pray. We must hold to what is certain, and abandon everything that is doubtful."

"But, the saints have such a feeling for us."

"Jesus has infinitely more. He is touched with the feeling of our infirmities. He knows us, altogether. No saint can have such a tender sympathy for us as Christ. He, alone, hath trodden the wine-press. He, only, is the Head of the Church. Let us not call ourselves after St. Paul or St. Peter; but, in Christ, let us be Christians. Let the servant pray only to the Master. Our prayers must reach the willing ear of God, or they are useless. Then, let them go up directly to him."

The soul of Farel was now shaken by conflict. Two views opened before him. In one he saw the vast array of saints, with the Church on earth; in the other, Jesus Christ, alone, with his beloved teacher. Now, he inclined to the saints, now, to the Saviour. It was his last error, and he must decide his last battle. He was almost carried over to those revered men and women, at whose feet thousands fell adoring. Had he also fallen there, he must have exalted Mary above her divine Son and Lord. But, God struck the blow for him; the spell was broken, the enchantment gone. The saints were in a cloud, and Christ appeared in his glory, as deserving of all adoration. Never could he render him reverence enough. And, why waste adoration upon the holiest saint in paradise? It was robbing the Lord of his right to all the tribute of the heart. Referring to this last conflict, when he for ever renounced the word of the Church, he wrote,—"Then, popery was utterly overthrown. I began to detest it as devilish, and the holy word of God had the chief place in my heart."

"It was necessary," he again wrote, "that popery should fall, little by little, from my heart, for it did not tumble down at the first shock. . . . . O Lord, would that my soul had served thee with a living faith, as thy obedient servants have done! Would that it had prayed to thee and honoured thee, as much as I have given my heart to the mass, and to serve that enchanted wafer, giving it all honour! I have known thee too late; too late have I loved thee!"

From the stormy sea, Farel had now reached the port, guided by the light of his aged friend; and no man, who ever exchanged a wrecked and sinking ship for the solid, healthy land, could have been more delighted with the new appearance of all things around him. Days of languor and disgust at sea give the traveller a keen wish for the fruits of the land; and, thus Farel, long soul-sick, but now having a firm footing on the shore of heavenly truth, craved and enjoyed the bread of life in the gospel. The desire for holy truth gives to it an enduring newness, for love never permits its object to seem old. "Now," said he, "everything appears to me under a new aspect. The Bible has a new face, Scripture is cleared up, prophecy is opened, the apostles shed a strong light on my soul. A voice, till now unknown—the voice of Christ, my Shepherd, my Master, my Teacher—speaks to me with power. So great a change has come over me, that, instead of keeping the murderous heart of a ravening wolf, I have come back quietly, like a meek and harmless lamb, with my heart entirely withdrawn from the pope, and wholly given to Jesus Christ."

Drawn from the abyss of popery, he must now go deeply into the Bible, enriching himself with its treasures. With absorbing interest he began the study of Greek and Hebrew, without neglecting his other studies, on which he set a just value. In order to hide the word of God in his heart, he read it daily, and God gave him increasing light and life. Now, he gave the Scriptures just the meaning which was apparent in them; what conflicted with them he cast away; what agreed with them he held fast. No longer did he "keep to the interpretation of the Church, and, indeed, of the pope." No more did he think that his "degree in arts" must precede those degrees which the apostle—not the pope—Peter laid down,—"Grow in grace, and in the knowledge of our Lord and Saviour, Jesus Christ." "Giving all diligence, add to your faith, virtue; and to virtue, knowledge; and to knowledge, temperance; and to temperance, patience; and to patience, godliness; and to godliness, brotherly-kindness; and to brotherly-kindness, charity."

On the walls of many an old church in Europe, one sees a dial, whose only use consists in casting a shadow, that will mark the time of day. Any sort of light will give the hand a shadow. It may be that of a lamp, or of the moon. But only one light can give the right shadow. It must be sunshine, falling direct from the unclouded face of that glorious orb which rules the day. Thus it is with the Bible. We may read it in the light of its beautiful poetry and touching eloquence; in the light of science and theology; in the light of antiquity and history; in the light of commentaries and sermons; and, while the darkness is driven from the intellect, the soul may derive no spiritual benefit. No mark is there, telling its advance in the circle of Christian graces. Only one light can throw a saving impression of the Bible on the soul, and that is the light of the Holy Spirit. When he shines upon the gospel-page, he carries its power into the heart, and, instead of mere shadows, there are burning beams. The hand of God touches the soul, and, beneath every finger, a new grace is started, or an old one revived. These graces are the degrees of the Christian's dial. From the time Farel had first read the Bible, trying in vain to make it agree with the teachings of the Church, the mark on his soul had gone backward ten degrees. But, now, under the shining of the Spirit, he understands the word, he feels its transforming power, he believes, he rejoices, he grows. He loves the truth, and that love is a mark of his being face to face with the Comforter, and with the Sun of Righteousness, which had risen upon his heart with healing in its wings.

From the study of Church history he derived great benefit; for, by its facts, he uprooted many an error that had grown deep in his mind. He found that, in the early centuries, the Christians prayed to God, and not to the saints. They confessed their sins to Christ, and not to a priest. They knew nothing of the mass, the consecrated wafer changed into the very body of the Lord, the stations of the way of the cross, the gazing on pictures, the worship of images, the adoration of relics, the pope and his cardinals, the sign of the cross, the rosary, the holy water, the holy unction, the prayers for the dead, the merit which saints leave for sinners, and the doctrine of purgatory.

They were as ignorant of all these essentials of popery, as the devotees of the pope were of the simple spiritual life of the early Christians. The ancient Church was a field, sown thick with the good seed of the kingdom; but an enemy had sown tares therein. That enemy was Romanism. Both had long grown together, until the tares had choked the wheat, or overlaid it; and now the harvest was come, and the tares must be cast away, and the wheat gathered into the store-house of the soul, so empty that men were perishing for want of that bread which came down from heaven. Thus, Farel discarded great bundles of error.

Still, Farel needed a church, where he might publicly worship God. Where could he go? Lefevre could not make one for himself and his disciple. Not yet was there any organized Protestantism. The only hope, then, was to see Romanism reformed. Farel saw no other way but to attend the Romish churches, and there worship God in spirit, as Jesus did in the temple, where, in spite of his cleansing, there were all the errors of the Pharisees. But, what did he find there? Loud voices, long chantings, prayers in a dead language, smoke and formalities. There was the priest seen at the confessional; but, might not Christ be there, unseen, and ready to forgive sins? There was the corrupt liturgy; but, might not a pure, unwritten litany go up from his heart, acceptably, to the Hearer of prayer? There was the outward form of godliness, without the power; but, might not he have the inward power, without the form? God was everywhere, and he, even there, would worship him in spirit and in truth. Jesus had said,—"Lo, I am with you alway;" and, under cathedral roofs, that threw back the smoke of papal censers to the cold stone floors, he would adore the Crucified, without the pretended help of a cross, or "the elevation of the host." Nor, needed he the dove on the painted window, to assure him that the Spirit, who came down at Pentecost, could enter the church, and fill his soul with something better than a "dim religious light," kindle the heavenly flame in his heart, and give him the tongue of fire.

The stations had lost their charm. The images had no attraction. The altars drew not his knees to the ground. The confessional brought no sigh from his heart, nor gave him a quivering lip. Standing, one day, in a crowd that was gazing on pictures, or bowing to crosses, he lifted his eyes to heaven, and said,—"Thou, alone, art God! Thou, alone, art wise! Thou, alone, art good! Nothing must be taken away from thy holy law, and nothing added. For thou, alone, art the Lord, and thou, alone, wilt and must command."

To him, now, priests, and pope, and teachers, were mere men. Lefevre was only a man, loved and venerated still, but not standing as a mediator between him and Christ. The saints had been but men, many of them the best of the earth, yet fallen from the lofty height to which his imagination had raised them. The old Pantheon, in his heart, had crumbled to the dust. Christ was the one mediator, and God's word the supreme law.

These grand results were attained by slower steps than our pages have moved onward, but freedom came to the soul of Farel about the date 1520, when he was full thirty years of age. Luther was then making a powerful impression in France, notwithstanding the decisions of the Sorbonne. Let Luther have the credit of being the great workman of the sixteenth century, and the chief reformer. But we take nothing from him when we give their due to the Paris doctor and his disciple. Farel was not guided by Luther or Zwingle;* he and they were

* "I began," wrote Zwingle, "to preach the gospel in the year of grace,

struggling for light and for life about the same time. Lefevre was before them all, and hence Beza hails him as the man "who boldly began the revival of the pure religion of Jesus Christ, and as, in ancient times, the school of Isocrates sent forth the best orators, so from the lecture-room of the doctor of Etaples issued many of the best men of the age and of the church."

Although there was still in this bold teacher a tinge of the Sorbonne, yet "he is the first catholic in the reform movement, and the last of reformers in the (Roman) Catholic movement." D'Aubigne says farther, "The Reformation was not, therefore, in France a foreign importation. It was born on French soil; it germinated in Paris; it put forth its first shoots in the University itself, that second authority in Romish Christendom. God planted the seeds of this work in the simple hearts of a Picard and a Dauphinese, before they had begun to bud in any other country on earth. If we look only at dates we must acknowledge that, neither to Switzerland nor to Germany [Zwingle in the one and Luther in the other] belong the honour of having begun this work, although hitherto these countries alone have contended for it. This honour belongs to France."

The wonder is that in these three countries the light should break forth so nearly at the same time, when the watchmen saw not eye to eye, nor heard each other's voice, nor laid any plans in concert. It proves that each one acted under an unseen power, who had planned the movement on an extended scale. With no communication one with the other, all struck their

1516, that is at a time when the name of Luther had never been heard in these countries. It was not from Luther that I learned the doctrine of Christ; it was from God's word. If Luther preaches Christ, he does as I do; that is all." In these words Lefevre might have joined without robbing Luther of any honour.

blows about the same time, "as in a battle all the divisions of an army begin to move about the same moment, although one has not told the other to march," for the chief commander has given the same order to each one of them. This is a proof that God chose the time the places and the men, and the great movement of the sixteenth century was the work of God.

When about thirty years of age, Farel could no longer have a good conscience and remain in the Romish church. He forsook her communion, with a feeling of abhorrence toward himself and of the errors in which he had so long been enthralled. Not far from this time he was recommended by Lefevre and elected to a professorship in the celebrated college founded by Cardinal Lemoine, one of the four principal colleges of the theological faculty in Paris, equal in rank to the Sorbonne. He soon became the regent, an honour which had always been given to men of learning and eminence. He filled the office with great credit to all concerned, during the short time that a persecution was preparing, and his name was held in delightful remembrance by his colleagues and students.

CHAPTER IV.

A CIRCLE OF FRIENDS.

(1512-1520.)

WHEN one maple puts forth its leaves in the early spring, we may know that the sap is in all the trees of its kind, and they will soon be in full leaf. The new life in Lefevre and Farel was soon to be manifested by other souls of their class, whom we now introduce as opponents of many evils in popery, if all of them were not yet friends of the reformation. We may know more of Farel by the company he keeps and the stirring times in which he began his career.

James Allmain, in 1512, took a position of astonishing boldness, for one of the youngest doctors of the University. Thomas de Vio, who afterwards contended with Luther on two great moral battle-fields, Augsburg and Leipsic, had published the doctrine that the pope was the absolute monarch of the church. If Julius II. was his favourite specimen of a pope there was need of strong argument to make thinking Frenchmen believe that dogma. This man was supposed to have taken the name, Julius, with an eye to the military fame of the first of the Cæsars, and was soon involved in a war with France. This pretended "vicar of Christ," assumed to imitate the Blessed One by holding down his head when the multitudes applauded him, and once a year washing the feet of twelve beggars. But he was as unlike our Lord as darkness is unlike the day. He was high-tempered, profane, drunken and dissolute; cruel in war, weak in peace, and ambitious to extend the temporal power of the popedom. Yet he sought to command respect by the long beard on a face of sixty, and by wearing a tiara of massive gold, covered with costly gems. Under such a fallible pope the dogma of papal infallibility was firmly established. Thus at the very time when Anti-christ put forth most strongly his three claims of spiritual dominion, temporal power and infallibility, Christ was coming again to the world.

The troops of the French king, in whose service was the Chevalier Bayard at the time, gained a victory over this papal Cæsar. Louis XII., "the father of his people," was well prepared to doubt the dogma of Cardinal de Vio's book, when it was put in his hands. He laid it before the university. To refute it seemed a bold undertaking. Allmain, a man of profound genius and unwearied application, made the daring attempt. He read his essay before the faculty of theology, showed the falsity of the cardinal's assertions, and received the greatest applause. Such courage is contagious, and a fire was kindled in the hearts of many of the students. Before long, the brothers, Arnaud and Gerard Roussel, two fellow-countrymen of Lefevre, with several others, gathered to the newly-raised standard.

A greater than these was admitted into this growing circle of generous minds, Count William, of Montbrun, the son of Cardinal Briconnet.* After the death of his wife, he had entered the Church, given his heart to study, taken orders, and was now the Bishop of Meaux. Twice he was sent on an embassy to Rome, and, on his return to Paris, he was astonished

* Sometimes anglicised into *Brissonnet*.

at what had taken place. He was expected to have much to say about the gay entertainments and festivals of "the holy city;" but his thirst for the truth led him to more solemn and important matters. He renewed his former acquaintance with Lefevre. He passed many precious hours with him, with Farel, the two Roussels, and their friends. Illustrious as a prelate, he was, nevertheless, humble-minded, and was willing to be taught by the humblest Christian, and especially by the Lord himself.

"I am in darkness," said he, "awaiting the Divine goodness, to which I am a stranger, because of my demerits."

"Get into your heart more of that good Bible, which I have already recommended to you," said Lefevre. "It will give you light. It will lead you back to the pure Christianity of the early Church."

"I have read it. But my mind is dazzled by the brilliancy of the gospel. Free grace, free pardon, the free gift of eternal life and heaven offered freely to all who will simply believe in Christ,—these amaze me. The eyes of all men are not able to receive the whole light of this great sun."

"We need a great sun to chase away the night that rests on the world. It is the glory of Christianity that it causes our eyelids to droop before its infinite mercy."

The gentle bishop read still more eagerly, and the simple and weighty truth of salvation by faith charmed his soul. He found Christ; he found God, in Christ, reconciling sinners to their Father. "Such is the sweetness of this divine food," said he, "that it makes the mind insatiable; the more we taste it, the more we long for it." Again, representing himself as an house, too narrow for Jesus to dwell in, he says,—"But, the dwelling enlarges according to our desire to entertain the good Guest.

Faith is the quartermaster who alone can find room for him, or, more truly, who makes us dwell in him."

And, now, from the court of the king, comes a still greater personage, the Princess Margaret, the Esther of the palace. Let us notice her steps, as she walks softly in the dawn of that morning when God was renewing the world. The same "still small voice," which had been calling Lefevre and his band out of the night into the day, has prompted her to seek the light. We must go back a little, in order to understand her position.

Louis XII. had left some bright lines in his record. He had opposed the temporal power of the pope with a conquering army. He had resisted the papal pretensions to absolute rule in the Church, and probably was glad that Allmain had expossd their fallacy. He was no friend to the infallibility of such popes as Borgia and Julius the profane. All this must have been known among the princes. It is even said that he had a coin struck with the inscription,—*Perdam Babylonis nomen*,—"I will destroy Babylon." He knew that the Babylon of his day was Romanism. In the year 1501 he had made a journey through Dauphiny. It was at the time when the Waldeneses were exciting a needless alarm among the priests, and Farel was a child of twelve. Some of the nobles begged the king to rid their provinces of these teachers. He was curious to learn what evil they had done, and sent his confessor, Parvi, to visit the accused. The report brought back was so favourable, that Louis said,—"They are better Christians than we are." He commanded the goods taken from them to be restored, and the papers, which gave them authority to prosecute these "better Christians," to be cast into the Rhone.

Nor was this all. About the year 1510 Louis invited the French clergy to meet him in council at Tours. He seemed to anticipate a reform, and, had it taken place during his reign, the whole of France might have become Protestant. The council declared that he had the right to wage war upon the pope, and that all popes were under the authority of the general councils. From Tours came very much to talk about in the university,—the city and the court,—and a deep impression must have been made on the mind of young Farel, who had lately come to Paris. But, what would the courtiers, the royal heir, and a certain young princess, think of all this conduct of the king?

If a wicked woman deserves to go unmentioned, then Louisa of Savoy should be treated with that silence which condemns. The less written of her profane character the purer our page. The shame is that she had great influence in the kingdom. The honour is that one of her two children, growing up in the court of Louis, was so unlike her as to merit a place in church history. No thanks to her for this, but to the truth of God. Her son was a prince of tall stature, striking features, and so strong a will that the king often said "That great boy will spoil all." This was Francis, the cousin of Louis. "His beauty, and address, his courage and love of pleasure, made him the first knight of his time. He aspired, however, at being something more; he desired to be a great and even a good king, provided everything would bend to his sovereign pleasure. Valour, a taste for letters, and a love of gallantry, are three terms that will express the character of Francis and the spirit of the age." Learned men gathered around him, and the strange thing is, as we shall see, that he did not join with the reformers, for a tender and gentle being at his side held over him a guardian power.

This gentle being was his sister, two years older than himself, and so queenly in her personal excellence that all her titles seem to add nothing to her greatness. To be Margaret of Valois, then duchess of Alençon, then queen of Navarre, was little honour compared to that of being a fervent Christian, the protector of the Protestants, the patron of young Calvin, and the devoted friend of Lefevre, who passed the seven last years of his life in the refuge of her home, and there died at the age of nearly a hundred years.

But she is young now, and she does not dream of these honours. Her cousin Louis spares no pains in her education; her mother's example is warning enough against the temptations that beset a princess; her brother tenderly loves her, or rather sends back a tithe of the flood that pours upon him from her own heart, and all wonder that such a bad woman as Louisa could have so good a daughter as Margaret. What is it to be the most beautiful, intelligent, witty, amiable and influential princess of her time? What is it it to be gifted with poetry, accomplished in literature and exalted in station? What is it to be esteemed by scholars, visited by ambassadors, and consulted by her king? A happiness that thousands would covet and think worthy the risk of their souls. But she is intent upon something far better. To prevent evil and to do good is her ruling passion. And when the gospel comes it is hailed as good news from heaven, as bread to the hungry soul, and as her defence against the evils of a corrupt court. Certain ladies tell her of the new doctors; they lend her the new little books; they tell her of the ancient church and the word of God; she listens, reads and believes. She walks out to breathe the fresh air of the revival morning, and catches some glimpses of the Light of the world. She talks with Lefevre, Farel and Roussel; she is struck with their pure morals, their piety and their

A CIRCLE OF FRIENDS. 61

earnestness, and she is entered on the list of friends to the new movement. The bishop of Meaux becomes her guide in the path of faith.

Francis was crowned in 1515, and there was some hope that he would go beyond Louis, his father-in-law, and extend his shield to those brave men who were using spiritual weapons against popery. He invited learned reformers into his kingdom, and heard them talk with delight. He founded professorships of Greek and Hebrew, to the great joy of Beza. He listened to his affectionate sister and was almost persuaded to be a Christian. But the court thought it would never do for the king to lend his hand in turning the world upside down. These reformers must be treated with contempt, and even persecution might teach them silence. Margaret's new opinions were whispered to the courtiers; their surprise was great, their talk was loud, their ridicule was keen. "What! the sister of the king take part with these new people! It must not be!" It seemed for the moment that her doom had come. She was denounced to Francis I. He, as her brother, pretended to think that the charge was untrue. Then her noble character silently rebuked her reprovers. They could not resist the charm of her good deeds. Every one loved her, says Brantome; "She was very kind, mild, gracious, charitable, affable, a great almsgiver, despising nobody, and winning all hearts by her excellent qualities."

No preacher could have done what Margaret was doing among the better minds at the French court. Her life pleaded the cause of the gospel with that eloquence which consists in actions more convincing than words. The new doctrine was gaining upon the nobles of France. If the king had followed his persuading sister, the nation might have opened its gates to Christ, and Margaret's conversion saved it from those storms which afterwards drenched that beautiful land with the blood of the Huguenots.

Not that Margaret was a saint,—far from it. In her writings were blots, in her character blemishes, and in her devotion appear tinges of Romanism. But, even a clouded star was a wonder in that court of darkness. If she wavered between her brother and her Saviour, it was because she turned to the one in order to give him light, and to the other to receive life. We shall soon see how true were Beza's words, when he said that God raised her up to overthrow, as far as possible, the cruel designs of Louisa, Anthony Duprat, the chancellor of France, and their associates, when they excited the king against the so-called heretics.

When wounded by the arrows of sin, and by the thorns of the court, she fled to her lonely retreat, and laid bare her sorrows to the eye of her crucified Lord. Her poetry then became prayer.

"O Thou, my Priest, my Advocate, my King,
On whom depends my life—my everything;
O Lord, who first didst drain the bitter cup of woe,
And knowest its poison, (if man e'er did know,)
These thorns, how sharp, these wounds of sin, how deep!
Friend, Saviour, King, oh! plead my cause, I pray;
Speak, help and save me, lest I fall away."

The tramp of the forest explorer calls the hungry lion from his lair, and so the march of these French reformers brought out the most cruel foes to track them along every new path of truth. They needed not to be ferreted out by spies, for these friends were not hiding away, as if ashamed of their doctrines. All was open, and broadly proclaimed. They were well-known by the lamps which they held forth in the night of error. By their light we may see who were their bitterest foes.

Louisa, the mother of Margaret and the king, loved her iniquities so well, that she naturally hated the word of God, and all who set it above the traditions of the Romish Church. She was the more to be feared on account of her great influence over her son. But, she had a favourite even worse than herself, whom she had put forward as chancellor of the kingdom; and he was now the cruel power behind the throne. This was Anthony Duprat, represented as "the most vicious of all bipeds." He had enriched himself at the expense of justice, and then taken "holy orders," so as to get his hands upon the richest livings, and increase his wealth at the expense of religion. Two such depraved characters might well seek to wash away their own lust and avarice in the blood of the "heretics." Devoted to the pope, and pleading for his absolute power over the Church, they sharpened the sword and kindled the fire, and hoped to make short work of the reformers. This was the enmity of the state.

Still more fearful was the enmity of the Church. The dignified Sorbonne joined hands with the profligate court. It furnished bigots of every grade; but our eyes fix on the leader of the gang. The same Picardy that sent forth Lefevre to begin a reformation, also let slip Noel Beda to begin a persecution. He was "reputed to be the greatest brawler, and most factious spirit of his day." Always restless, he was a torment to all around him. He seemed born to fight, and, when he had no foes, he struck at his friends. He loudly declaimed against learning, and tried to make every new idea appear frightful. Many smiled while he blustered; but, there were enough to listen, and, by making himself a terror to all who differed from him, he gained a wide sway among the colleges. He "created heretics before any existed," and had called for the burning of Merlin, the vicar-general of Paris. "But, when the new doctors appeared, he bounded like a wild beast that suddenly perceives an easy prey within its reach." The cautious Erasmus wrote,—"In one Beda there are three thousand monks." But, where was the proper victim?

The suspecting eye fell upon Lefevre, for Beda had grown nervous over the renown of his fellow-countryman. To increase his own chance for making a noise, he would gladly have put the aged doctor to silence. He either could not see, or could not lay hold of the strong points in the new doctrines, and he scented out the grievous heresy of "the three Magdalenes." For Lefevre had asserted that Mary, the sister of Lazarus, Mary Magdalen, and the woman who anointed the feet of Jesus, were three different persons. This set Beda and his host in motion. The whole Church was aroused, and, as a specimen of her infallible judgment, she declared that these were but one person, an opinion which no priest would be likely now to affirm. Lefevre was condemned by the Sorbonne, and prosecuted by the parliament as a heretic. But Francis, glad to strike a blow at the Sorbonne and to humble the monks, rescued him from their violent hands, and saved him from the scaffold. Perhaps the thanks are due to Margaret. Beda was enraged at seeing his victim snatched from his grasp, and he resolved to take more caution with the next one, whom he was about to select from the nobility.

At the court was a gentleman of Artois, about thirty years old, named Louis de Berquin. He was frank and open-hearted, pure in his life, tender toward the poor, warmly attached to his friends, and wished to have no enemies. He had fairly won the title of "the most learned of the nobles." He had a horror of everything called heresy by the church, and devoutly observed the fasts, festivals, confessions and masses. It created surprise to see so much devotion at court.

There seemed to be nothing to incline such a man toward the new doctrines. But Beda disgusted his generous spirit. Not wishing to injure any one, he could not bear to see others injured. As he did nothing by halves, he spoke freely, wherever he went, about the cruelty of this rough tool of the Sorbonne, and he attacked "in their very nests, those odious hornets who were then the terror of the world." Nor did he stop here, as if it were enough to oppose the persecutors. He sought to learn what the persecuted had to say for themselves. He wished to know that Bible, which was "so dear to the men against whom Beda and his creatures were raging, and he scarcely began to read the book, before it won his heart."

Berquin lost no time in seeking admission to the circle of reformers, in which was the delightful company of Margaret, Lefevre, Farel, Briçonnet, and the Roussels. Any one who loved the word of God was now a brother, and all sat at the feet of the Master. Nor was the young noble yet satisfied. He wished all France to know the truth. He showed all the zeal of Beda in the other direction. He began to use the pen in order to resist Beda's sword.

In 1520 the noise about Luther had reached France. His writings came soon after with the east wind. His victory over Dr. Eck gave joy and courage to the company of reformers. Many of the Sorbonne doctors found striking truths in the little books of the monk of Wittemberg. They were watched by their colleagues, and if one of them uttered a reasonable sentiment, the loud cry arose, "He is worse than Luther." The more boisterous priests seemed to gain the day, and became the willing recruits of Beda and his satellites. The more silent doctors read and thought for themselves.

Berquin translated several of Luther's writings. This was too much; he was now one with the German monk who had dared to set himself against the pope. Death was too good for Luther; it was good enough for his translator; and Beda resolved to bring him to the scaffold. There was this argument, the University had condemned the German writings to be publicly burned. An appeal was sent to Francis, who was then pleasuring through the land. Margaret whispered in his ear. His eyes were opened. He saw that the "heretics" were simply men of learning. The grave deputies were sent back, crestfallen and in great wrath, with this reply from the king, "I will not have these people molested. To persecute those who teach us, would prevent able scholars from coming into our country."

Among those who were thus shielded were many of Luther's disciples. They had crossed the Rhine in advance of his writings, and found a welcome among all the Bible-readers, whose new doctrines were often called "the sentiments of men of genius." "In a short time," says a Jesuit author, "the university was filled with foreigners, who, because they knew a little Hebrew and Greek, acquired a reputation, insinuated themselves into the houses of persons of quality, and claimed an insolent liberty of interpreting the Bible."

And that the king should allow them to stay! This was an awful calamity to the church. But if Beda and his troop could not erect scaffolds or pile up the fagots, there was another sort of persecution which might be employed. They could annoy the reformers, vex them, slander them, cry out against them, and make the people believe that the church was in danger.

They might hiss and hound them out of society, or provoke them to say and do things in self-defence, on which they could found such charges as would bring down the wrath of the king. Beda was bold to declare that he would wage war upon them to the bitter end; if the king consented well, but if not his majesty must make the best of it. The aged Lefevre felt tormented by these ignorant zealots, and began to look for some retreat where he might be free from the strife of tongues. Where should he find it? Where be out of the reach of the man in whom there were three thousand monks?

CHAPTER V.

A BUSY BISHOP.

(1520–1523.)

"COME to me, good father Lefevre, and find rest from your troubles," we seem to read in a letter from Briçonnet, the Bishop of Meaux, who is now at home, with his flock, in the beautiful country of the river Maine. "Our city will afford you an asylum."

"Shall such a man as I flee?" we think Lefevre responds, in the spirit of Nehemiah.

"Come over and help us," urges the bishop; and the call to work proves stronger than the invitation to rest. Lefevre goes, and finds a busy bishop, who needs help and counsel. Let us see what has been going on at Meaux.

After Briçonnet had opened his heart to the "good Guest," he returned to the diocese, and, with the zeal of a Christian, began the work of a faithful bishop. He visited every parish. He inquired into the doctrines and lives of the preachers, as one who had an account to render unto the great Master. He summoned witnesses, who had a sad story on their lips.

"At collection-time," they said, "the Franciscans of Meaux begin their rounds. A single preacher will visit four or five parishes in a day, always delivering the same sermon, not to feed the souls of his hearers, but to fill his mouth, his purse, and his convent. When their wallets are replenished, their end is gained; there are no more sermons, and the people see the priests no more in the churches until the next pay-day comes."

"These shepherds make it their only business to shear the sheep," declares the bishop, who pities the shorn flocks, and is indignant against the monks. "But, where are these hirelings?"

"They get their money, and then go to Paris to spend it," reply the parishioners.

"Alas! are they not traitors who thus desert the service of Jesus Christ?"

The bishop resolved upon a sifting process. He called all his clergy together in 1519, and took account of them. Many, who cared for little else than the charms of Paris, urged that they had employed curates to tend their flocks while they enjoyed the city. What, then of these curates? Were they as bad as the priests who held the livings? One hundred and twenty-seven of them were examined, and only fourteen of them were approved by the bishop! The rest were weak, ignorant, worldly and selfish.

The next year the bishop published a mandate, in which he declared "traitors and deserters all those pastors who, by abandoning their flocks, show plainly that what they love is the fleece;" selected others, who were found to be qualified, and set them over the sheep, ransomed by the most holy blood of Jesus Christ. He now was convinced that, if he would have able ministers in his diocese, he must train them himself. He therefore resolved to establish a theological school at Meaux, under the direction of pious and learned doctors. He must find good teachers; and, without meaning it, Beda was providing them.

Lefevre had left Farel and the Bible-band at the capital, hunted everywhere by the secret detective police of the Sorbonne.

Farel did not preach, for he was not yet ordained; but he talked with students and citizens, argued with professors and priests, and boldly proclaimed the cause of the reformation at the university and in the city. Some, however, fired by his example, openly preached the gospel. Martial Mazurier, president of St. Michael's college, and eloquent in the pulpit, threw aside all reserve, and painted the disorders of the times in the darkest but the truest colours. It was almost impossible to resist the wisdom with which this earnest Stephen spake. Beda and his recruits were raised to the highest pitch of anger, and declared,—"If we tolerate these innovators, they will invade the whole body, and all will be over with our teaching, our traditions, our places, and the respect felt towards us by France and the whole of Christendom."

All had, indeed, been over, long ago, with the respect which the Sorbonnists claimed. They had forfeited it by their bigotry and intolerance. They stood accused, before all true Christendom, of the great crime of persecuting the men who would have saved France from darkness and blood. On them was fixed the lasting dishonour of having refused the true light, because their deeds and doctrines were evil. They were blinding their own eyes, and were fighting against God. To them, these excellent men, of whom Paris was not worthy, might have said, as Paul and Barnabas declared to certain persecutors,—"It was necessary that the word of God should first have been spoken to you; but, seeing ye put it from you, and judge yourselves unworthy of everlasting life, lo, we turn to the Gentiles." Never was there a more solemn hour to that capital city, in which was concentrated all France. Never were the destinies of that nation more delicately hinged on an event, small in the eyes of men, but great in the sight of God. That event was the persecution of those who held forth the word of life! Paris then decided her history for centuries; she sent Christianity into exile; she set up Romanism in her heart, and there it has remained, causing, in one age, a St. Bartholemew's day of blood, and, in another, an infidel revolution of horror.

The bishop of Meaux learned how fierce was the enmity against Farel, the Roussels, Mazurier, and their co-labourers, and how all their zealous efforts were thwarted. He entreated them to come and join Lefevre. They saw only a hopeless conflict before them if they remained, and thought it important to be united together in one solid and sacred phalanx for the triumph of the truth. They accepted the bishop's invitation, and went to Meaux. They went into the neglected parishes to feed the flocks that had been fleeced by the priests and curates. They laid no tax upon the rich; they gave generously to the poor. The bishop was like that ancient "son of consolation," who laid his money at the apostle's feet. "His fortune equalled his zeal; never did man devote his wealth to nobler uses, and never did such noble devotedness promise, at first, to bear such glorious fruits." The new teachers gathered a goodly company around them, and Meaux has the honour of being the first city in France in which grew up a protestant congregation. In this "cradle of the French reform" a protestant church was established in 1546. Beza wrote of it, "the little flock of Meaux has not only served as an example to all the churches of France, but has also begotten to the Lord several other churches, and that too of the greatest. What is more, it may boast of having offered martyrs to God as its first fruits, since the restoration of the gospel."

The voice of Lefevre was heard crying aloud, "Kings, princes, nobles, people! all nations should think and aspire after Christ alone. Every priest should resemble that archangel whom John saw in the apocalypse, flying through the air, holding the everlasting gospel in his hand, and carrying it to every people, nation, tongue and king. Come near ye pontiffs, come ye kings, come ye generous hearts. . . . Nations, awake to the light of the gospel, and inhale the heavenly life. The word of God is all sufficient."

This all-sufficient word must be in all houses, in all hands, under all eyes, and become the book of the people. Lefevre wished to see it read by every class and in every language. During the next three years (1522—1525) he published the entire New Testament in French, and a version of the Psalms. In private and in families the Bible was read; conversations about its truths became more frequent and public, and the Holy Word proved itself to be from God by the light which it cast into the corrupt heart and the dark home.

Erasmus, by publishing the Greek Testament, reached chiefly the learned, and this was a result too great for time to estimate. Lefevre, by publishing the French version, not only drew educated minds to the Bible, but he sent it into the abodes of the poor, the lowly, the illiterate and the toiling. The city of Meaux was largely inhabited by artisans and dealers in wool. The fullers and weavers, says an old chronicler, "took no other recreation, as they worked with their hands, than to talk with each other of the word of God, and to comfort themselves with the same. Sundays and holidays, especially, were devoted to the reading of Scripture, and inquiring into the good pleasure of the Lord." The bishop was delighted to see the good work thus going on, for piety was taking the place of superstition in his diocese. An old Romish annalist lays a heavy charge upon Lefevre for using his great learning to "so cajole and circumvent Messire Guillaume Briçonnet with his plausible talk, that he caused him to turn aside grievously, so that it has been impossible, up to this day (1560,) to free the city and diocese of Meaux from that pestilent doctrine, where it has so marvellously increased. The misleading of that good bishop was a great injury, as until then, he had been so devoted to God and to the Virgin Mary."

Not only into the factories, but into the fields, went the glad tidings, and thence still farther out into the world. Near to the city were rich crops, and at the harvest time, a crowd of labourers came from the surrounding regions. They reaped until they needed rest, and then while resting they talked with the townpeople about other seed-times, other soils, and other harvests. When their work was ended, they went home with the gospel in their hearts. They told the wonderful news, and in one instance, the peasants of Landouzy carried back with them the gospel, and persevered until an evangelical church was formed in their district, and it still stands, we believe, as one of the oldest protestant churches in France. Thus "in this diocese an image of the renovated church was seen to shine forth."

Nor was the king forgotten. The light must reach him. The court must be gained to Christianity, if possible. The bishop sent to Margaret (now the Duchess of Alençon) "the epistles of St. Paul translated and splendidly illuminated, most humbly entreating her to present them to the king, which cannot but be the most pleasing from your hands." Thus, probably, the word of God was placed under the eyes of Francis I. and his mother Louisa. If they opened it, they closed it without receiving any lesson for their hearts. Perhaps too much was hoped from the conversion of the king, should he avow himself the patron of Christianity.

7

"The gospel is already gaining the hearts of the great, and of the people," said Lefevre one day, in the fervour of his heart, when certain of the Romanists were talking with him and Farel. "In a short time, spreading all over France, it will everywhere throw down the inventions of men."

On a sudden, a Franciscan monk, named Roma, started up to resist the animated doctor, whose eyes sparkled, and his worn-out voice grew musical with the promise of refreshing times. "Then, I and all the other religioners will preach a crusade," cried Roma. "We will raise the people; and, if the king permits the preaching of your gospel, we will expel him from his kingdom by his own subjects."

It might have been ill for the monk, but well for the truth, had the knightly king heard this last threat. He might have taught Roma a lesson on loyalty. No reformer was proposing to drive the monarch from his throne, if he did not favour the gospel. If such a threat was a crime, where were Beda and Duprat? If they were on the hunt for an offence, there was one, far greater than any committed by the reformers. The Franciscans applauded the words of Roma. They began to feel alarm; their craft was in danger; their livings were reduced; they could not shear the sheep, and their convents were in need of supplies. They went about, mourning and clamouring, as if their fall was a sign that the world was coming to an end. They tried to rouse the people against the new teachers. Then, with bolder face, they went to the bishop, and impudently declared to him,—"Crush this heresy, or else the pestilence, which is already destroying the city of Meaux, will spread over the kingdom."

The bishop, at first, stood like an oak against the storm. He had a contempt for the selfish monks, who sought to lord it over him. He went into the pulpit and defended the aged Lefevre, and called the monks Pharisees and hypocrites. It had been well for his name had he been slain at the very onset of this gathering battle, and buried as the first Protestant who fell in France. But his courage failed. He trembled, wavered, and became a frail reed in the wind. He was only a bishop, and the monks could crush him. He took alarm when he saw them posting off to the capital, to lay their complaints before the higher powers. They entered Paris; they were closeted with Beda and his gang; they were a joy to Duprat, and they easily gained the ear of parliament. They charged the bishop with the immense mischief done at Meaux. His palace was a fountain of heresy, and it must be sealed. The Sorbonne and the parliament agreed in waging a war upon the reformers.

Poor Briçonnet! holding out a flag of truce at the very hour when a victory was at hand. He would not surrender everything, but he would yield enough to satisfy Rome. He would keep the gospel, but give up Luther's writings. He would allow Mary to be invoked, along with Christ. The compromise was made. In 1523 he issued three mandates; the first enjoined prayers for the dead and the invocation of the saints; the second one forbade any one to buy, borrow, read, or carry about with him, any of Luther's works, and ordered them to be torn in pieces, scattered to the winds, or burnt; the third asserted the doctrine of purgatory. But this was not enough. If he would save himself, he must sacrifice those who had trusted him, and whom he had sheltered. It was hinted that the gospel-teachers must not be allowed to leave Meaux, for they would only carry their doctrines into other places. An end must be made of them. This was too horrible a work for the bishop, and it was thought best to entrust it to surer hands. He was asked to forbid their preaching in the parishes, and he did it. He also began to visit the churches, in company with Andrew Verjus, the first president of the parliament of Paris, so that this zealous dignitary might see and hear for himself. It was hard, but the bishop laboured to "weed out the heresies that were there shooting up." Verjus and his brother deputies returned to the capital, fully satisfied. Briçonnet had fallen. They said he had returned to the faith, and risen to his proper place in the Church.

The aim was now taken at the faithful Lefevre. His writings were searched by Beda and his detective police. They pointed out intolerable heresies to the Sorbonne. "Does he dare to recommend all the faithful to read the Scriptures? Does he not tell therein that whoever loves not Christ's word is not a Christian? and that the word of God is sufficient to lead to eternal life?" The Church must never endure this, for it puts all her interests in danger. Romanism cannot stand if the Bible be the book of the people.

The secret whisperings in the Sorbonne, the plots of their detectives, and the noise of the monks, were of little avail unless the king would give the order to crush the heresies and force men into the faith of the church. And what did Francis say to all this uproar? He appointed a commission to investigate the matter; Lefevre appeared before it, justified himself, and came off from this attack with victory on his banners of truth. Yet flight was wisdom, and he soon after left Meaux for a time. It seems however that he returned and was secretly harboured by the bishop.

Farel could not hope for protection, since his host had turned against the invited guests. He left the city where there were still many firm adherents to the gospel, and where martyrs were soon to seal their testimony with blood. It seems that he went at first to Paris, and with unsparing words attacked the errors of Rome, until he put his life in jeopardy. Thence he probably went to Dauphiny, anxious to bear the good news to his native land. It has been supposed, however, that he spent several months at Metz, where the gospel standard was being lifted high, and to it were gathering some of the most worthy chieftains of the French reformation. Let us see them flocking to this ancient city, the old Divodurum of Tacitus, built where the Seille adds its waters to the blue Moselle.

Before the bishop fell, and his chief guests departed, the Lord raised up a lowly disciple to be a pastor to the little flock at Meaux. John Leclerc heard his fellow wool-carders talk of the gospel, and hid the good word in his heart, for it must not be mentioned at home to his father, who was blindly led by the monks. His mother and his brother Peter joined with him on the side of the new preachers. He read the Bible and the "little books;" he grew strong under the teachings of Lefevre and Farel, and became a ready expounder of the Scriptures. When the teachers were exiled, the Christians looked to him as their shepherd.

This wool-carder went from house to house comforting the disciples. His zeal outran his prudence, and he sought to give popery such a blow as only a Luther had strength to inflict. He wrote a proclamation against the pope, declaring that the Lord was about to destroy Anti-christ by the breath of his mouth. He took the "placards" and boldly posted them on the gates of the cathedral. Hundreds gathered on the spot to read the strange words. Soon all were in confusion; the disciples were amazed; the priests were angry; the monks were outrageous, and they demanded that, at least, one example should be made to terrify the people. Who would be a better one than this wool-carder? The king would not call him "one of his learned men," and treat him with favour. Leclerc was cast into prison.

He was hurried through a trial, under the eyes of the fallen bishop. He was condemned to be whipped through the streets of the city on three days, and to wind up the cruelty, his forehead was to be branded with the mark of a heretic. No time was to be lost. The poor carder was led through the city, with his hands bound and his shoulders bare, while the blows fell and the blood flowed. An immense crowd followed in the gory tracks of the victim; some yelled with rage against the heretic; others gave clear signs of their tender compassion. One woman lent him her eyes and her voice; the sufferer took courage; she was his mother.

At last, on the third day, when the scourgings and marches were over, the fortieth stripe not being spared, the procession halted at the usual place of execution. The hangman prepared the fire, heated the iron, and branded the brow on which the name of Jesus was written. A loud shriek was heard, but it came not from the tormented disciple. It was that of the mother, who shouted, with a voice that made the persecutors tremble, "Glory to Jesus Christ, and to his witnesses!" Such boldness, at such a moment, was a crime worthy of severe punishment, but she had appalled both priests and soldiers. An unseen hand controlled their fury. She turned away, the crowd respectfully parted, the monks and town-sergeants gazed unmoved, and she slowly walked to her humble dwelling. None dared to arrest her. Leclerc was then set at liberty, and passed some months at Rosay, about twenty miles from Meaux. He was recovering for a greater work in a new field.

The foes of truth were elated with their victory; the friends of the Crucified hid under the shadow of the Almighty. An old chronicler says, "The Cordeliers, having recaptured the pulpits, propagated their lies and trumpery as usual." But the poor workmen would not go to hear them. They "began to meet in secret, after the manner of the sons of the prophets in the time of Ahab, and of the Christians of the primitive church; and as opportunity offered, they assembled at one time in a house, at another in some cave, sometimes also in a vineyard, or in a wood. There he, who was most versed in the Holy Scriptures, exhorted the rest; and this done, they all prayed together with great courage, supporting each other with the hope that the gospel would be revived in France, and that the tyranny of Anti-christ would come to an end."

On other plains the light was breaking. At Metz* there dwelt a man, described as "a marvellously learned clerk, of small stature, who had spent much time in travel, who spoke every language, and had studied every science." This was Master Agrippa, now chief magistrate of the city. He had read

*In the thirteenth century Metz drew the attention of Christendom. Certain Waldenses brought to that city translations of several books of the Bible, which were scattered through the diocese, and eagerly read by the people. Societies of Bible-readers were formed. These Christians began to separate themselves from the Roman church. The priests endeavoured to put a stop to their meetings. The bishop reported them to the pope, who advised gentle measures. But they were forbidden to hold their meetings. They refused to give up the Bible, even if the pope should demand it. They pointed out many Romish errors, and said that the Bible gave them better light than the ignorant clergy. At length, they were accounted heretics, quite akin to the Waldenses; their assemblies were broken up, their Bibles burned, and a synod at Toulouse, (1229,) uttered its warning against all translations of the Scriptures into the language of the people.—*Neander's Church History, vol. iv.*

Luther's works, and loaned them to his friends. Many of the clergy, nobility, and citizens were gained over to the cause of truth. In 1522 some one had pasted, on the corner of the bishop's palace, a placard, whose large letters extolled what Luther had done. The public attention was excited. Master Agrippa had enough to do in answering questions and preserving the peace.

Leclerc went to Metz in 1523, and there, like Paul at Corinth, he worked at his trade and persuaded the people. He talked with the labourers, and the "Lutheran business" was on every lip. The flames, partly smothered, now broke out afresh. Every opposition was useless; the people would inquire, discuss, and believe. Many of the more learned among them took the side of the Reformation, and the gospel began to be preached. Another helper came to the work of the Lord.

John Chatelain, an Augustine monk, had been brought to the truth at Antwerp. He came to Metz, says the chronicle, "a man declining in years, and of agreeable manners, a great preacher, and very eloquent, a wondrous comforter to the poorer sort; by which means he gained the good-will of most of the people, (not of all,) especially of the majority of the priests and great rabbins, against whom the said friar, John, preached daily, setting forth their vices and their sins, saying that they abused the poor people, by which animosity was stirred up." And yet the truth from his eloquent tongue did not fall with such power as it did from "the lips of a poor artizan, who laid aside the comb, with which he carded his wool, to explain a French version of the gospel."

There dwelt in the city a devout woman of the middle class, named Toussaint, who often talked with her son, Peter, in a serious strain, while he was at play. She, like all the towns-people, expected something wonderful to occur in those times. One day the child was riding on a stick in his mother's room, while she was conversing with her friends on the things of God. She said to them, in an earnest tone,—"Anti-christ will soon come, with great power, and destroy those who have been converted at the preaching of Elias." These words, often repeated, were fixed in the child's memory for life.

Peter was no longer a child when the new preachers were declaring the gospel in Metz. His genius led his relatives to hope that he would one day fill an eminent place in the Church. An uncle was the dean, and Cardinal John of Lorraine a warm friend. Peter, although but a youth, obtained a prebend, when the gospel came to his ear. He listened, and wondered if the preaching of Chatelain and Leclerc was that of Elias. Antichrist was arming against it in every quarter. He believed in the coming of the Lord, and prepared to enter his service. He saw the chevalier Esch, his uncle's intimate friend, casting his lot with the reformers, who gave him a hearty welcome. Peter called him "the knight, our worthy master," adding, with noble candour, "if, however, we are permitted to have a master upon earth."

Cheering was the progress of the gospel in the city, when it was suddenly arrested by the imprudent zeal of Leclerc. The affair of the placards, at Meaux, had not cured him of rashness. He saw with grief the idolatries of the people. One of their great festivals was approaching. It was the habit of the people, on a certain day, to make a pilgrimage to a chapel, about three miles distant, where were images of the Virgin, and of the most celebrated saints of the country. They worshipped these images, in order to obtain the pardon of their sins.

The eve of the festival came; Leclerc's pious soul was agitated.

He seemed to hear a voice, saying,—"Thou shalt not bow down to their gods; but thou shalt utterly overthrow them, and quite break down their images." As the night came, he left the city, and went to the chapel. There he sat a while, silent, before the statues. He wavered in his purpose; but he thought how, in a few hours, the whole city would be bowing down before blocks of wood and stone. He rose up, took down the images, brake them in pieces, and scattered the fragments before the altar. Then he returned to the city, just at daybreak, and, almost unnoticed, entered the gates.

All Metz was on the move; the bells were ringing; the brotherhoods were assembling; the procession was forming with an array of greater and lesser clergy in the lead. The multitudes recited prayers and sang praises to the saints whom they were going to adore. Crosses and banners were displayed, drums were beaten and sweeter music filled the air. After about an hour's march they reached the end of the pilgrimage. The priests advanced, with their smoking censers, to render the early homage. But what a sight! the images they had come to worship were shattered and the fragments covered the ground. The monks recoiled with horror. They announced to the crowd what a sacrilege had been committed. Suddenly the chanting ceased, the instruments were silent, the banners were lowered, and an intense excitement prevailed. Their leaders inflamed the minds of the people, insisting that search be made for the criminal and his death demanded. One cry burst from every lip,—"Death, death to the sacreligious wretch!" In haste and disorder they returned to the city.

All fixed upon Leclerc. Many times he had said that the images were idols. A few remembered that they had seen him at daybreak, coming from the direction of the chapel. He was seized. He confessed; he claimed that the deed was not a crime, and exhorted the people to worship God alone. To adore what a mere man could so easily destroy was absurd. But no argument could cool the rage of the crowd. In their fury they wished to drag him to instant death. When led before the judges, he declared boldly that Christ alone should be adored. He was soon convicted, sentenced to be burnt alive, and taken to the place of execution.

Here everything horrible in fire and heated irons was prepared for him. Wild yells rose from the monks and people, but he was firm, calm, unmoved. They began to torture him in ways too cruel for description. His body was being torn to pieces, but his mind was at rest. With a loud voice he recited the 115th Psalm, "Their idols are silver and gold, the work of men's hands. . . . They that make them are like unto them: so is every one that trusteth in them." The voice and the sight of such fortitude daunted the enemies and gave strength to the faithful. The people, so angry before, were now touched with compassion. But the priests saw him burnt by a slow fire, and thus turned the festival into an awful funeral. Leclerc was the first martyr among the French reformers.

Not yet were the priests satisfied. They had tried to persuade Chatelain to renounce the gospel, but were obliged to say, "He is deaf as an adder, and will not hear the truth." He was arrested, carried away, and shut up in the castle of Nommeny. The officers of the bishop degraded him; they stripped him of his priestly garments; they scraped his fingers with a piece of glass, saying, "By this scraping we deprive thee of the power to sacrifice, consecrate, and bless, which thou receivest by the anointing of hands." Then throwing over him a layman's dress, they surrendered him to the secular power, and another martyr perished in the flames. But the fires of truth were not thus to be quenched with blood. Even the historians of the Gallican church, approving of this severity, admit that "Lutheranism spread not the less through the whole district of Metz."

The dean was in trouble lest his nephew, Toussaint, should perish in the storm of persecution. He had not taken an active part against the first two French martyrs, but he dare not throw his shield over his brother's son. Peter's mother felt a still greater alarm. Not a moment must be lost. The liberty and life of every one who had lent an ear to the glad tidings of free pardon were endangered. The taste of blood inflamed the rage for more, and other scaffolds and other fires would soon threaten the faithful. The only safety seemed to be in flight. Peter Toussaint, the knight Esch and many others fled in haste and sought refuge in Basle.

Thus the north of France rejected the gospel, and the gospel gave way for a time. But the great "Captain of our Salvation" was only changing his forces to new fields. He, who retreated from Nazareth, appeared again in Capernaum, Samaria, and Jerusalem. The Reformation only changed its ground: we shall see it again in the south-east of France, and in Switzerland. For, as in the days of the apostles, "They that were scattered abroad went every where preaching the word."

CHAPTER VI.

FAREL A WANDERER.

(1523-1524.)

HOME, unvisited for years, attracted Farel to its refuge, at the foot of the Alps, when he was driven from Meaux and shut out of Metz. Time, study, truth, and grace had greatly changed him since the day when his father wished him to be a knight, like the brave Bayard. He was something far better,— a good soldier of Jesus Christ, enduring hardness. It was not simply home, with its old scenes and comforts, that was drawing him; he seemed to hear a voice, saying,—"Return to thy house and thy kindred, and show what great things the Lord hath done for thee."

His brothers had reason to wonder that he was still alive. They feared to have him come. In their eyes he was an apostate, a heretic, a fanatic. Rumours of what had taken place at Paris and Meaux filled them with a certain degree of terror. But William got their ear and their heart as he told them of the new and admirable things in the gospel. He entreated them, with all his fiery zeal, to believe and embrace it. He won three, if not all of them, to the truth. They did not at first abandon the Church of their fathers; but, when persecution came, they had the courage to sacrifice friends, property, and country, for the sake of liberty in Christ.

Farel thus kindled a new fire on the hearth at home; but he was not content until he had declared the truth to his friends and relatives in the neighbourhood. There are some who assert that he was invited, by certain of the clergy, to preach in the churches; others declare that he did not yet assume to enter the pulpit. However this may be, he taught in such a way as to cause great agitation. The multitude and the priests wished to silence him. "What new and strange heresy is this?" they asked. "Must all the practices of piety be counted vain? He is neither monk nor priest; he has no business to preach." Of this, Farel was the better judge, and upon his labours came the blessing of heaven.

It was a time when several Frenchmen of that region were gained over to the gospel. Among them was a young gentleman from Dauphiny, the Chevalier Anemond de Chatelard. Even in his Romish piety he was a foe to relics, processions, and the dissipated clergy of his acquaintance. From Farel he received the truth, gave it a deep place in his heart, and soon was very zealous for it. He disliked forms in religion, and gladly would have seen all the ceremonies of the church abolished. "Never," he declared, "has my spirit found any rest in externals. The sum of Christianity is comprised in these words,—*John truly baptized with water, but ye shall be baptized with the Holy Ghost;* ye must put on the new man."

Anemond could not be idle, for he had all the vivacity of a Frenchman. If a celebrated doctor was to be heard, he wished to be present. If a door was open to the gospel, he was waiting to enter it. His father was dead. His elder brother was harsh, haughty, and bigoted, and repelled him with disdain. His younger brother, Lawrence, with all his love, could but half understand him. Anemond, finding himself rejected by his own kindred, sought to be of service in another quarter. Only laymen had yet been converted in Dauphiny, and Farel, with his friends, had wished to see a priest at the head of the movement, which already gave some promise of shaking the Alps. God had his finger upon the man.

There lived at Grenoble a Franciscan priest, Peter Sebville by name, a preacher, of great eloquence, a man of a good and honest heart. He sought infallibility in Romanism; it was not there, and yet it must be somewhere, if man had any religion on which he could depend. He took up the long-neglected book, and found it in the word of God. He resolved to preach the word "purely, clearly, holily." His eloquent voice was heard in the province. Farel was delighted, and Anemond felt at liberty to visit Luther and Zwingle. He willed his property to his brother Lawrence, who, probably, thought the chevalier was going forth on as foolish an errand as that of many a knight in the olden time.

And, perhaps, Luther thought likewise, when the young Frenchman first met him at Wittemberg. His plans were on the largest scale, and his hopes of seeing all France converted were the brightest, if Luther would only go himself and take the glorious prize. But the Saxon doctor could not enter the field across the Rhine. "Then write to the Duke Charles, of Savoy," earnestly said Anemond, who thought that Francis I. might be reached through his uncle. "This prince feels a strong attraction toward piety and true religion, and loves to converse with certain persons at his court about the Reformation. He is just the man to understand you, for his motto is this,— *Nothing is wanting to those who fear God*, and this is yours also. His heart stands in need of God and his grace; all he wants is a powerful impulse. If he were won to the gospel, he would have an immense influence on Switzerland, Savoy and France. Write to him, I beseech you."

"Assuredly," replied Luther, "a love for the gospel is a rare gift, and an inestimable jewel in a prince." Although Luther knew that the success of the gospel did not so greatly depend upon the favour of princes as his friend supposed, yet he wrote a most touching letter to the duke. We know not the result. Anemond, in his ardour, would have rejoiced to possess the power of rousing all France.

Farel hardly expected the German champion to come over the Rhine. He laboured on until the civil and ecclesiastical powers of Gap combined against him. They thought him an agent of that sect which the Sorbonne denounced. Beda hunted and Duprat was ready to burn. "Let us cast this firebrand of discord far from us," they exclaimed. He was summoned to appear, was harshly treated, and violently expelled from the city. But he was still a "voice crying in the wilderness." He knew the country of his youth, when his rashness had led him to explore the mountains, and now, if closely followed, he could hide in the forests, caves, and clefts of the rocks. He went about preaching in private houses, secluded hamlets and lonely fields, and found an asylum in the woods and on the brink of torrents. In this school God was training him for future labours and endurance. The poor heard the truth from his lips, and the solitary places were glad.

Letters came to him from Anemond, and he greatly desired to see the reformers of Germany and Switzerland. The valleys of his native land were narrow; perhaps he might find a broader, as well as a safer, field. France was offering him nothing but fire and sword; perhaps some other country would offer him a large harvest to reap. But how was he to get away?

Foes hung upon every path, neither willing for him to teach the people nor to leave them to themselves. Following by-roads, hiding in the forests, now losing his way and now finding some other way, he evaded the pickets of the enemy and escaped. He reached Switzerland early in 1524, and found Anemond at Basle.

Farel was received at Basle as one of the most devoted champions of the gospel. There was honour in the hospitality extended to him. He was the guest of Œcolampadius, one of the most genial of the reformers. Scarcely any two men were more unlike in their natures. The host charmed his hearers by his mildness; the guest carried all before him by his impetuosity. It was Peter in the house of John, and that most remarkable friendship in the apostolic band was reproduced in the union between these two reformers.

Œcolampadius had been preaching in Basle as a pastor, but his words seemed to fall like gentle snow-flakes upon a rock. He was discouraged and greatly depressed. He had said to Zwingle, "Alas, I speak in vain, and see not the least reason to hope. Perhaps among the Turks I might meet with greater success. But I lay the blame on myself alone." These sighs rose in Farel's ear, and called forth his sympathy and his heroic words of good cheer. The bold man fired up the courage of the timid. An undying affection grew up in the heart of the host, and he must declare it. "Oh, my dear Farel, I hope that the Lord will make our friendship immortal, and if we cannot live together here below, our joy will only be the greater when we shall be united at Christ's right hand in heaven."

There were many refugees in the city, who had escaped from the scaffolds of France. They formed a French church. Among them were Anemond of Dauphiny, Esch and Toussaint of Metz,

Du Blet of Lyons, and others of lesser note. These all held Farel in high esteem, and he was not backward to maintain his reputation. His courage, learning, and piety soon won the hearts of all who could appreciate his influence. He was the rising man, and to him were the honours paid.

There was, however, one man who felt slighted. He was sensitive to neglect. He had not come to Basle to be overlooked. He had made a noise in the world. It had been the affair of his life to send a storm upon the schoolmen and the monks, and his scathing satires had made his name a dread to all who did not please him. His learning was acknowledged in all the great universities. As a pioneer, he had hoped to prepare the way for the reformers; but the wisest of the reformers had made the painful discovery that he was trying to castle himself on the half way-ground, between popery and protestantism, and shot the arrows of wit at both parties. His levity of mind was like that of his body—a puff of wind might bear him away. He could expose error, but he lacked the moral courage to stand up for the truth. Yet he had drawn the gaze of Christendom; for he was Erasmus, the prince of scholars. Thousands were ready to crouch at his feet and do him reverence, coveting one kind look, one brotherly word from this master of the age.

And yet Farel had not come near him, as a young noble, wishing to be made a knight by a blow of the sword, and the words, "Rise, sir," from his king. The young Dauphinese refused to go and pay homage to the old sage of Rotterdam, because he despised those men who are only by halves on the side of truth. The commentaries of Lefèvre had caused no little debate among the guests, at their simple entertainments, where it was well-known that Erasmus had said harsh things of the good doctor, who had excelled him in making the New Testament the book of the people. The lines were drawn—some taking sides with the commentator, and some with the severe critic. Farel was valorous for the old teacher, who had shown him the spiritual stations on the way of the true cross. He was ready to break a lance with the cavilling Erasmus. What greatly annoyed him, was the treatment given to the lovers of the gospel. Erasmus had shut his door against them. Farel was not the man to go and beg for admission. The favour of the old sage was of little account to him. He would not fawn for his sarcastic smile. More than all, if Erasmus had given a pledge to the pope to write against Luther, he would have nothing to do with such a spy in the camp.

No doubt Farel said more than was proper, and the illustrious scholar was nettled at his independence. Princes, kings, doctors, bishops, popes, reformers, priests, and men of the world were ready to pay their tribute of admiration to the Rotterdam philosopher; even Luther had treated him with a certain forbearance; and now this young Frenchman, unknown to fame, and an exile, dared to brave his power and beard the lion in his den! Such insolent freedom was more annoying than the homage of the whole world was pleasant. Hence Erasmus took every occasion to vent his ill-humour on Farel, and on all the French refugees in Basle, whose frankness and decision offended him. They had little respect to persons, and cared not for the man who "knew what was right, but had not the courage to avow it," however exalted his genius. We may wish them more gentleness, but, if we admire the vigour of the old prophets, we must credit them with a brave love for truth when they would not bow down before that which the world adores. It was evident that a face to face engagement was soon to take place between the bold Dauphinese and the learned Dutchman.

One day Farel was talking with several friends on the doctrines of Christianity, in the presence of Erasmus. The former had, perhaps, heard that, instead of being called Farellus, the name *Fallicus* had dropped often from the lips and pen of the satirist; thus giving to one of the frankest men of his day the epithet of a cheat and deceiver. The latter had heard that he had been called a *Balaam*, as if the presents of the pope had induced him to curse the people of God. If he had been heated before, he was now boiling with wrath to chastise the author of this reproach.

"Why do you call me Balaam?" inquired Erasmus, rudely interrupting the conversation.

"I have not given you that title," replied Farel, at first astonished by so abrupt a question.

"Then name the offender."

Farel declined, tried the virtue of mild words, explained his own position, but yet felt himself pressed.

"It was the merchant, Du Blet, of Lyons," said Farel.

"It may be he who made use of the word, but it was you who taught him." And then, ashamed that he had lost his temper, Erasmus quickly turned the conversation. "Why do you assert that we ought not to invoke the saints?* Is it because it is not enjoined in Holy Scripture?"

---

* Farel might have read him a passage from his "Praise of Folly," to show that Erasmus regarded the worship of the saints as an absurdity. "Do we not see every country claiming its peculiar *saint?* Each trouble has its saint, and every saint his candle. This one cures the toothache; that assists in sickness; a third restores what a thief has stolen; a fourth preserves you in shipwreck; a fifth protects your flocks. There are some who have many virtues at once, and especially the Virgin, in whom the people place more confidence than in her Son. . . . . . The mind of man

"Yes."

"Well then; I call upon you to prove by Scripture that we ought to invoke the Holy Ghost."

Farel made this simple and true reply. "If he is God, we must invoke him."

Some accounts represent the discussion as going on through a long line of arguments, not because Erasmus doubted the divinity of the Holy Spirit, or the duty of praying to him, but solely for the sake of worrying the young reformer. But Erasmus wrote, "I dropped the conversation, for the night was coming on." He evidently confessed himself baffled.

From that day, whenever the name of Farel fell from his pen, he represented him as a hateful person, who ought to be shunned. He was clearing himself, in the eyes of the Romanists, from all suspicion of heresy, by employing the most bitter abuse of the reformer and his countrymen. He wrote to the pope's secretary, "Some Frenchmen are still more out of their wits than even the Germans;" and hinted that they were prompted by Satan to "have five expressions always in their mouths; the gospel, God's word, faith, Christ, and the Holy Ghost." This was high authority in proof of the sound teaching of these "Frenchmen." The same charge might have been brought against the apostles John and Paul. Thus the sage's abuse was the reformer's praise. No wonder Farel declared that Erasmus was "the most dangerous enemy of the gospel," and yet his letters are full of moderation in regard to the satiric scholar. The gospel in its most fiery temper is milder than mere philosophy, a fact

is so constituted that imposture has more hold upon it than truth. If there is one saint more apocryphal than another, (a St. George, St. Christopher, or St. Barbara,) you will see him worshipped with greater fervency than St. Peter, St. Paul, or even than Christ himself."

still illustrated by those who take shelter under the broad wing of the church while they hurl their reproaches against her men of truth and zeal.

In the meantime the forces were gathering for a contest in a larger field. Basle had its university and its senate. In both there were many friends, but more enemies of the gospel. The doctors opposed it to the utmost of their power. They sought to suppress it by public disputations. Œcolampadius was ready to take them at their word, and use their own weapons. He posted up four theses and invited all who took offence at his doctrines to refute them, or yield to the force of his arguments. He defended them, adopting the new plan of speaking in the German language, so that all the people might understand. The doctors did not appear, not even with their Latin essays; and the general respect for the gospel preacher increased. The people felt more interest in such discussions, and knew that the reformers were not afraid to expose their doctrines to the light.

Stephen Stoer, the priest of Liestal, had taken a wife, believing that the laws of the Bible were better than the decrees of Rome. The papists thought it a scandal to their pretended sanctity, and wished the senate to send this priestly husband into disgrace. But he was loved in his parish; and the people asked the senate to permit him to defend the step he had taken by an appeal to Scripture in a public debate. The doctors tried hard to prevent it; but a disputation, in the German language, was held in the University hall. Five theses were defended, but no deputies from the bishop, nor any of the professors came to hear or answer. All they had to say was to express their mortification at seeing the five theses approved by the majority of the preachers and even by the friars.

The doctors thought they had enough of debate, but Farel thought it his duty to give them a little more, and profess in Switzerland, the doctrine set forth at Paris and Meaux, that "the word of God is all-sufficient." He asked permission of the University to maintain certain theses, as he said "the rather to be reproved, if I am in error, than to teach others." The University refused. Its leading professor was the intimate friend of Erasmus.

Farel then applied to the senate, submitting to it thirteen propositions, from which the following sentences are taken:

"Christ has given us a perfect rule of life, which we are not at liberty to alter, either by adding to it, or taking from it.

"No one should impiously regard the precepts of Christ simply as good advice; nor exalt the advice of his fellow-men to a level with Christian precepts.

"We ought to pray most earnestly for what the Holy Spirit can impart to us. Christians must present their offerings to God alone."

The senate granted the request, and issued a public notice that a Christian man and brother, named William Farel, had drawn up certain articles in conformity with the gospel, and they had given him liberty to maintain them in Latin. The doctors saw that they could not arrest the discussion, for the University must yield to the senate. But their wits suggested another scheme. They asked the Vicar-general to interfere. He at once issued an order to all the priests, students, and others, forbidding them to attend the disputation, on pain of excommunication and banishment. Farel might declaim to the walls.

Not so, thought the senate; jealous of its supreme authority, they issued an edict making it a duty to give Farel an audience, and a crime to stay away. It ran, "the pastors, preachers, priests, students and other persons connected with the University shall attend the disputation, under penalty of being deprived of their benefices and the protection of the laws." The day came, and an audience with it. Farel spoke in Latin, and Œcolampadius translated it into the language of the people, so that the French accent of the debater might not prevent the understanding of every word.

"It is my opinion," said Farel in beginning, "that every Christian cannot do better than make himself thoroughly acquainted with the truth, which Christ has declared himself to be." He did not attack, by name, any particular men or doctrines. His two leading ideas were a return to the word of God and to faith in Christ. The opposers were frequently invited to reply, but not one of them appeared. They contented themselves with boasting in private how much they could have done had they been there! The interpreter said, "These sophists act the braggart—but they do it in dark holes and corners."

One effect of the disputation was, that the priests and members of the University sank in the estimation of the people, for they wished to suppress the truth and dared not defend their own doctrines. Another effect was, that Farel rose in the esteem of all the reformers, as a champion in the good cause. They were delighted to see a Frenchman exhibit so much knowledge with his zeal, and piety in his courage. "He is strong enough," said they, "to destroy the whole Sorbonne singlehanded." Conrad Pellican, a learned Franciscan monk, was confirmed in the faith, and became a valuable ally of the great Reformation.

Farel had learned a lesson concerning himself. He found that he needed more of the dove in his nature. His zeal had betrayed him into language which fell like hail where the soft and gentle rain would have been more effective. In the pleasant home of his friend, he was kindly admonished of this fault. They mutually agreed to cultivate meekness and a tenderness of speech. Yet his friend regarded his ardour as a virtue, for without it the world could not be moved nor the church aroused from sleep. He wrote to Luther in a letter of introduction, afterwards, "There are certain men who would have his zeal against the enemies of the truth more moderate, but I cannot help seeing in this same zeal an admirable virtue, which, if seasonably excited, is no less needed than gentleness itself." This the impetuous Luther could appreciate, coming as it did from one of the gentlest of men.

Farel visited the land of Zwingle and Myconius, who welcomed him with a kindness never forgotten. On his return to Basle he found Erasmus and other enemies at work, stirring up the senate against him. As his freedom of speech was not on their side, they insisted that the people could not bear it, and disturbances would arise if he was not ordered away. In vain did his friends urge that this was an abuse of all custom and law; for their city took pride in being an asylum for the persecuted. Farel bade adieu to Basle. "It is thus we exercise hospitality," said his indignant host, "we true children of Sodom!"

With the chevalier Esch he set out for Germany, with letters for Luther and Capito, and he was commended, by his friend of the warm heart and home, as "that William who has toiled much in the work of God." It does not appear that he went as far as Luther's Wittemberg.

The opposers of the gospel in Basle became more arrogant than ever; and by public mandates or secret intrigues, endeavoured to suppress the truth and crush its adherents. But

Œcolampadius had caught something of Farel's spirit, and he no more wished himself among the Turks. In a letter to the bishop he reproached them for being so noisy after refusing to appear in defence of their faith, and for claiming the exclusive right to teach a people who were not allowed to understand their doctrines. The flock would go where they were best fed; the priests were despised as cowards and hirelings who did not care for the sheep, and the reformers were counted as their best friends and pastors. Thus the gospel was working with power at Basle.

CHAPTER VII.

A NEW FIELD.

(1524.)

IN strange ways God can open new fields of labour. The young Duke Ulrich had lost his estates in Wurtemberg by the Swabian league, in 1519, and taken refuge in Montbeliard, an earldom in France, which still belonged to him. In his dark days he had met with the reformers in Switzerland, and found the cheering light of the gospel. The once violent and cruel prince now seemed to be a lamb, seeking the fold of Christ. The priests led him in barren pastures, and his eye was attracted to a little flock that, in some way, had been gathered at the chief town in his domain. They wanted a pastor, and the duke promised to aid and protect them in sustaining a man of their choice. They laid their case before Œcolampadius, and he saw that the hand of God was extended to lead back the chief of the exiles to France. He sent word to Farel to come to him from Strasburg.

Farel was bold enough to go to Basle, and wise enough not to expose himself to those who had lately driven him away. There were hidden paths and dark nights, of which he could take advantage, and he secretly entered the old city. He was safely concealed in the house of his former pilgrimage, and we seem to hear the mild voice of his friend rising into earnestness, and his own louder voice toned into greatness.

"I have sent for you," says the host, "to urge you to preach the gospel. You have refrained from entering fully into the service of the Church. It is now your duty, for there is in you all that may constitute you a minister of the Lord."

"I have considered my weakness," replies Farel, "and I have not dared to preach, waiting for the Lord to send more suitable persons. If I could have a clear call, I would not hesitate."

"You have a three-fold call. God, in his providence, has opened the way for your return to your country. All France calls you, for, behold, how little is Jesus Christ known to those who speak the French language! Will you not speak to them in words which they can understand? And the people of Montbeliard invite you among them, and the duke gives his assent."

"It does not seem lawful for me to resist; I must obey, in God's name. I accept the charge; but I am not yet ordained."

"Extraordinary times demand extraordinary measures. You must here, in this house, be set apart to the ministry."

The step was a bold one, and is not an example to be followed. Whether any of the preachers in Basle were invited to be present, we know not, but Œcolampadius ventured upon a private ordination. He solemnly set Farel apart to the ministry, calling upon the name of the Lord. Let the success of the minister be considered in evidence of the Lord's approval.

"Now, go and feed the flock of God," said his friend; "and guard your own nature. The more you are inclined to violence, the more you should practise gentleness; temper your lion's courage with the meekness of the dove." This needed counsel was received by Farel with all his heart.

In July, 1524, he entered upon his labours at Montbeliard, and the first promise of success was astonishing. The seed was hardly sown when the harvest began to appear. The duke and his court were much in his favour. Most of the people were eager to hear the word of God; a few, who regarded themselves as of the higher class, were disposed to treat him with contempt, or dread his presence as a source of disturbances. There are always some who fear lest the world will be turned upside down by the gospel. Chevalier Esch was his companion, and, doubtless, was of service at the court of the duke. Farel had written to his gentle friend at Basle, with no little exultation, and now another chevalier proposes to join him.

Anemond, delighted with the good news, ran, with his usual vivacity, to Peter Toussaint, saying, hastily,—"I shall set off, to-morrow, to visit Farel."

"Good! I am just finishing a letter to him. You must be the bearer."

"Gladly will I be so; and I am to take one also from Œcolampadius." At the time appointed the chevalier set out, and in a few days was at Montbeliard, where his face and the letters were appreciated.

Œcolampadius wrote,—"It is easy to instill a few doctrines into the ears of our auditors, but to change their hearts is in the power of God alone." Toussaint wrote,—"I am glad that the duke and court are on your side; but there is need of watchfulness, for you well know that the destroyer of our peace never slumbers. He employs every weapon to overcome his opponents, and the more so whenever any extraordinary attack is made upon his kingdom." These were but little drops of caution in cups overflowing with encouragement.

The advice was timely, for Farel was already attacked by the destroyer of peace. The city was in commotion. Many of the nobles were alarmed, and said, as they looked in contempt at the new preacher, "What does this sorry fellow want with us? Would that he had never come! He cannot stay here, for he will ruin us all, as well as himself." But the worst opposition came from the Romish clergy.

On a certain Sabbath Farel had just begun to preach, when the priests, sent there for the purpose, called him a liar and a heretic. In an instant the whole congregation was in an uproar. The people rose up and made the confusion still worse by crying out for silence. Word was sent to the castle; the duke hurried to the spot, and found that the disturbers were led on by the dean of the priory and the guardian of the Franciscan convent at Besançon. They and their pack had come over to cry down the gospel-preacher. The duke reprimanded the dean, who took it in good part and retired from the scene. But not so the guardian. He went to another church in the afternoon, gave the lie to Farel, abused his sermon, and did all he could to excite a tumult in the town. The duke arrested both Farel and the guardian, requiring the latter to prove that the sermon was heretical, or to retract what he had said about it. He chose to retract, and confessed publicly, from the pulpit, that Farel had spoken the truth, and that the opposition to him arose out of a bad temper. Farel was set at liberty. An official account of the affair was published, so that no false reports might be circulated.

Farel, whose very nature had fire enough, was now burning with zeal. He thought it his duty to unmask the priests who had been so active in all this riotous business, and with vigour he plied the sword of the word. He had been preaching what their guardian had admitted to be the truth, and now he exposed their errors.

'How fares it with Farel's meekness?" inquired Œcolampadius of one who had come from Montbeliard; probably Anemond. The strongest testimony was borne to his faithfulness, energy, and success, although he had shown too much violence in attacking the priests for their errors concerning the mass. His gentle friend wrote him and reminded him of the resolutions which he had formed at Basle. He advised meekness and modesty. "Mankind must be led, not driven."

During the winter a friar, of the order of St. Anthony, came into the neighbourhood and employed a monk to proclaim from the pulpit that he had some relics for sale. The monk gave the wares a hearty commendation. There was at Montbeliard a disciple of Luther, named John Gailing, who first preached the gospel in Wurtemberg, and was now the court-preacher to the duke. He had, doubtless, rendered great assistance in the work going forward, and he knew that the sale of these relics was only a trick to divert the minds of the people from the gospel. Farel and Gailing appealed to the senate to put a stop to such imposture, representing in strong terms how this traffic had destroyed souls, robbed the poor of their savings, and God of his glory. But the senate had not courage to act in the case, and declared that such matters belonged solely to the duke. To the duke they went, asking him to send away the friar, unless he could prove from Scripture that it was right to sell relics. This gave the monk and friar a fine chance to defend themselves by that all-sufficient word, by which Farel would test everything, as well as to show that the relics were genuine. But the impostors dared not accept the challenge, and made no further noise.

A report of Farel's labours and success came to the ears of the old sage, Erasmus, and mightily annoyed him. He hinted to some spy in the camp at Montbeliard, that severe measures should be employed against the zealous preacher. He wrote at once to his Romish friends that an exiled Frenchman was making a great disturbance in those regions. Farel knew of all this, but had enough to engage his attention in spreading the truth far and near. He was, at Montbeliard, "like a general on a hill, whose piercing eye glances over the field of battle, cheering those who are actively engaged with the foe, rallying those ranks which are broken by an impetuous charge, and animating those who hang back through fear." Behind him were Basle and Strasburg, as a base of operations, whence he drew his supplies of tracts and books.

The refugees at Basle were forming a Tract and Bible Society, and raising up colporteurs to scatter the truth through France. The presses then were constantly occupied in printing French books, and these were sent to Farel, who put them into the hands of book-hawkers, and these simple-hearted men passed through the country, calling at almost every door. Anemond was a true chevalier in this good work, which was moving forward with such strength that Erasmus was on the rage, and the Sorbonne in alarm. He sent to Farel all the useful books he could get; and one of his large plans was for Farel to use the pen, while he raised a fund and a force to work the presses, day and night, and thus flood all France with the truth. He was anxious to see the New Testament printed in French, and widely circulated in the provinces.

The Chevalier happened one day at the house of a friend, where his eye fell upon a new edition of Lefevre's French Testament. He was overjoyed. But how came the needed prize so near at hand? Vaugris, a merchant of Lyons, who had fled to Basle, had secured its publication in October 1524. The edition was limited. "Lose no time in reprinting it," said the earnest Anemond, "for there will be a call for a great number."

At the urgent advice of his friends Farel wrote several small books, among which was "A summary of what a Christian ought to know, in order to trust God, and serve his neighbour." The last one passed through several large editions, and was widely circulated.

This same year Lyons was the centre of a movement in which Farel took a deep interest, if not an active part. The merchants Du Blet and Vaugris had taken the lead in the reformation at this old city where four centuries before, Peter Waldo had preached, and by his sermons had shaken all France. Preachers were again needed, and the raging of nations was to bring them. Francis I. was leading an army against Charles V. of Spain, and passed through Lyons on the way to Pavia. Margaret the Duchess of Alençon came also leading the spiritual soldiers of the Lord, and they halted at this point, while the other hosts went on to Italy. She caused the gospel to be publicly preached at Lyons. Her preacher, Michael D'Arande, drew large crowds to hear him, and with courage he declared a pure gospel. Anthony Papillon, a friend of Erasmus, and "the first in France for the knowledge of the gospel," was present to support the efforts of the duchess. Nor were these labours confined to the city. Into all the region round about, the Christians went with the good word. There was at Lyons a monk named Maigret, who had been boldly declaring the new doctrine in Dauphiny, and had been driven out by the priests. One of Farel's brothers had written to Chevalier Anemond, painting the state of things in the gloomiest colours, and asking for Farel and the knight to come to the help of their native land. Anemond thought of going, but the Lord sent more efficient workers. Maigret urged Papillon and Du Blet to repair thither, and they went.

We have not forgotten Sebville, whom we left preaching the word, "purely, clearly, holily" in Dauphiny. A violent storm had just broken out against him, and the monks, who were angry because Farel, Anemond and Maigret had escaped their grasp, now called for Sebville's arrest. The friends at Grenoble felt that they could not have him taken from them. They appealed to Margaret, and she had him rescued from the fury of his persecutors.

But the mouth of Sebville was closed for a time, for he must choose between silence and a scaffold. He wrote Anemond, "Silence is imposed upon me under pain of death." Many gave way; but Amadeus Galbert, a cousin of Anemond, gathered a faithful band around him, and clung to the truth. These Christians met Sebville secretly at their own houses, and if there was none to preach, there were many to talk of the good word. They crept away to some retired spot; they visited some brother by night; they prayed in secret to Christ, and though often alarmed were not arrested. The threat was that if they dared to speak the word in public their lot should be the stake.

Thus stood affairs when Papillon and Du Blet went to Grenoble. They may not have done much in Dauphiny, but they put Sebville upon a new mission. "If you cannot preach at Grenoble, you can at Lyons. The Lent is coming on, and there will be crowds in the city." He went, and met with a kind reception from Margaret. It was proposed that Michael, Maigret, and Sebville should lead on the gospel army. There was to be a gospel Lent in Lyons. The rumour of it went abroad far and near. Anemond wrote in joy to Farel, "Sebville is free, and will preach the Lent sermons." Maigret was already

A NEW FIELD. 107

preaching "God manifest in the flesh." The priests raged, but the duchess protected him. At last, however, they seized the bold preacher, dragged him through the streets, and cast him into prison. Vaugris left for Basle, spreading the news on the way. One thought still cheered the reformers, "Maigret is taken, but Madame de Alençon is there: praised be God!"

The work of the spiritual army was greatly disturbed by the defeat of the royal army at Pavia, in February 1525. The king was taken prisoner and was on the way to Madrid. The duke of Alençon had proved a coward, and he came to Lyons to die of shame and grief. All France was full of mourning, and the Romanists began to declare that this great disaster was provoked by Heaven, because the new doctrines had been tolerated in the kingdom. The "heretics" must be expelled, "People and parliament, church and throne, joined hand in hand "to banish the gospel. The preachers at Lyons were dispersed. Soon after this Du Blet sank under persecution. Papillon died in such a way that it was reported, even among his enemies, that he had been poisoned. Sebville, probably, did not preach his Lent sermons. Michael D'Arande was threatened with death. Margaret thus saw her plans for the spread of the gospel at Lyons end in sad disappointment. The camp was broken up; the forces scattered, and the cause seemed to be lost.

Nor was this all. Another strong force was leaving the field where there had been such great success. Farel was pulling up his stakes at Montbeliard. The defeats at Pavia and Lyons could hardly have influenced him, for he removed before these sad tidings could have put him in fear. It has been hinted that Erasmus, whose anger still burned against him, may have done much to excite a persecution too bitter for him to endure. But another reason has been given by those who lament that Farel's warlike zeal sometimes carried too far, and brought unnecessary opposition against him.

One day, about the time of the king's defeat at Pavia, Farel was walking on the banks of a little river that runs through Montbeliard, beneath a lofty rock on which the citadel is built. It was the day of the feast of saint Anthony, and when he came to the bridge he met a procession which was crossing it, reciting prayers, and headed by two priests bearing the pretended image of the saint. Farel suddenly found himself face to face with these superstitions, without seeking it. A violent struggle took place in his soul. His blood boiled at the sight of such a delusion practised upon the people. Should he give way? Should he hide himself? Should he gaze and be silent? He could not be a coward, and would not let his silence give consent to the imposture. He knew that he was exposing himself to the fate of Leclerc, yet he boldly advanced, grasped the image of the holy hermit from the arms of the priest, and tossed it over the bridge into the river; as bold a deed as that of the Chevalier Bayard when he stayed an army at the bridge of the Garigliano. Then turning to the awe-stricken crowd he exclaimed, "Poor idolaters, will ye never cease from your idolatry!"

The priests stood confused and motionless. With the loss of their saint, they lost their presence of mind. Their superstitious fear seemed to rivet them to the spot. But some one cried out, "the image is drowning!" The priests recovered from their stupor. The multitudes shouted in rage, and gazed at the image floating away. Farel let them gaze and rave, and taking advantage of their devout attention to the saint, he escaped their violence. For a time he hid himself among his friends.

The duke and his court soon left the city, and having no strong arm to defend him, Farel had an additional reason for leaving Montbeliard. In the spring he took a secret refuge at Basle. He always took an interest in the church he had left, as a minister will ever do in the flock where were gathered the first-fruits of his labours. We will meet Peter Toussaint in this field.

CHAPTER VIII.

MOURNING AND MADNESS.

(1525-1526.)

SAD tidings came to Farel at Basle. His friend, the Chevalier Anemond, was sick at Schauffhausen, where the Rhine presents one of the finest waterfalls in Europe. The Chevalier had wandered from place to place, to recruit his failing health. He had hoped to preach the gospel, and still cherished plans, almost romantic, for urging forward the reformation. Farel sent him four gold crowns. A messenger came to tell him that his warm-hearted compatriot was dying. Before he could set out to visit him, a letter was received from Myconius, announcing the death of the young knight, "who was in himself an host," and who had made many sacrifices for the truth.

Farel applied to the senate of Basle once more to sanction his return, but without success. He went to Strasburg, and, for about fifteen months, was engaged in preaching to a small church of French exiles. If we cast an eye upon France, we can see a reason why this brave man kept beyond her borders.

There was a loud wail throughout France over the disasters of Pavia. The king was carried away to Spain; the national power was humbled; the bravest of many an house had been slain, and ruin seemed at hand. The Romanists saw that it was their hour. They made the most of their time. They declared that *heresy* was in the land; it was the cause of all the troubles, and it must be crushed. The blame was thus laid upon those who were most innocent. There was a loud cry for blood.

Louisa was now the regent—the ruler—the Jezebel of the kingdom. She wrote to the pope, and he gave orders for the introduction of the inquisition into France. This delighted the cruel Duprat, who was made a cardinal, and who was given an arch-bishopric, and, in the bargain, a rich abbey. The parliament thought that the king had erred in tolerating the new doctrines, and the members said to Louisa,—"Heresy has raised its head among us, and the king, by neglecting to bring the heretics to the scaffold, has drawn down the wrath of Heaven upon the nation."

She wished to enlist the Sorbonne. They ordered Beda to return her an answer. He advised that all "writings of heretics be prohibited by a royal proclamation; and, if this means does not suffice, we must employ force against the *persons* of these false doctrines; for those who resist the light must be subdued by *torture* and by *terror*."

Everything was arranged for a vigorous campaign against the "heretics." Meaux was chosen as the first point of attack. The bishop, Briçonnet, had not yet fallen so far as to return fully to popery. But, how should they manage him? It might not be wise to burn him; those in sympathy with him would only cling the more stoutly to his doctrines. But, if he could be induced to recant, the effect would be bettter for the persecutors. There was an agent at hand to bring him to terms.

The eloquent Mazurier, whom we left among the reformers at Meaux, had been so zealous for the new faith that he had once broken to pieces an image of St. Francis. He was sent to prison. He was in fear of the stake. He saw that he was not with the popular party; Rome must conquer in France. He basely recanted, and became a Jesuit.

This man visited Briçonnet, and endeavoured to make the bishop fall, as he himself had done. The plot succeeded. The earliest supporter of the gospel in France denied the glad tidings of grace, because he was artfully persuaded that, if he did not, he would lose his influence over the court, the church, the nation. He was deceived with the notion that Rome would permit him to be a reformer still! He found, however, that he must labour to undo all that he had done for the gospel. He restored the invocation of the saints, and put away every sign of "Lutheranism," as the new doctrine was now called. Poor man! His fall is, perhaps, the strangest of all that occurred in those times. He died in 1533; in his will he commended his soul to the Virgin Mary, and ordered twelve hundred masses for its repose.

Such was the first triumph of the Sorbonne. It was one that went to the hearts of all his old friends, and caused them to trust less in men and more in God. But, this must be speedily followed with another victory. It was not hard to decide upon the victims. It was the man who had led the bishop into the "heresy," and who had been so long harboured at Meaux. Beda's eye had long been upon this man, who was once a doctor of the Sorbonne—Lefevre. His accusation was soon drawn up, and the parliament condemned nine doctrines found in his commentaries, and placed his French Testament on the list of prohibited books. This was but the prelude, as Lefevre well knew, and he recalled the words of his Lord,—"When they persecute you in one city, flee ye into another." He quitted Meaux and went to Strasburg, under a borrowed name. The persecutors had missed their victim, but they consoled themselves by thinking that France was rid of the father of all heretics.

This was something for the Sorbonne; but still there were no *tortures*, and nothing to terrify the people. There was yet one man, who had vexed them more than the bishop or Lefevre. This was Louis Berquin, a more decided man than either of his two masters. He had unmasked the monks, exposed the priests, and done much to enlighten the people. He was one of the noblest of the nobles of Artois. He went zealously among the cottages of his estate, and taught that there is salvation in Christ alone. He crossed into Picardy, and, in the fields and towns, declared the true way of life.

Every day some noble, priest, or peasant went to the Bishop of Amiens, and told him what was said or done by this Christian gentleman. The bishop called a council. Suddenly, he started for Paris, and had a word with the Sorbonne. Berquin was just the man they wanted. They went to his quarters in Paris, seized his writings, and, "after the manner of spiders," drew from them certain articles, out of which "to make poison, and bring about the death of a person who, with simplicity of mind was endeavouring to advance the doctrine of God."

Beda, probably, never read anything more eagerly in all his life. He had a remarkable talent for discovering in a book what would ruin its author, and he pored day and night over the seized volumes. He found enough to satisfy the inquisitors, who required but little, and Berquin's death was decided upon by the Sorbonne and the parliament. An officer was sent to arrest him in the name of the law. The dwellers on his estate, who were devoted to him, would have risen up to defend him, but he restrained them. He was thrown into prison, "entering it with a firm countenance and an unbending head."

Some months after this, three monks entered his prison as his judges, and reproached him for having taught that salvation is not dependent upon priests, and that the gates of hell could not harm a believing soul. "Yes," answered he, "when the eternal Son of God receives a sinner who believes in his death, and makes him a child of God, the divine adoption cannot be forfeited." To these monks this joyful confidence was mere fanaticism. The strength of the prisoner was admitted by the fact of an increasing force being brought against him. Two or three priors, "monks of all colours, imps of Anti-christ," says the chronicler, "gave help to the band of the Sorbonne, in order to destroy by numbers the firmness of Berquin."

"Your books will be burnt," said the pope's delegates.

"I cannot help that," thought the accused.

"You will make an apology, for only in this way can you escape. If you refuse what is demanded, you will be led to the stake."

"I will not yield a single point," said the man of heroic faith.

"Then it is all over with you," exclaimed the whole party, more in exultation than pity. Berquin remained in prison, calmly waiting for their threats to be fulfilled. We shall hear of him again, through the kind interventions of the duchess Margaret.

Thus one protestant leader had surrendered, another had left the field, and a third was a prisoner. Who next should receive a blow? The name may surprise us—Erasmus. To punish him would throw the reformers into terror. If such a trimmer could not escape, how could those who had gone the whole length of the new movement? True he had courted the favour of the Romanists, but was he not still in the camp of the reformers? He had written against Luther, but had he not stung the monks? One of those solitary Carthusians in the woods near Paris, had sent forth from his retreat a hot shell filled with all manner of slanders against the "heretics." But his name Sutor (cobbler,) even when polished into Le Couturier, raised a laugh, and by his meddling with things which he did not understand, the old proverb was suggested, "Let the cobbler stick to his last."* Erasmus cared little for such a missile as he had sent up in the air.

Beda came to the attack. He ordered Erasmus to lay down his caustic pen. The old sage must not write that the blunders and calumnies in Beda's book against Lefevre were so gross that "even smiths and cobblers could have pointed them out." He must not say of the articles on which Berquin was condemned, "I find nothing impious in them." He must not declare of the Sorbonne doctors and tools, "they employ every device to excite the anger of the nation. They vomit fire and flame against their adversaries, and heap upon them the most scurrillous abuse. All means are good in their eyes; they pick out a few words here and there, neglecting the text, that may explain the passage quoted; they insert expressions of their own, and omit or add anything they please to blacken the characters of those whom they suspect."

This scathing pen of the great scholar must be dropped. Beda grasped for it and thought he had it in his hand. He made a collection of all the calumnies that the monks had invented against the illustrious philosopher, translated them into French, and circulated his book through the court, the city and the land, striving to rouse all France against him. This was the signal for a great army to march upon the works and char-

* Ne Sutor ultra crepidam.

acter of a solitary man, who disdained to be counted with the reformers. Erasmus was assailed from every quarter. He was a greater heretic than Luther! He was an apostate and Berquin was his follower! Erasmus' books should be used to burn Berquin!

Astonishment took hold of Erasmus. Was this the result of all his trimming, his half-way policy, his courting all parties, and even his hostility to Luther? Better be a thorough reformer. He would not lay down his pen. He would turn the point of it against the worst of all his foes, those in his rear, whom he had imagined to be friends. He fell upon the whole pack of those who were hounding him to death. He wrote to the Sorbonne, charging Beda and his fellows with a conspiracy, and with betraying the soldier who was fighting in their interest. He complained to the parliament, that Beda and Sutor were allowed to attack him from behind while, at the order of the emperor, the pope and the princes, he was leading on the charge against "these Lutherans." He appealed to the captive king, touching upon a tender point, and warning him that his descendants would suffer from the Sorbonne, for its doctors "aspire to tyranny even over princes." This prophecy was to be fulfilled in the very next age, when the house of Valois was put under the ban of the priests. He invoked the protection of Charles V., saying, "Certain persons, who, under the pretence of religion, wish to establish their own gluttony and despotism, are raising a horrible outcry against me. I am fighting under your banners and those of Jesus Christ. May your wisdom and power restore peace to the Christian world."

Thus was this prince of the pen drawn away from the war against the reformers, and enlisted against the persecutors. His appeals were heard by the king and emperor. The danger was averted, for those who had attacked this one man found that the great powers of the world were leagued on his side. The vultures thought their prey was in their talons, but now they must drop it and turn their eyes to another quarter. We shall see them again in Lorraine, the country of the Guises, who are rising into terrible power.

Where was the Duchess Margaret all this time? The nation knew that she was toiling for the deliverance of the captive king. He was a sick prisoner at Madrid. She made a heroic journey thither; found him—a dying man, pale, worn, and helpless; was the agent of restoring him to life, and of securing his liberty early in 1526. The reformers knew where her heart was, and they had reason to bless God for her voice and her hand. She was in Spain when she heard of the fierce movement going on against "her brethren, the reformers." She poured into her brother's ear the most earnest entreaties for those who were in exile or in prisons. Words were not enough; she must show her love by her works. The thought of poor starving exiles, who knew not where to lay their heads, haunted her imagination while in the splendid palaces of Spain. She sent four thousand pieces of gold to be distributed among the sufferers.

She was too noble, too generous, too patriotic, and was doing too much for the nation, to be attacked by those who had grasped the sceptre and the sword in order to wage war upon the best men in the kingdom. But there was one person on whom they might wreak vengeance—Margaret's secretary, Clement Marot. They threw him into prison, and he consoled himself by composing little poems. They did not dream that his poems would one day stir all France, when his version of the Psalms should be in the mouth of every Huguenot, and sung in the palace of the king.

Let us see how it fares with the two young gentlemen who fled from Metz after the burning of Leclerc. Peter Toussaint was often talked of in the mansion of the Cardinal of Lorraine. The many who met there with Peter's uncle, the dean, deplored the sad fate of the young prebendary, who had promised so fair. He had been led away by those heretics, Chatelain and Leclerc! "He is at Basle," they would say, with deep pity, "in the house of Œcolampadius, living with one of the leaders of this heresy!" The lamentable thing was that he could not see what an error he had committed, and what evils were shadowing his path.

They wrote to him as earnestly as if they thought him exposed to eternal death. These letters pained him, because he knew they were prompted by sincere but mistaken affection. One of his relatives, probably the dean, urged him to remove to Paris, to Metz, or to any other place in the world, where he would be far away from the reformers. This relative supposed that Peter felt exceedingly indebted to him, and would at once comply with his request, but, when he found his efforts useless, his love changed into violent hatred.

These men were so determined to win back the young Toussaint to the Romish Church, that they went to his mother, who was "under the power of the monks," and wrought upon her mind. The priests crowded around her, frightening and persuading her that her son had committed crimes that they could not mention without shuddering. She wrote a touching letter to her son, "full of weeping," (said he,) in which she set forth her misery in heart-rending language. "O wretched mother! O unnatural son! cursed be the breast that cherished thee! . . ."

The unhappy Toussaint was almost distracted. What should he do? He could not return to France. To go to any of the

German cities would only add to the sorrow of his relatives. Œcolampadius advised a middle course. "Leave my house," said he. "Live with some one who is not attached to the reformation." He went, with a sad heart, and made his home with an ignorant and obscure priest—one whose religion might have satisfied his relatives. It was a change that cost him much self-denial. He never saw his host, save at meals, and then they were constantly discussing matters of faith. As soon as the meal was over the debate was postponed until the next meeting, and Toussaint retired to his lonely room, where he carefully studied the word of God. "The Lord is my witness," said he, "that in this valley of tears I have but one desire—that of seeing Christ's kingdom extended."

One event greatly cheered his heart. He persuaded the Chevalier Esch to return to Metz and encourage the trembling converts in that city. They were in peril. The Chevalier obtained some books from Farel, who was still at Montbeliard, and, traversing the forests, reached Metz early in 1525. The priests knew why he came, and watched all his movements.

It seems that in June of 1525 Toussaint and Farel made a journey to Metz,* intending to take a firm stand in that field. They requested a hearing before their lordships, *The Thirteen;* this being refused they appealed to the highest civil authority. But it was discovered by them that the agents of Beda were on the ground. They had exposed themselves to a masked battery. Plans were already laid for seizing and casting them into prison. Seeing the danger they quickly left the city and travelled all

---

*So D'Aubigne. Hist. of the Reformation, vol. iii., bk. xii., ch. xiv. No little difficulty has been found in harmonizing all the dates in reference to these two men, especially this visit of Toussaint, and his sojourn at Paris, where he was imprisoned, as stated hereafter.

night, lest they should be overtaken. It was a timely escape, for the heresy-hunters were sweeping down upon Lorraine.

The Chevalier Esch had not been able to escape the eyes and suspicions of the priests in Metz. They discovered that he kept up a communication with the gospel Christians; and this was enough. They arrested him and threw him into a prison at Pont-a-Mousson, about five miles above Metz, on the banks of the Moselle. Others were seized in the neighbouring parishes. Among them was the pastor, Schuch, of St. Hypolyte. A guard of brutal men brought him to trial, and the judge heaped abuse upon him. The pastor made no reply to these epithets, but, holding in his hands a Bible, all covered with notes, he meekly, and with great power, faced the inquisitors with the truth. They were amazed and enraged, and, tearing from him his Bible "like mad dogs," says the chronicler, "unable to bite his doctrine, they burned it in their convent." He was afterwards sent to the stake, where he continued to recite a passage until the smoke and flames stifled his voice.

The refugees could not receive letters from their friends, nor write to them, without exposing some hidden believer to danger. An intercepted letter might betray him. One man, however, dared to carry tidings from France to Basle, by sewing a letter, which bore no signature, in his doublet. He escaped the bands of detectives, and laid before the exiles the sad account of what was going on in the kingdom. At Paris, Meaux, Metz, Lyons, everywhere that any trace of the Christians could be found, there was persecution to the death. "It is frightful," Toussaint wrote to Farel, "to hear of the cruelties inflicted."

Yet these strong-hearted exiles and their persecuted friends kept up their courage. The gates of hell should not prevail against the true church of God. "In vain were all the parliaments on the watch; in vain did the spies of the Sorbonne and of the monks creep into churches, colleges, and even private families, to catch up any word that might fall unwarily; in vain did the soldiers arrest on the highways everything that bore the stamp of the Reformation;" for some would escape, and others confound their inquisitors with shame and defeat. These Frenchmen had faith in better days to come. But not from man had the refugees any hope. "Those who have begun the dance," said Toussaint, "will not stop on the road." They could only trust that God would end their "Babylonish captivity."

The Chevalier Esch escaped from his prison and met his friend at Strasburg. This fact soon was known to Toussaint, who immediately wrote to Farel, saying, "For the honour of God, endeavour to prevail on the knight, our worthy master (if it becomes us to have any master on earth,) to return to Metz as speedily as possible, for our brethren have great need of such a leader." Esch therefore went back, to expose himself to the wiles of his enemies.

It was not Toussaint's disposition to send others to the battle and not join it himself. He was eager to engage in the cause, although Œcolampadius said, "I wish my dear lords of France would not be so hasty in returning to their own country, for the devil is spreading his snares on every side." But the young exile felt that a prison could not be much worse than the house of the ignorant and contentious priest with whom he lodged. He turned his eye toward Paris. There the youthful James Pavanne of Meaux and the aged hermit of Livry had been burned, and the fires were still smoking. There no one could name the reformation without risking his life. But was not this a reason why he should go? Thither, it appears from his letters, he went, and he entered the university. Instead of the rioting which held sway in the college while Farel was a student, he found an intense fanaticism for popery. He sought to form an acquaintance with some of the brethren who were secretly imitating Farel's example, especially in the college of Lemoine where he and Lefevre had taught. But this only exposed him to danger.

One day certain officers arrested him. A duke and an abbot, who are unknown now, had pointed him out to the agents of Beda as a heretic. He was cast into prison. While in chains he prayed to God, and dwelt on the names of his friends, Roussel, and Lefevre, and Farel, and Œcolampadius, that gentle father, said he, "whose work I am in the Lord." Death seemed hanging over him, and his mother, his uncle, the dean of Metz, and the cardinal of Lorraine, made him the most lavish offers if he would recant. But he could not thus be moved. "I despise them," said he; "I know they are a temptation of the devil. I would rather suffer hunger. I would rather be a slave in the house of the Lord than dwell with riches in the palaces of the wicked." Then boldly confessing his faith he exclaimed, "It is my glory to be called a heretic by those whose lives and doctrines are opposed to Jesus Christ." He signed his letters to Farel, "Peter Toussaint, unworthy to be called a Christian."

The date of his release we cannot find. It seems that he soon after resolved to go to Metz, not to yield to his uncle and mother, but to assist the Chevalier Esch. On reaching Louvain he was betrayed, and arrested by his former friend, Theodore Chamond, the Abbot of St. Anthony. This abbot was well known as a cruel, violent, merciless man. He was not touched by the youth, the candour, nor the weak health of his victim. He threw him into a horrible dungeon, full of abominations, where the young evangelist could hardly stand. With his shoulders pressing against the wall, and his feet planted on the only spot which the water did not reach, and almost stifled by poisonous vapours, he called to mind the cheerful house of his uncle, the dean of Metz, and the gorgeous palace of the cardinal of Lorraine, where he had once been so kindly received while he believed in the pope. What a contrast now! And how cheaply might he buy it all back, and flourish again in the homes of the great! Only renounce his religion and all would be happy. But no! If he did not suspect that such a course would gain him only penances and humiliations at the hands of those who wanted to make a terrifying example of him, he knew that he would bring his soul into the deepest wretchedness. But where were the days, when, as a child, he learned from his mother to say, "Anti-christ will soon come and destroy all who are not converted?" He thought that time had arrived. His imagination was excited. He saw himself dragged to punishment. He screamed aloud, and was near dying of fright. All who saw him were interested in one so young, so feeble, and scarcely able to bear his weight on his feet. He was so mild, so child-like, so harmless, that even the cruel abbot knew not how to justify his death.

This persecutor thought that if he could search Toussaint's books and papers, he might find some excuse for burning him. One day the monks came to his vile pit, and led him out to see the abbot. "Write to your host at Basle," said the crafty Romanist, "and tell him that you want your books to amuse your leisure, and beg him to send them to you." It flashed upon the mind of the young man, that the books were ordered for a far different purpose. He hesitated, and the abbot gave utterance to most terrible threats. The almost helpless hand penned the letter, and he was sent back to his pestilential den. There he must wait, without knowing that the duchess Margaret would appear as his deliverer.

CHAPTER IX.

FAREL'S TURNING-POINT.

(1525–1526.)

NO exiles met on foreign shores with greater joy than did the aged Lefevre and Farel, his disciple at Paris, his co-worker at Meaux, his dear son in the faith. The wrinkled hand of the one had first guided the steps of the other, and after a separation, in which months were as years, they both poured out their hearts together. But the disciple was now really in advance of his master, for Lefevre had not entirely separated himself from the Romish church. He and his patron, the bishop of Meaux, had hoped to aid a reform in that church, and see it brought back to apostolic purity. The bishop had been subdued, the doctor expelled.

"Do you remember," said Farel, "what you once told me when we were both sunk in darkness, saying,—'William, God will renew the world, and you will see it?' Here is the beginning of what you foresaw."

"Yes," answered the pious old man. "God is renewing the world. My dear son, continue to preach boldly the gospel of Jesus Christ."

It delighted this man, who had first lifted his voice in Paris and found it would not be heard, to listen to the preaching at Strasburg. It was just what he had intended to teach! "He seemed to have been born a second time to the Christian life." The French refugees had formed a church, and Farel was the preacher, whom none heard with a more joyful heart than the former doctor of the Sorbonne. Such Christian society lessened the pain of exile.

An aged man, who had taken the name of Anthony Pilgrim, was often seen walking cautiously through the streets, as if he wished to be unknown. But he could not be hidden. In a short time the whole city knew that he was the illustrious Lefevre, who was the translator of the Bible into the Gallic tongue, and the very children saluted the venerable Frenchman with respect. Gerard Roussel, (Le-Roux,) took the name of Tolnin, so fearful was he lest he should be found by the enemies who were upon his track. Master Cornelius Agrippa, who had loaned Luther's works and started men to thinking in Metz, was there "taking his tone and tuning his voice" in harmony with the reformers.

The house of Capito was like an inn, where all were sure of a welcome. These refugees met with Zell, who, as priest of St. Lawrence, had been among the first to preach that "man is saved by grace." A nobleman of this city, Count Sigismond, of Hohenlohe, was touched by the preaching of Zell and the heroism of Luther. He was not one of those nobles, so numerous then, who followed the Saviour as a secret disciple. He made it his business to help Luther's writings over the Rhine and forward them to the Duchess Margaret, who called him "her good cousin," and felt herself greatly benefited by his influence.

The dews of Christian love had often been shed upon Farel, in order to moderate his flaming zeal, and he had taken kindly the gentle advice. But he thought that, while he might be over-hasty, some of his friends in Basle were too slow in acting fully up to their knowledge. They tolerated too many Romish practices. It was very offensive to him that Pellican should still attend mass and wear the dress of a monk. He remonstrated; but one of his friends, who had done the same thing to no purpose, only reminded him that it was a hard task to change a monk into a Christian. Farel requested Luther to use his influence with Pellican. The next year he had the pleasure of seeing his friend cast off the badge of popery and teach the word of God in Zurich.*

To this zealous man was given the work of a peace-maker. A controversy had arisen in respect to the Lord's Supper—some holding with Luther and some with Zwingle. It was likely to disturb the pleasant meetings of the preachers in Strasburg. They requested Farel to be an agent in reconciling the parties. He did much to bring Luther and Zwingle into a more friendly style of discussion, and, when their letters came, they were

* Many years after this Pellican was deeply wounded by a report that Farel had used some harsh terms concerning him. Calvin's letter to Pellican throws such light upon Farel's character that we condense a part of it. "That which is reported to you about Farel is to me so utterly incredible, that I would venture, even at the peril of my life, to be answerable for it, that no such expression had ever fallen from him; for I know that he both loves and reveres you. . . . If it had been said that he had made you wince a little, and without any more serious outrage, I would admit that the report might have been believed. But, only consider how monstrous it is to suppose that he, who has been so closely allied to you, who at this very time reveres and loves you, had given utterance to such reproachful expressions as would be reckoned extreme even among the most deadly foes. Besides, it is altogether inhuman that any man should be condemned unheard. Such persons do wrong Farel when they do not acknowledge him to be such a man as they have ever truly found him by experience to be."—*Calvin's Letters, No. ciii., A. D.* 1543.

found to be quite nearly agreed on most of the points at issue. The friends at Strasburg resolved to fix upon the important meaning and benefit of the ordinance, and hold "to the main point—faith and love, or to the remembrance of Christ for the invigoration of our hope, since Christ must be internal and invisible, and not necessarily connected with what is external, be it a sign or anything else."

The fellowship at Strasburg was bearing good fruit. Men, raised up here and there, as they had been, and each struggling almost alone with the faith, needed such a school. Doctrine had been the great thing hitherto; discipline had been too much neglected. The energetic Farel, the learned Lefevre, the spiritual Roussel, gifted with opposite natures, were now to act upon each other. Farel learned gentleness, Roussel gained courage; the one imparted the overplus of his peculiar traits to the other. The soft iron became steel; the steel had the rough wire taken from its edge. In other days these brethren remembered how they dwelt together in unity. "We carefully put out of sight all that might interrupt the harmony between brethren. The peace that we tasted, far from being without savour, like that of the world, was prepared with the sweet odour of God's service."

In the spring of 1526, a shout of joy was heard rolling through France from the Pyrenees to Calais. Strasburg heard it, and was behind no city in its gladness. The duchess Margaret had secured the release of the king. He was on the way to Paris. Louisa must resign her fearful power. Duprat must learn that he has a master. Beda may find that he has not the church of France in his hands.

None were more joyous than the friends of the gospel. Some of them determined to go and meet the king and petition him on behalf of the exiles and the prisoners. They felt sure that he would put himself at the head of a party which Charles V. his detested rival and captor was persecuting. But he had a secret hatred of "the evangelicals," and, although Margaret uttered a cry in favour of the miserable, he kept the most cautious reserve. She had hoped to see the Count Sigismond come from Basle to Paris, and give his talents to the work of restoring the gospel in France. He was delaying for the king to send him an invitation.

One day Margaret took courage, and asked her brother to invite the Count; he was not ready. He knew Count Sigismond well, and thought his gospel principles exaggerated. Besides, if there was to be any change in France, he meant to make it alone. And what would the pope and the emperor say, if the count were in Paris, preaching at the court, in the churches, and in the open air perhaps? He did not fully tell his sister what he would do, but to her suggestions he replied, "Not yet," and she turned away bitterly disappointed.

Again she pleaded her cause. "I do not care for that man," said Francis, sharply. This was not true. He cared for him when he wanted him. When he needed three thousand soldiers, then it was "my very dear and beloved cousin of Hohenlohe," highly esteemed for "his loyalty and valour, his nearness of lineage, love and charity." But where the gospel was concerned it was quite a different affair. The usual "Not yet," was again heard. The Count Sigismond did not come to France.

Thus one of Margaret's plans failed. But she had another. The king must call back the exiles, and open the prisons. Already had she entreated for one sufferer, saying to the king, "If you do not interfere, Berquin is a dead man." He did interpose, and wrote from Spain that he would make the first president answerable for Berquin's life, if he dared to condemn him. The president halted, the monks hung their heads, and Beda and his pack "were nigh bursting with vexation." And now the returned king resolved to save Berquin from "the claws of Beda's faction." He said to the parliament, only a few days after his return, "I will not suffer the person or the goods of this gentleman to be injured. I will inquire into the matter myself." The king sent his officers to take this Christian captive from his prison, and put him into a more commodious chamber. They were still to keep watch over him, but he should be well treated. He took courage, and set about forming plans for the triumph of the truth.

Good news for Strasburg; the king was inquiring into matters himself; he was making the prisoners more comfortable; he was listening to the importunate Margaret; he was despising the monks and vexing Beda, and now one step more, and the exiles would be permitted to return to France. One day the duchess urged him to put an end to the cruel exile of her friends. He granted it. The glad tidings went to Strasburg, and France was open to her refugees. Nay, not all of them. There was one exception, unaccountable to us, and mysterious in the providence of God. This we shall see to be the earnest William Farel.

What joy! the aged Lefevre, the fervent Roussel, are recalled with honour. These are nearly the words of Erasmus, who did not regard the two men as "Lutherans," nor so far gone out of the old Romish church as Farel. The Strasburgers bade them farewell with tears, and they took the road to France, happy that they were going to the land of their birth, one to die there, and the other to preach the new life. Others followed; all believed that the new times were come.

Lefevre and Roussel hastened to their protectress. Margaret received them kindly, and lodged them in the castle of Angoulême, where she was born, on that smiling hill near "her softly flowing Charente." She had a project in her mind. It was to make Blois, which had been the favourite residence of the house of Valois, a refuge for the persecuted, and a strong-hold of the gospel. The first of June Roussel went to this city, built about a hundred miles south-east of Paris. Lefevre joined him there on the last of the month. One was the eloquent court-preacher; the other was the teacher of the king's third son, and the keeper of the castle library. Chapelain, the physician of the duchess, and Cop, who was too near the truth to remain a doctor in the Sorbonne, were also there. All of them felt grateful to Francis I., and were contriving means to impart "something of Christianity to the most Christian king," which was in truth very necessary both for him and the people.

The amiable Peter Toussaint was still in the horrid den into which the cruel abbot of St. Anthony had thrust him. His host at Basle had not sent the books which the treacherous priest had forced him to order; no doubt the man saw through the trick, and knew in whose hands the life of his young friend was placed. Margaret heard of him through such men as the merchant Vaugris, who had interceded in vain for his release. She went to the king, as persistent as ever, and gained her suit. In July 1526 the order came for his deliverance. The officers charged with this pleasing task went down into the gloomy dungeon, and raised out of his stifling den, a young man, thin, weak, and pale as a faded flower. His eyes were pained by the light of day, and his mind seemed bewildered with joy. He was as much less than the Toussaint of former days as a merciless tormentor could make him.

At first he knew not where to go. Hoping for some pity, he applied to certain old acquaintances, but they were afraid to shelter a heretic who had barely escaped the stake. He had not Berquin's energy; his delicate sensitive nature needed a support, and in the free air and the wide world, he was almost as much alone as in a dungeon. "Ah," he exclaimed, "God our heavenly Father has delivered me, in a wonderful manner from the hands of the tyrants; but alas! what is to become of me? The world is mad, and it spurns the rising gospel of Jesus Christ!"

"The duchess of Alençon alone can protect you," said some timid and well-meaning friends. "There is no asylum for you, but at her court. Make application to a princess, who welcomes with so much generosity, all the friends of learning and of the gospel; and profit by your residence at her court, to investigate closely the wind that blows in those elevated regions." Toussaint laid hold of such a hope. Timid as he was he went to Paris, under an assumed name.

Margaret was not there, but was soon expected. He kept himself closely concealed. When she arrived he asked permission to see her alone; she received him with great kindness. What an exchange! Just from one of the lowest dungeons, and snatched as a lamb from the claws of a monster, but now in the palace of St. Germain, and in favour with the most elegant and brilliant personage who lent her grace to the court. What charmed him most was her piety.

"The most illustrious duchess of Alençon," he wrote to Œcolampadius, "has received me with as much kindness as if I had been a prince or the person who was dearest to her. I hope that the gospel will soon reign in France."

The duchess was touched with the faith of the young evangelist. She could share in his hopes and sympathize in his fears. She invited him to come again the next day. He went, and he went yet again. They had long conversations.

"God by the light of his word," said he, "must illumine the world, and by the breath of his Spirit must transform all hearts."

"It is the only thing that I desire," she replied, believing in the final victory of truth. "It is not only myself that longs for this triumph. Even the king wishes for it. . . . The king is coming to Paris to secure the progress of the gospel; if, at least, the war does not prevent him." Not the war, but the wickedness in high places, and the fear of the Romish powers, pope, Sorbonne and all, were to prevent him. Toussaint learned that much of the piety displayed at the court was a mere pretence for the sake of gaining office. When with Margaret, the priests who were applicants for favours, were almost reformers: when with some scoffing noble they threw off the mask and were not even good Romanists. "Alas!" wrote he, "they speak well of Jesus Christ with those who speak well of him; but with those who blaspheme, they blaspheme also." What could be expected of Francis I., who lent his ear to such priests and courtiers? His sister saw only his best face.

Toussaint had another joy. Lefevre and Roussel came to Paris. Young, impetuous, and full of respect for them, he hastened to tell them of his vexations, and wished them to unmask these hypocrites, and preach the gospel in this perverse court.

"Patience," said the two scholars, each rather temporizing in his disposition. "Patience; do not let us spoil anything; the time is not yet come."

Toussaint burst into tears. "I cannot restrain my tears,"

said he. Perhaps he wished that Farel was there. "Yes, be wise after your fashion; wait, put off, dissemble as much as you please; you will acknowledge, however, at last, that it is impossible to preach the gospel without bearing the cross." These words, from an honest heart, reveal one of the dividing lines between the reformers of France. One party, clustering about the duchess, would not do anything to injure the old fallen church; the other would leave the Romish church and seek a new one—or, rather, return to that one which had existed long before Rome introduced her perversions. Toussaint had already cast his lot with the thorough reformers.

He said, plainly, to Margaret,—"Lefevre is wanting in courage; may God strengthen and support him." She did her utmost to keep the young evangelist at her court. She offered him great advantages, and advised him to be more moderate. She wished for men who would exhibit a Christian heart and life, but who would not break with the church. He repelled all these gracious advances. He was sick of the court air. Admiration gave way to disgust. "I despise these magnificent offers," said he. "I detest the court more than any one has done. Farewell to it."

The cardinal of Lorraine appeared now as his friend. He advised Toussaint to be cautious, for, as a heretic, he was never secure of his life. But his courage rose with the perils of his situation. He requested Farel to address him without any concealment, since he was not ashamed of his own name, nor of his correspondence, nor afraid of the consequences of its being known. Since no one else had invited Farel to France, he did it, assuring him of protection among certain friends in Paris. But Farel wished an invitation from a higher authority.

Margaret begged him not to leave France, and commended

Toussaint to one of her friends, Madame de Centraigues, a noble lady, who abounded in charity for the persecuted evangelists, and gave them a home in her chateau of Malesherbes, in the Orleans district. He, fearing that a terrible struggle was coming, besought his friends to pray that France would show herself worthy of the word of God. He also prayed that the Lord would send to this people a teacher to lead them in the true paths of life, and went to his new home, to wait there for more favourable days.

Who would be the reformer of France? Not Lefevre, for he was old, timid, and wished not to separate from the Romish church. Not Roussel, for he dare not always go as far as his convictions prompted him. "Alas," he wrote to Farel, "there are many gospel truths, one-half of which I am obliged to conceal." He was just the man for the duchess; he would advance the Christian life without touching the institutions of the church.

Would it be Berquin? We left him in a comfortable chamber of his prison, forming large plans for the conquests of the truth. Margaret had not dared to visit him, but she tried to send him a few words of good cheer. It was, perhaps, for him that she wrote the "Complaints of the Prisoner," in which he thus addresses his Lord,—

"But yet where'er my prison be,
  Its gates can never keep out Thee,
  For instant where I am, Thou art with me."

She did not rest here; she was unwearied in her petitions to the king. The Romish party knew that if Berquin was free, he would deal hard blows, which they could not resist, and they did all they could to prevent the bolt from being drawn. But Margaret had a hand on that prison bolt, and, at length, in

November, 1526, he left his guarded chamber to enter upon the plans he had formed for rescuing France from the hands of the pope. He was then thirty-five years of age, pure in his life, charming in his character, devoted to study, flaming with zeal, and indomitable in his energy. His enemies feared him; Beda said to himself that Berquin would be the Luther of France.

But Berquin could not advance a great system of gospel-truth. He could preach duties, but could not raise up a fortress of doctrines into which the trembling might flee and be safe. His work was to resist Beda and the "three thousand monks" that were in him, and to die such a noble martyr that one of the executioners would say publicly, to the great vexation of the judges,—"No better Christian has died for a hundred years than Berquin."

Was the reformer of France to be Farel? He was then her greatest light. Toussaint was waiting for him to appear, and let us see how it was that this most fervent, most eloquent, most intrepid and persevering of the French reformers before Calvin, came not back to his own country, but went to Switzerland, to set the western Alps on fire.

When the king recalled the other exiles Farel was left behind. He saw his friends returning to their country, wondered why he must remain alone in exile, and, overwhelmed with sorrow, cried to God for resignation. He still remained at Strasburg, with one foot on the border, waiting for a call, but the order did not come. The king and his sister did not wish so bold a man in the land. They were afraid of him. The court had no taste for his style of preaching; they "wished for a softened and perfumed gospel in France."

There were Christians in the land, who saw that the men at Margaret's court would stop half way in the work, and accomplish nothing permanent. In their view, France needed a man of artless nature, fearless spirit, powerful eloquence, and ability to give a new impulse to the work which Lefevre had begun. They thought of Farel, but his coming seemed to depend upon the duchess. Roussel knew her fears. He knew that Farel would be a preacher and not a courtier, and he would never agree with her policy. Still the noble and devout Roussel felt that such a man was greatly needed, and he tried to open the way for him to put forth his mighty labours in some of the provinces. "I will obtain the means of providing for all your wants," he wrote on the 27th of August, 1526, "until the Lord gives you an entrance, at last, among us."

This, also, was Farel's earnest desire. He was not then invited to Switzerland. His country possessed his heart; day and night his eyes were turned toward the gates which were so strangely shut against him; he went up and knocked. None came to open them. He was depressed and he exclaimed, "Oh! if the Lord would but open a way for me to return and labour in France!" Suddenly there was a prospect that his greatest wishes would be realized.

On the day of a grand reception at court, the two sons of Prince Robert de la Marche came to pay their respects to the king's sister. Margaret, ever intent on winning souls, said to Roussel, her eyes indicating the persons meant,

"Speak to those two young princes; seize I pray, this opportunity of advancing the cause of Jesus Christ."

"I will do so," replied the willing chaplain. He approached the young noblemen, and began to converse about the gospel. They showed no astonishment, but listened with a lively interest. Finding that they were not strangers to the good word, he urged them to extend the truth among their subjects.

12 *

They gave their fullest assent to his words, but felt that they were too weak for the task of making known the gospel. Roussel now thought he had found a field for the pining exile, and he said to the young nobles, "I know of but one man fitted for such a great work: he is William Farel. Christ has given him an extraordinary talent for making known the riches of his glory. Invite him."

"We desire it still more than you," said the young princes. "Our father and we will open our arms to him. He shall be to us as a son, a brother, and a father. Let him fear nothing; he shall live with us; yes, in our own palace. All whom he will meet there are the friends of Jesus Christ. We ourselves will be there to receive him. Only bid him make haste; let him come before next Lent."

"I promise you that he shall," replied Roussel, and he began to think how he should lay all this before Farel. Toussaint wrote and added his entreaties; "Never has any news caused me more joy; hasten thither as fast as you can."

Thus was a plan laid for Farel to come into almost the centre of France. So confident were the young princes of his coming, that they undertook to set up a printing establishment in order that he might circulate the truth by means of the press, not only in La Marche, but throughout the kingdom.

"Farel would have been the man fitted for this work," says D'Aubigne. "He was one of those whose simple, serious, earnest tones carry away the masses. His voice of thunder made his hearers tremble. The strength of his convictions created faith in their souls; the fervour of his prayers raised them to heaven. When they listened to him, 'they felt,' as Calvin says, 'not merely a few light stings, but they were wounded and pierced to the heart; and hypocrisy was dragged from those wonderful and more than tortuous hiding-places which lie deep in the heart of man.' He pulled down and built up with equal energy. He was not only a minister of the word; he was a bishop also. He was able to discern the young men who were fitted to wield the weapons of the gospel, and to direct them in the great war of the age. Farel never attacked a place, however difficult of access, which he did not take. Such was the man then called into France, and who seemed destined to be her reformer." The letters of Roussel and Toussaint were on the way; but already Farel had another invitation before him. Let us see whence it came.

On the shield of an ancient Swiss city was the figure of a bear,* and the wits called its people the "bears of Berne." It was the centre of a little republic, whose freemen caught the spirit of the great awakening, and as early as 1518 held out attractions to literary men. Berne, whose soldiers had won renown, must have its scholars as well as Basle and Zurich. The next year appeared among them a young man of twenty-one, named Berthold Haller, who had been a fellow-student with Melancthon. Haller won the hearts of the people and soon became the preacher of the cathedral. The gospel which Zwingle was

---

* The old Germans called a bear a "bern," and for centuries he has been the favourite of all pets in that city. His image is still upon sign-posts, fountains, and public buildings. Living specimens were kept in the town at the public expense, and when the French army, in 1798, carried the bears captive to the gardens of Paris, the people lamented their loss. But when the ancient order of things was restored, one of the first cares of the citizens was to replace their ancient pensioners, and secure for them an endowment. The visitor who does not pay his respects to the bears may expect to be regarded as very disrespectful by the Bernese. They are "the lions" of the city.—*Murray's Handbook for Switzerland.*

teaching came to the city, and Haller examined it, believed, and began to declare it. But the "bears" were not lambs, willing to be led in the new pastures of truth, without making enough resistance to discourage the meek and timid shepherd. He wished to see Zwingle and talk to him as a son to a father. So, taking with him his burden of trials, he paid a visit to Zurich. He was kindly received by this "first of the reformers," whose gentleness imparted a charm to his manners. Zwingle was pleased with this young man of about twenty-eight years, tall, artless, candid and diffident, but who gave fair promise of being the reformer of Berne.

"My soul is overwhelmed," said Haller one day; "I cannot support such unjust treatment. I am determined to resign my pulpit and retire to Basle, to employ myself entirely, in Wittembach's society, with the study of sacred learning." This desire for study was strong in the first reformers.

"Alas!" replied Zwingle, "and I too feel discouragement creep over me, when I see myself unjustly assailed; but Christ awakens my conscience by the terrible stimulus of his terrors and promises. He alarms me by saying, 'Whosoever shall be ashamed of me before men, of him shall I be ashamed before my Father.' He restores me to tranquillity by adding, 'Whosoever shall confess me before men, him also will I confess before my Father.' Oh my dear Berthold, take courage! Our names are written in imperishable characters in the annals of the citizens on high. I am ready to die for Christ. Oh, that your fierce bears would hear the gospel; then they would grow tame. But you must undertake this duty with great gentleness, lest they should turn round furiously and rend you in pieces."

Haller took courage, went home, laboured gently, and then

wrote to his friend, "My soul has awakened from its slumber. I must preach the gospel. Jesus Christ must be restored to this city, whence he has been exiled so long. "The timid young preacher rushed," as Zwingle described it, "into the midst of the savage bears, who, grinding their teeth, sought to devour him."

The cause gained strength as the years passed, and Haller declared, in confident hope,—"Unless God's anger be turned against us, it is not possible for the word of God to be banished from the city, for the Bernese are hungering after it."

The Bernese had certain districts in Roman Switzerland, where the people spoke the French language, and a French missionary was needed. Farel was the man to carry the gospel into these new regions, and Haller gave him the most urgent invitation. What should Farel do? France was shut; no one opened its gates; not a word yet from thence inviting him to return. France had rejected him. Switzerland was open; a voice was calling him thither; it must be the voice of God, who took Paul away from the Asia in which he proposed to labour, and sent him over into Macedonia. He could not hesitate. He left Strasburg on foot in December, grieved as he cast an eye toward his native land that now disowned her son, but cheered as the prospects of success in new regions rose upon his vision. He was on the road when the messenger of Toussaint and Roussel arrived at Strasburg. It was too late. His friends sent the letters on to Berne; but even there they did not overtake him. In his zeal he had made haste to enter upon his new field. In a little Alpine village he had fully settled down, when he received the invitation of the lords of La Marche. Might he not even then return? Should he put aside the call of the lords of Berne, and the call of God's providence, and obey the voice of the young princes? In his soul there was a fierce struggle. He was only a lowly school-master in a little village of the Alps. In France he might be a reformer in a great field, using princes in pushing on the good work, perhaps enlisting the king, and making the throne, the court, the capital, a centre of power on the side of the gospel. If this invitation had only reached him at Strasburg! But, no! It was too late. The hand of God had drawn him away for some purpose yet to be disclosed. He will remain at the humble desk in his little school, and have an experience which invites our further attention.

Thus France lost the reformer whom many Christians thought had been raised up for her deliverance. But God had wisely planned these events. Farel would have been a powerful evangelist; but he was too much a soldier and too little a scholar for that great nation. He was a general who could urge forward a movement against error, but not the guide who could lead men to the full system of truth contained in the Bible. A greater than Farel was about to appear, who would combine all the excellencies of his predecessors in the French reformation. He was then a student of seventeen, in the college of La Marche, at Paris, working his way, as Farel had done, into the clear light of the gospel. His was that great name—John Calvin. Farel knew him not; but it was yet to be the work of this Alpine school-master to lay the foundation in Roman Switzerland, to open the gates of Geneva, and be the forerunner of Calvin, whose voice should shake the world and roll on through the centuries.

"O Lord, I know that the way of man is not in himself; it is not in man that walketh to direct his steps." "The steps of a good man are ordered by the Lord, and he delighteth in his way. Though he fall, he shall not be utterly cast down; for the Lord upholdeth him with his hand." What was true of Jeremiah and David was to be true of William Farel, who had passed the delicate turning-point in his eventful life.

CHAPTER X.

THE ALPINE SCHOOL-MASTER.

(1527–1528.)

ON the banks of the "Great Water," a narrow stream that falls in thunder from the rugged glaciers of the Diablerets, lies the small town of Aigle,* (Ælen,) about ten miles from Villeneuve, at the upper end of Lake Leman. A rail-road now passes through it, and, from the cars, at this point, one may see the sublime Dent du Midi rising on the south, and the proud Dent de Morcles on the north, both crowned with snow; and between them, a quiet, smiling valley, whose picture will not soon fade from his memory. There the laurel blooms beside the most exquisite grapes; and, yet, hanging almost above them, are vast glaciers, near to which, in summer, the shepherds lead their flocks for pasture. If this be his first gate of entrance, the traveller begins to think that he is amid the grandeur of Switzerland.

To this small town, in December, 1526, a man was making his way, on foot and in the rain. He wished to conceal his name, for he was one whom persecution had made an exile from France. He was of middle stature, with red beard, quick eyes, fearless face, and the step of a native mountaineer. If he met any of the villagers, he was likely to give them the whole road, and speak kindly to them in purer French than they employed; but,

---

* The old Latin Aquilea, now containing about 1650 inhabitants.

if he met a haughty priest, he was ready to claim his full share of the path, and look back at him with indignation after he had passed. The wonder is that he did not tear down some of the crosses along the way, and dash in pieces the images that exacted devotion from the superstitious traveller.

With him walked a single friend. Night closed around them, and the rain fell heavy and cold. They lost their path, a very dangerous thing for Alpine travellers on whom the snow might be falling before morning. Drenched and chilled, they sat down almost in despair. "Ah!" said the chief one, "God, by showing me my helplessness in these little things, has willed to teach me how weak I am in the greatest, without Jesus Christ."

"It is no little thing to be lost," we imagine the other replying. "We shall perish if we stay here."

"Let us perish then trying to find our way." Then rising, they bent forward on their dark journey, feeling for stepping places among the rocks, plunging through bogs, wading through the waters, crossing vineyards, fields, hills, forests and valleys, and, at length, dripping with rain and covered with mud, they reached the village of Aigle.

In this desolate night the exile received a new baptism. His natural energy was somewhat softened. He was so subdued that he felt more timidity than he needed, and anxious to be wise, he overstepped his mark. He assumed a new name, hoping, as he afterwards said, "by pious frauds to circumvent the old serpent that was hissing around him." He represented himself to be a school-master—Ursinus—and he waited for a door to be opened that he might appear as a reformer.

He looked about upon the people, and saw ignorance and degradation as the fruits of Romanism. The priests fleeced the flocks, and then left them to be pastured by curates who played the hireling, and only confirmed the people in their rudeness and turbulence. The best way to bring the priests into watchfulness was to teach the villagers the gospel. Awaken thought among them, and the jealous clergy would rush to the spot to smother it. He cared not, however, how far they kept away from the field.

Ursinus gathered the children and began his work with no fixed salary. His modest lessons were mingled with new and strange doctrines. His scholars wondered when he told them of the good book and the great God who gave it; the true cross and the Lord of glory who died upon it. They had something to believe, to tell, to expand their minds and elevate their souls. The teacher was encouraged; by feeding the Saviour's lambs, he would soon have sheep to feed.

When the day's work was done, Master Ursinus left the school-room and the primers, and took refuge in his poorly furnished lodging-place. It became a palace, for the Bible was the light thereof. He applied himself, with absorbing interest, to the Greek and Hebrew Scriptures, and the few works of learned theologians that he had brought with him. The debate between Luther and Zwingle was still going on. He examined anew the entire ground on which they wrestled, and asked to which of these champions he should attach himself. The case was decided; he clung to the Zurich reformer.

Master Ursinus went a step farther in his work. He cautiously set about teaching the parents as well as the children. He showed them that purgatory was a mere invention, there was no such place. Then he exposed the delusion practised in the invocation of the saints. "As for the pope, he is nothing," said he, "or almost nothing in these parts; and as for the priests, if they annoy the people with that nonsense, which Erasmus knows so well how to turn into ridicule, that is enough for them."

Thus he went on teaching in a quiet way for some months. A flock gathered around him, loving the good man, who did more for them than any one had dreamed of doing before. If they were puzzled by the thought that one so great should come among them in their out of the way corner, it was all explained by his simple goodness of heart. And he told them of Him who condescended from heaven to earth; from the throne to a manger; from the crown to the cross; and they understood and believed. He thought the looked-for moment had come, and he might tell them who he was, and what was his mission.

"I am William Farel, minister of God," said he one day. The villagers thought none the more nor any the less of him for that. It was to them like any other unheard-of name. But the priests and magistrates were in amazement and terror. They had heard of William Farel. They now saw among them that very man whose name had already become so fearful. They dared not do anything but let him have his way. Nor did he consult with flesh and blood. He had quietly taken the tower; now he would take the town by a bold movement. He ascended the pulpit, and openly preached Jesus Christ to the astonished multitude. The work of Ursinus* was over; Farel was himself again.

The council of Berne, in the month of March, commissioned

---

* Ursinus from *ursa*, the bear; an allusion to the fact that he came as a Bernese. Whether he went from Basle to Berne and then conferred with Haller and the lords of that city does not appear. It seems that he took no commission with him; if so, he did not show it, or thought that the gospel preacher needed no other commission than that of Christ.

Farel to explain the Holy Scriptures to the people of Aigle and its neighbourhood, and to preach until the incumbent of the benefices, Nicolas Von Diesbach, should appoint a suitable minister, a thing that Nicolas was not likely to do. At the same time a fresh order was issued against the immorality of the clergy and laity, and measures were taken to punish offenders. This new order was galling to the priests, who had lived so long in the freest and loosest way that they could not bear to be restrained. They saw that Farel would have the law on his side, and become bolder than before in attacking the general vices and superstitions. The rich and lazy incumbents, with the poor and ignorant curates, were the first to cry out. "If this man continues preaching," they said one to another, "it is all over with our benefices and our church."

The civil power also opposed this first preaching of the pure gospel in these regions. The bailiff of Aigle, and Jacques de Roverea, the governor of the four parishes, Aigle, Bex, Ollon, and the Ormond valleys, felt proud of their "brief authority." They would not support their Bernese lords, nor accept the minister they had sent. They took the side of the priests, and said,—"The emperor is about to declare war against all innovators. A great army will shortly arrive from Spain, and assist the Arch-duke Ferdinand."

Farel stood firm, and fearlessly went on in his work, avoiding to excite opposition by imprudent vehemence, or by exposing too many of the errors of Romanism. He boldly declared the truth, having patience with the rude and ignorant people. This enraged the bailiff and the governor. They forbade "the heretic" to give any kind of instruction, whether as minister or school-master. Thus they hoped to starve him out or send him away. But they did not know their man, nor their excellencies of Berne. Great was the displeasure of the Bernese lords when they learned what had been done. They sent a new decree, dated July 3d, and ordered it to be posted on the doors of all the churches in the four parishes. The people read that "all the officers of the state must allow the very learned William Farel to preach publicly the doctrines of the Lord."

This new proclamation was the signal for a revolt. On the 25th of July great crowds assembled at Aigle, at Bex, at Ollon, and in the Ormonds, crying out,—"No more submission to Berne! Down with Farel!" From words they soon proceeded to riots. At Aigle they were headed by the fiery bailiff, and they tore down the edict, and prepared to fall upon the reformed people. Farel was soon summoned by his friends, who resolved to defend him. The firm countenances of the Christian converts checked the rioters, and they dispersed. Farel left the town for a few days, and, like a general who flanks an enemy, he entered upon a new movement.

The traveller, who comes from Geneva in a steamer to Lausanne, will expect to find the beautifully situated capital of Vaud repay him for his visit. He may be puzzled by its crooked streets and wearied with its three hills, but he will be interested in its history and its antiquities, especially in the cathedral, founded about the year one thousand. If Farel's voice of thunder could have been heard therein, he would have started up a nest of as dissolute canons and priests as all Rome could furnish. Although they had a bishop over them, they were drunk at the inns, they gambled in public, they fought in the churches, they kept the vilest company, they were fathers without being husbands, and sent their children out to beg bread; they disguised themselves as soldiers, and came down from the cathedral-hill at night, roamed the streets with swords in their hands, and surprised, wounded, and sometimes even killed worthy citizens. Yet they were "ministers of the Virgin," whose image drew hosts of pilgrims to the great church. There was a power in that city which aimed to keep the whole country at the feet of the pope. Even the trumpet-voice of Farel could not have prevailed in the streets of Lausanne. He knew it, and did not propose thus to storm the strong-hold.

A more quiet way showed itself. The bishop had a chaplain named Natalis Galeotto, a man of elevated rank and the most polished manners. He was fond of learning and of learned men, but yet very zealous about fasts and the rites of the church. Farel thought that, if this man could be gained over to the gospel, Lausanne, "slumbering at the foot of its steeples," and amid the noise of its monks, would perhaps awaken, and all the country with it. True, he had denounced Farel's zeal against fasts and formalities, as absolutely immoral; but yet there was some hope that a man of his intelligence and character might be won to a purer faith.

Farel wrote to Natalis. He modestly introduced himself and gave some account of his former struggles, and the means by which he had found the true light. He urged the gospel upon the chaplain, and entreated him to use well his talents, to warn the wicked, to lose no time in publishing the praises of God, and to "preach Christ as our great pattern, both in speaking and acting." Then he referred to the evils which were best known, and which none could deny. "Alas! alas! religion is now little better than an empty mockery, since people who think only of their appetites are the kings of the church." But Natalis made no reply.

Again Farel wrote, urging upon him "that we should renounce everything for Christ's sake, even our dearest friends and relatives," if they were in the way. "No loss, trial, or affliction should be shunned on this account, and the Christian ought to go wherever the Lord calls him, though the whole world should rise up against him." Farel might properly give this advice; he was following it himself. Then, perhaps, referring to some late conduct of Natalis, he wrote,—"Knock, cry out with all your might, redouble your attacks upon our Lord." But still Natalis kept silence. He would not come out of his entrenchments.

The third time Farel returned to the charge. He urged that "the manifestation of the love of God to men through Christ ought to excite every one to gratitude." He dwelt still longer upon the doctrines which he believed, and called upon Natalis to explain his own views with the same frankness, to agree with what he considered true, and point out what was erroneous. The chaplain ordered his secretary to break the silence.

The reply showed no signs of a friendly disposition, but was full of abuse. The writer asserted his own belief in all the Romish observances, and reproached Farel for undervaluing them. To this the reformer made a calm reply. The correspondence came to an end. If it did not secure its object, it proved the union of gentleness and energy in a man too often supposed to have been made of only explosive materials. The depth of his piety was evinced by the sufferings he endured; and, if his requirements from others were strict, they were no stricter than his own example enforced. For a time Lausanne was shut against him.

After this skirmish with a priest, came a face to face conflict with a monk. A mendicant friar, who did not dare to oppose the reformer at Aigle, crept slyly into the village of Noville, built where the Rhone pours its waters into the Lake of Geneva.

The friar went into the pulpit and made his attack upon Farel. He exclaimed,—"It is the devil himself, who preaches by the mouth of this minister, and all those who listen to him will be damned." Having thus vented his feelings he felt courageous enough to go back to Aigle. He did not, however, propose to appear there against Farel, whose powerful eloquence terrified him. There was a greater attraction than a combat with the weapons of truth. With a meek and humble look he went to beg, in behalf of his convent, a few barrels of the most delicious wine in all Switzerland!

He had not walked very far into the town before he met the minister whom Berne was resolved to keep in the field. At this sight he trembled in every limb. There was no mob of priests now in the streets to drive away the man of fiery eyes and fearful voice. Farel advanced and in a friendly tone asked,—

"Did you preach against me at Noville, saying that the devil spoke through me?"

"I did," whispered the monk in Farel's ear, not wishing to attract public attention.

"Would the devil preach the gospel, and will those who listen to it be damned?"

"Certainly not."

"Then, why have you publicly spoken against me in such terms? I request that you will point out and prove the errors which I am charged with preaching; for I would rather die than teach false doctrine to the poor people, whom Christ has redeemed by his blood. May the Lord never permit me to preach any doctrine that he does not approve."

"I have heard say that you are a heretic, and that you mislead the people by your doctrine," answered the priest, who would have been glad to turn away and look after the wine.

"That is not enough," replied Farel; "you must make good what you said in your sermon, for I am ready to stake my life in defence of my doctrine."*

The monk now began to bluster, and said, angrily,—"What have I preached against you? Who has heard it? I am not come hither to dispute with you, but to collect alms. You ought to know best whether you have preached sound or erroneous doctrine."

Farel then represented to him that the truth was of the utmost importance, and that he was in a place where he would be certain of meeting with justice. "If you have spoken the truth," said he, "I cannot injure you. If you are right you should defend your sermon. If you have misled the people you should lead them back to the true path."

"You are the false teacher; you mislead the people," said the friar, growing very uneasy and starting down street as if he would shake off his undesirable companion, and "turning now this way, now that, like a troubled conscience." A few citizens gathered to the spot, and Farel knew them.

"You see this fine father," said the reformer, pointing to the monk. "He has said from the pulpit that I preach nothing but lies, and that you will perish if you listen to me."

"Prove what I said," cried the friar in a passion, and still trying to move away. "Where are your witnesses?"

"The Omniscient One is my witness. Come, now prove your assertions."

---

* This was no empty boast; it was a matter of conscience and true fortitude. In a later letter Farel wrote,—"I must be prepared to suffer death if I should teach anything contrary to the doctrine of piety. I should be most worthy of any punishment whatever, if I should seduce any one from the faith and doctrine of Christ."

Then the monk, blushing and stammering, began to speak of the offerings of the faithful (the precious wine of Yvorne, for instance, that he came to beg!) and he said that Farel had opposed them. The crowd increased. The reformer, who only sought for an opportunity to proclaim the true worship of God, exclaimed with his loud voice, "It is no man's business to ordain any other way of serving God than that which he has commanded. Let us worship God alone in spirit and in truth; the true offerings are a broken and a contrite heart."

The people looked intently upon the two actors in this scene, the monk with his wallet, and the reformer with his glistening eye. When the friar heard Farel say that there was a better worship than the holy Roman church prescribed, he turned pale and flush by turns, trembled and seemed quite out of his senses. At last, raising his hood and taking off his cap, he flung it on the ground and trampled it under foot, and cried out, "I wonder that the earth does not open and swallow us up!"

"Listen to him as he has listened to you," said one of the by-standers, as he took the monk by the sleeve.

The monk now ceased to stamp on his cap, and to "bawl like one out of his wits," and he seemed to himself already half dead with fright. Venting his wrath against him who held his sleeve, he said, "Thou art excommunicated, and dost thou lay hands on me." "What!" replied the villager, "are all excommunicated who touch thy cowl? Hast thou a different God? or art thou baptized into a different name? Art thou not to be spoken to?"

The friar was silent, although furious; and the little town was in an uproar. Farel gave the poor wine-beggar some good advice, while he also took advantage of the crowd to declare some of the most solemn truths of the gospel. It was, probably, his first chance since the cry, "down with Farel," had been raised in those streets and perhaps by those very people who now looked on amazed and confused. At length a magistrate appeared, ordered the monk and Farel to follow him, and he shut them up in prison, "one in one tower, and one in another."

On the Saturday morning, Farel was brought to the castle, where the court was assembled, with the monk already before them. He reminded his judges that they were sitting in God's stead, and that they should not have respect to persons or rank. He was willing to be punished if he had preached anything contrary to the word of God. He wished to obey the lawful authorities, but as for this friar, "let him make good his charges, or if he cannot, let the people hear the gospel." The violence of the monk was over. He was now ready to make matters up as best he could. He fell on his knees in alarm.

"My lords," said he, "I entreat forgiveness of you and of God. And Magister Farel, (turning to him) what I preached against you was grounded on false reports. I have found you to be a good man, and your doctrine good, and I am prepared to take back my words."

"My friend and brother," said Farel with deep emotion, "do not ask forgiveness of me, for I am a poor sinner like other men; I put my trust in Jesus. Before I saw you I had forgiven you as well as others who have spoken against me and the gospel. I have prayed to God both for them and for you."

One of the lords of Berne came up at this time, and the friar, imagining that he was on the brink of martyrdom, began to wring his hands, and to turn now to the Bernese councillor, and now to the court, and then to Farel, crying, "Pardon, pardon."

"Ask pardon of our Saviour," said the reformer, who begged that the monk might not be punished any farther. The gospel was now defended, and that was all he wished. He hoped that neither the monk, nor any of his brethren, would henceforth say anything behind him which they could not prove before his face.

"Come to-morrow and hear the minister's sermon," said the Bernese lord to the friar. "If he appears to you to preach the truth, you shall confess it openly before all; if not, you will declare your opinion. Give us your hand in this promise."

The monk held out his hand and the judges retired. But he made the best of his Saturday, and was not to be found on the Sabbath. Farel wrote the account of the affair,* closing thus,—"Then the friar went away, and I have not seen him since, and no promises or oaths were able to make him stay."

This was much more than a private and personal strife. It was a contest between truth and error, between Romanism and the Reformation. The future success of the gospel seemed to hinge on the triumph of the monk or of the minister. The good cause won the day. French Switzerland was to have the word of God.

The preaching of Farel brought back the priests to the parishes, for their craft was in danger. And, as if they were not enough against one lonely reformer, certain Romish agents came to their aid from Savoy and Valais. They assembled the people, they discussed measures which were dangerous and revolutionary; but they took care not to meet Farel in debating

* For the benefit of the nuns of St. Clara, at Vevey, whom the monks often visited. They thus learned something more of the truth of religion from Farel's letter than they were likely to receive in any other way. After the triumph of the gospel in this region, they removed their convent to a more monkish district.

ten theses, which a large council of reformers at Berne had appointed him to defend. He was fresh from this conference, held January, 1528, where he had met several of the distinguished divines in Zurich, Basle, and Strasburg. He was ready for the priests, being armed with an ordinance which declared "that the return to the Scriptural faith and the free use of the Bible was a right that belonged to the people, and that the churches of the cantons should follow the example of Berne." But the agents of Rome were afraid of arguments. Their only hope was in outward resistance. Berne had no business to sanction the late innovations, and "the bears" would find the world at war against them! They would treat Farel only with slander, ridicule, threats, and violence; they would set at naught the decrees of those who sent him. The proclamations were torn down from the church doors. Troops of citizens paraded the streets. The drum was beaten to rouse the populace against the reformer. Sedition and riot everywhere prevailed.

Farel knew what was threatened, but he was fearless in duty. On the first Sabbath after his return, February 16, he went into the pulpit and began to preach, having, probably, a Bernese senator present to secure him a peaceful hearing. Riotous bands collected about the gates of the church, uttered savage yells, raised their hands in tumult, and compelled the minister to break off in his sermon. The papal party were carrying matters too far, and their noise should be heard across the mountains. They should hear again from Berne. The senate discussed the late events, and ordered that Farel should not be molested in his preaching. Envoys came and called a meeting of the four parishes. Bex declared for the reform. Aigle, less decidedly followed the example. Ollon left the case with the women; the peasants did not dare to maltreat Farel; they, however, excited their wives to rush upon him and beat him with their fulling-clubs. The parish of the Ormonds felt calm and proud at the foot of its glaciers, and signalized itself by resistance. The senators were patient with the ignorant people of these last two parishes, and gave them more time to decide upon their course. But, meanwhile, they must hear the word of God, and allow no one to speak from their pulpits against the late orders. And Farel must superintend the preaching.

At Ollon there was no little disorder. While Farel was preaching, one Jajod fell upon him, and roused others to join in the assault. The commission of senators were surprised at this outrage. They ordered the governor to arrest the rioters and to protect the preacher. The people must hear his side as well as that of the priests, and thus be able to come to a fairer decision. Farel sent one of his helpers into the field. But the inhabitants would not hear him.

Claude, one of Farel's co-workers, went to the Ormonds. When preaching there one day, with great animation, he was suddenly disturbed by the ringing of the bells, "whose noise was such that one might have said all hell was pulling at them." At another time the shepherds rushed down the mountains like an avalanche, and fell upon the church, crying furiously,—"Let us only find these sacrilegious wretches who tear down our altars, and we will hang them, we will cut off their heads, we will burn them, we will throw their ashes into the 'Great Water.'" It is no wonder that the gospel made slow progress among mountaineers, who seemed to take their angry spirit from the storm that roared through their lofty valleys with a fury unknown to the people of the plain.

At Bex and Aigle the good work met with more rapid success. The senate was glad to know that some churches had given up the mass, removed or burned the images and torn down the altars. The curates, still leading immoral lives, were loath to yield to the order of the senate requiring them to give up their offices to the reformed preachers. Farel was often interrupted at Aigle, and once the pulpit was overturned. But the Bernese senators felt that they must take care of a poor dying people who were too ignorant to banish the wolves and receive the kind shepherds sent to the flocks. They must employ their authority in securing a fair hearing for the gospel.

A new governor was appointed over the four parishes, Hans Rudolf Nageli, a man favourable to the reformed doctrine. Deputies went with him, and by their prudence and firmness great changes were quietly effected. The stormy Ormondines were, at length, induced to forsake their ancient superstitions, and let their altars be destroyed, their images be burned, their Romish paintings be defaced, and their depraved curates be dismissed. The preachers were found to be more attentive to the flocks than the priests, and the doctrines which they had so fiercely opposed were seen to be the pure truths of that good word which God had revealed for their salvation.

The Elijah of the Alps had received the call to return to France, but he was in his element, and would not be tempted nor even driven from the parishes of a poor and misguided people. Impetuous as the streams that broke down the mountain sides, he was still prudent as the shepherd who would have his flock to love him, and at the sound of his voice, follow him up to the glaciers. For months he stood alone, but the Bernese authorized him to secure helpers in his work. From Berne and Basle and France there came devoted fellow-labourers. Yet not all of them were blameless. One Christopher Ballista did him much evil. This man had been a monk at Paris, and had written to Zwingle; "I am but a Gaul, and a barbarian, but you will find me pure as snow, without any guile, of open heart, through whose windows all the world may see." And the world did see that the monk knew not himself. Zwingle sent him to Farel, who was calling loudly for labourers in Christ's vineyard. The fine language of the Parisian at first charmed the people. But his words were the best things about him. He had been disgusted with popery, but not truly converted from it. He found the work too hard for one who was brought up to a soft, lazy, gluttonous life. Plain fare, rough journeys, Alpine storms, patient labours and an ignorant rude people were not to his liking. The people began to distrust him, and then he became, as Farel wrote, "like a furious monster vomiting wagon-loads of threats." Thus ended the toils of Ballista.

Often did Farel's heart turn to his native land. To some one he thus wrote, with force and beauty; "Let us scatter the seed everywhere, and let civilized France, provoked to jealousy by this barbarous nation, embrace piety at last. Let there not be in Christ's body either fingers, or hands, or feet, or eyes, or ears, or arms, existing separately and working each for itself, but let there be only one heart which nothing can divide. . . . Alas! the pastures of the church are trodden under foot, and its waters are troubled! Let us set our minds to concord and peace. When the Lord shall have opened heaven, there will not be so many disputes about bread and water [an allusion to the debates about the real presence in the Lord's supper and on baptism.] A fervent charity—that is the powerful battering-ram with which we shall beat down those proud walls, those material elements, with which men would confine us."

During most of this time Farel had lived at his own charge. On one visit to Berne he received many presents, and the senate, no doubt, gave him a salary afterwards. Important movements were going on in the canton of Berne, but we cannot turn aside to see "this great sight." The language of that canton was German, and the history belongs to that of the German-Swiss reformers. The work there was not much affected by the influence of Farel the Frenchman.

CHAPTER XI.

THE ROMANCE OF PREACHING.

(1529–1530.)

THE valleys now promised a cheering harvest for their Lord, and Farel turned his eyes to another quarter. He was supported by Berne. The cantons of Berne and Friburg held, in partnership, the parishes of Morat, Orbe, and Granson; they also had alliances with Lausanne, the capital of Vaud, and with the cantons of Neufchatel and Geneva. The Bernese senators saw that it was both their interest and their duty to have the gospel preached to as many of their allies and subjects as they could reach. They commissioned Farel to carry it among them, provided he could obtain the consent of the respective governments. This was granted him.

The visitor at Friburg may be shown the ancient trunk of a Lime tree, which supports a legend. The story runs that, on the day of the battle at Morat in 1476, a young Friburger, who had fought bravely, ran home to tell the good news in the city, how Charles the Bold of Burgundy was defeated and disgraced by the loss of 15,000 men. The courier reached this spot, losing breath and blood, and falling down utterly exhausted. He could barely say, "Victory," and then he died. He carried a branch of lime in his hand, and this was planted on the spot where he expired. It grew into the old tree which now is propped up by pillars of stone. Farel was to wage a moral battle at Morat with Friburg against him, and, as bold as the once routed duke, he was to win a better victory than Charles lost. It was for him to bear the palm of victory, and to plant in this very town that little seed which should grow into the mightiest trees of righteousness.

One day he went to Morat and preached the truth at the foot of those towers which had been thrice attacked by some of the greatest armies of Europe. If we mistake not, the bishop of Lausanne had been at this place a few years before, and in his avarice, had attempted to impose a tax on the people at the celebration of the mass. This they had not forgotten. In a short time the new preacher gained the willing ears of a large class of people, and certain of the priests became obedient unto the faith. The reception of the reformed doctrines was to be decided, after a fair hearing, by the majority. The general vote was still in favour of the pope, and Farel quietly withdrew and went to Lausanne, where a considerable number of people had already abandoned popery.

The bishop and the clergy opposed the reformer and drove him from Lausanne. He soon reappeared bearing a letter from the lords of Berne to the authorities of the city. They read the bold words; "We send him to you to defend his own cause and ours. Allow him to preach the word of God, and beware that you touch not a hair of his head."

This was a shell thrown into the camp and might burst. The council was in great confusion. There was the bishop on the one side and Berne on the other. It was a very serious business. The council of Twenty-four referred it to the council of Sixty, but their honours excused themselves from touching it, and sent it up to the Council of Two Hundred (Nov. 24,

1529.) But they could do nothing. They gave it back to the Smaller Council. No one wished to have anything to do with it.

True, there was need of a reform. The citizens were complaining of the priests and canons and monks, saying "that their lives were one long train of excesses." But the faces of the reformers looked too austere. They seemed too strict and rigid for those who sought mere gentle decency rather than earnest devotion. The new preachers would carry the people over to the other extreme. Besides how dull would the city be if deprived of her bishop, his court, and the dignitaries about him! No more pilgrims to the image of Our Lady; no more great fairs for the sale of relics and indulgences; no more purchasers in the markets, nor boon companions in the taverns; no more suitors in the church courts, nor gay processions on her festivals; no more masses in the great cathedral which Pope Gregory X. had consecrated two centuries and a half ago! It was painful to think of the change which the Reform would make. The city would become a desolate widow, beholding no more the noisy throng of her people, who were her wealth and her glory! "Better a disorder that enriches than a reform that impoverishes!" It would raise an uproar. It would turn everything upside down. It must not be permitted. Berne must not send her preachers there. Farel must depart; and he departed.

He returned to Morat. The word gained over the hearts of the people. Merry bands were upon the roads on festival days, who said to one another, laughingly, "Let us go to Morat and hear the preachers." Then slily cautioning each other, they said, "Be careful not to fall into the hands of the heretics." They entered the church, smiling; they soon grew serious, glancing no more at each other, but riveting their eyes on the preacher, or dropping them to weep. Truth had her firm grasp upon them. They went home, some in deep silent thought, some in spirited talk about the doctrines they had heard, some to pray, and many to believe the glad tidings. The fire sparkled among the people, and spread in every direction. This was enough for Farel; he found a welcome for the truth. His eye was turned to another stronghold among the ridges of the Jura, and on the borders of France.

At a short distance from Morat was one of the fortresses of popery, the earldom of Neufchatel, with its six or seven delightful valleys, and its chief town of the same name, built on a hill that slopes down to one of the most charming lakes of Switzerland. Its chateau had been the old home of princes, and now belonged to Joan, the widow of Louis of Orleans. She had inherited the earldom from her ancestors, and lost it when her husband aided the French king (1512) in a war against the Swiss; but now (1529) she had just received it back as a present from the Swiss cantons.

The princess was now at Paris, in the suite of Francis I., "a woman of courtly style, vain, extravagant, always in debt, and thinking of Neufchatel only as a farm that should bring her in a large revenue," and devoted to the pope and popery. Twelve canons, with several priests and chaplains, made up a powerful clergy, having at their head the Provost Oliver, the brother of the princess. This main army was flanked by a strong array of auxiliaries. About half a league distant, on one side, was the abbey of Fontaine-Andre, regarded with great veneration. The monks, who founded it in the twelfth century, cleared the ground with their own hands, and became powerful lords in the world. On the other side was the abbey of the Benedictines of the Isle of St. John, whose abbot had lately been deposed by the Bernese, and, burning with vengeance, he had taken refuge in his priory at Corcelles, where a third entrenchment was thrown up.

To march right into such a stronghold, held by such an army, and having such reserve forces on each side, and demand its surrender, looked as foolish as the wildest dream of the old knight-errants of the Rhine. Even Farel would not thus attempt to take the fortress. The papists had done all they could to make it difficult of access. They dared not weaken their own cause by instructing the people; they hoped to strengthen it by amusing them. Pomps and shows took the place of sermons. "The church, built on a steep rock, was filled with altars and images of the saints; and religion, descending from this sanctuary, ran up and down the streets, and was travestied in dramas and mysteries, mingled with indulgences, miracles, and debaucheries." The higher clergy were rich, influential, and corrupt; the people untaught, rude, superstitious, and warlike; the princess was ready to crush any new movement, and the governor, George de Rive, was zealous for the ancient system of worship. It seemed that the place could be taken only by a wise strategy.

On a December day a frail boat left the southern bank of the lake, and carried a Frenchman of ordinary appearance, who steered for the Neufchatel shore. Quietly landing under the walls, he walked to one of the gates, near which had grown up the little village of Serrière. He inquired for Emer Beynon, the priest of the place, whom he had learned "had some liking for the gospel." Parson Emer received him with joy, for the visitor was no other than Farel, who had planned his campaign, and had entered upon it. But what could he do? Farel had been heard of and feared, and he was forbidden to preach in any church whatever in the earldom. The poor priest suggested that no injunction was laid upon the rocks nor the open air. Farel mounted on a stone, still pointed out, in the cemetery, and, turning his face away from the church, preached to the wondering people who came at his call. This rock was the corner-stone of protestantism in the canton of Neufchatel. The whole town became his church, and many came to hear him.

Very soon the rumours of this bold movement went in at the gates, and filled all the capital. A great commotion was seen in the streets. On one side the government, the priests, and the canons cried "Heresy!" On the other "some inhabitants, to whom God had given a knowledge of the truth," flocked to the preacher's pulpit of stone. Already was there a small protestant force in Neufchatel. The soldiers, who had been with the Bernese army, had just returned, bringing back the liveliest enthusiasm for the reformed doctrines. They hailed with delight the man who had thus planted himself at the very gates of the city. These, and others, who longed for the glad tidings of salvation, could not repress their joyful hopes. "Come," said they to Farel, "and preach to us in the town."

They were almost disposed to carry the preacher in their arms. They assumed to be his body-guard; they entered the gate of the castle; they passed the church and in front of the canon's houses; they descended to the narrow streets, inhabited by the citizens, and reached the market-cross. There Farel mounted a platform and addressed the crowd which gathered from all the neighbourhood; "weavers, vine-dressers, farmers, a worthy race, possessing more feeling than imagination." Grave was the preacher's countenance; weighty truths hung on his lips; his speech was energetic; his voice like the thunder; his eyes, his features, his gestures, all showed that he was a man of intrepidity. The citizens, accustomed to run about the streets after mountebanks, were touched by his powerful language.

The very first sermon won over many of the people. If they could have had their way, scarcely a finger would have been lifted against the messenger of glad tidings. If the people in the sixteenth century had been left to their own choice, the reformation would have gained all Europe. The same would be true now. But never and nowhere would the priests let them alone. At this first sermon of Farel, certain sly and crown-shaven monks glided among the hearers and began to excite them to do what they would never have thought of doing. Some of the ruder class were thus aroused to obey their masters and attempt violence. "Let us beat out his brains," cried some. "Throw him into the fountain," cried others. The fountain was near at hand (and is still shown,) but the undauuted preacher was neither to be beaten nor drowned. None of these things moved him.

In vain had there been a decree that this "heretic, William Farel," should preach in no church in the Canton. He needed none. Every place was a church, every stone or bench or platform was a pulpit. He preached in the streets, at the gates, in the public squares, and the dwellings of the monks echoed his powerful voice. No matter if the snows and winds of December were forbidding the people to hear him; or if the cheerful fire-sides were tempting them to remain within doors, they would crowd about the man who cared for their souls. The canons made a vigorous defence, and the "shorn crowns" rushed out into the cold weather, shouting, crying down, rousing up, begging, threatening, and making a furious ado, but it was all useless. No sooner did this Frenchman rise up in any place and in trumpet tones declare his message, than the monks found all their labour lost. All eyes were fixed on him; with open mouth and attentive ear the people hung upon his words, and forgot the winter's cold, and the rage of the priests. And scarcely did he begin to speak when as he exclaims, "Oh! wonderful work of God! this multitude believed as if it had but one soul."

Thus at the first assault the gospel carried the town. For several days the multitudes increased. They came from the neighbouring districts; they invited him to their homes and villages; they scarcely knew how to leave him. It seemed to him that Jesus Christ was walking, almost visibly, through the streets, opening blinded eyes and softening hardened hearts. Wearied and yet stronger than ever, he bowed down in his humble lodging, and thanked God for his marvellous power, and then he sent a message to his colleagues at Aigle. "Unite with me in thanking the Father of mercies for so graciously enlightening those who were oppressed by the greatest tyranny. God is my witness, that I did not leave you, with whom I would gladly live and die, from a wish to escape bearing the cross. The glory of Christ and the love shown to his word by the disciples of this place, enable me to bear the greatest sufferings."

But during all these days what were the strong forces of the pope, here gathered, attempting to do? Was the winter shutting them up in their comfortable quarters?

We must not follow the worst of them into their resorts of revelry, lust and shame, nor ask for the fathers of those children which crept out of dens of infamy to be taken up and supported at the public expense. A plain blunt age made and preserved the record which now cannot bear the light. We have opened it far enough, unless we may turn from their baser crimes to their cruelties. In a house near the city were placed some poor lepers, who were barely able to keep soul and body together by the funds arising from the sale of certain offerings. The rich canons made their feasts more sumptuous by taking these proceeds, and thus they robbed these helpless sufferers of the bread of charity.

These canons had been at open war with the monks of the Abbey of Fontaine André. Encamped on their two hills, they claimed each other's property, wrested away each other's privileges, launched at one another the coarsest insults and criminal charges, and even came to blows. "Captor of silly women," cried the canons to the abbot of Fontaine, and "he returned the compliment in the same coin." These quarrels disturbed the whole country. Such was the boasted purity and unity in the Romish church, at that day, in the canton of Neufchatel.

On a sudden these quarrels ceased, the fighters shook hands. A strange event was taking place in the city. The word of God was there preached. The canons, from their lofty hill, could not look down on the crowds in the streets with contempt. They were startled, affrighted, and aroused to league together all their forces. The monks of Fontaine should be mustered into service. The report had reached the abbey. All there were astir. They would now be brothers to the canons. Hatred to the gospel united these parties. They joined their strength against the reformer.

"We must save religion," said they, who had so long been destroying it. They meant that they must save their livings, their tythes, their banquets, their scandals and their privileges. It would be folly for them to oppose a single doctrine preached in their streets. They must resort to insult. At Corcelles, these opposers went farther. A voice was one day heard proclaiming the gospel under the windows of the priory where the deposed abbot of Fontaine had taken refuge. The monks looked down upon a listening crowd: Farel was there. What an interruption of their peace! a public disturbance indeed! They rushed forth, not to call a magistrate in the legal way, but to fall upon the heretic. Among them was the prior Rodolph, increasing the tempest, and creating a real public disturbance. One writer affirms that he had a dagger in his hand. Farel escaped with difficulty.

This was not enough. The civil power must be brought against the reform. Popery has always taken this course. The state must assist her in persecuting the teachers of truth, in keeping back the Bible from the people, and in maintaining her power in the land. The canons, the abbot, and the prior, now the best of brothers, appealed to the governor, George de Rive. He was prompt in marshalling all the forces of church and state to put down the new movement. On every side Farel saw himself surrounded. He was called "to endure sufferings, greater than tongue can describe." Before long he was compelled to yield for a time. He again crossed the lake of Neufchatel; but, on looking back, he could see the gospel fires, kindled at so many points, burning in a flame of glory.

He went to Morat. The people urged him to stay and pass the Christmas with them, but the senate of Berne wished him to visit Aigle, and thither he pressed. He was not now the strange Master Ursinus. He was the good missionary, the first shepherd the people ever had, the lovely man who had led them to the bishop of their souls. It was a Christmas when Christ was honoured in that village as never before. But soon a messenger came to bid him away.

Great events were passing at Morat. On the 7th of January,

1530, a second vote was taken there, and the majority were in favour of the reform. But the Romish minority, long urging that the majority should rule, were disposed to revolt. They began a course of insult and violence. One man was needed, and the voters for the gospel cried for Farel. Berne heard the voice and sent for him.

A few days after this, Farel and the Bernese messenger were scaling the magnificent mountains above Vevay, and catching indescribable views of Lake Leman, with its waters of marvellous blue. They entered upon the estates of John, the knight of Gruyere, who was in the habit of saying,—"We must burn this French Luther." The darkness came on them at St. Martin, where they took lodgings. The curate and two priests prepared to insult them in the morning. They said the messenger's badge was an infernal mark, and pointing to Farel, cried,— "Heretic! devil!" They knew he was not the latter, or they would have been silent enough. The curate was as cautious as Shimei, and the knight stayed close in his castle. Farel passed on, leaving the revilers to take comfort from their impudence.

On reaching Morat Farel brought to nothing the schemes of the popish minority, and gave strength to the growing cause. Not spending time and breath to defend himself, he hastened to preach in the adjoining districts. He filled all Mittellach with his doctrine. He crossed the little lake of Morat, and entered into the villages of the valley, lying between it and Lake Neufchatel. There, on the beautiful hills, he planted that heavenly vineyard, better than the earthly ones that covered them. The effort was fully successful. Friburg objected to the movement. Berne replied,—"Let our ministers preach the gospel, and we will let your priests play their tricks. We desire to force no man. The majority should rule." Farel was raising up the majorities. The people began to find true liberty in that religion which is its source, its regulator and its defence. It was about this time that he wrote his powerful letter "To all lords, people and pastors."

The reformer took all the margin that was on his commission. The Bernese senate reminded him that his special field was now Morat, and that he should remain where his instructions were so eagerly received, unless sent for by others who were willing to hear him. But he thought it his duty to sow, and God would take care of the harvest. He went into the northern part of the canton of Berne, awakening the people of the valleys and the villages.

One day, in April, he entered the church at Tavannes, just as the priest was saying mass. Farel went into the pulpit. The astonished priest stopped. The minister preached until the people were so moved that it seemed as if an angel had come down from heaven. "The poor priest, who was chanting the mass, could not finish it." He fled from the altar. The people were so roused that they demolished the images on the spot, and pulled down the altars. They were putting down popery in a shorter time than the priest had spent in its most pretentious rite. The other ministers came to the work. The whole valley was soon disposed to adopt the reformation, in spite of the protests from the bishop of Basle. The parish afterwards was favoured with a settled pastor.

On a cold day in 1529, some Bernese soldiers were trying to pass away their time, while they were defending the city of Geneva from the army of Savoy. With them were some young men from Neufchatel, and the talk often ran upon what a good work Haller and his friends were doing. The young Bernese were shivering and it was proposed to have a fire. Where could dry wood be got? Some of them knew; for every Romish church had its idols. They went to the Dominican church, and brought away arm-loads of the sacred trash, saying, "Idols of wood are of no use but to make a fire with in winter." The young men of Neufchatel returned home wiser than they left it, and it was their delight to recount in their jovial meetings the exploits of the campaign, and the way they kept warm at Geneva.

These young men were to cause an uproar in Neufchatel. They were waiting for Farel to return. He reappeared about the middle of the year 1530. Being master of the lower part of the city, he raised his eyes to the lofty cathedral and castle. The best plan, said he, is "to bring these proud priests down to us." His young friends hit upon a scheme that had cost more than one man his liberty. They went here and there through streets, one early morning, and posted up large placards bearing these words, "All those who say mass, are robbers, murderers and seducers of the people." There was no lack of readers, talkers, clamourers and agitators. The noise grew louder. The town began to shake. The canons summoned the people, called together the clerks, and armed a large troop with clubs and swords. Then marching at their head, they descended into the city, tore down the placards, cited Farel before the court, as a slanderer, and demanded ten thousand crowns damages.

The two parties appeared in court, and this was all that Farel desired. "I confess the fact of the placards," said he, "but I am justified in what I have done. Where can be found more horrible murderers than these misleaders, who sell paradise, and thus nullify the merits of our Lord Jesus Christ. I will prove my assertion by the gospel." He began to open his Bible,

"The common law of Neufchatel," the canons cried out, flashing with rage, "and not the gospel is in question here. Where are the witnesses?"

"Here are witnesses enough in this Holy Word." Farel was not to be cried down. He persisted in the testimony of the Scriptures against his accusers, and proved that the canons were really guilty of the charges on the placards. To make good such a proposition was to ruin popery. The court were perplexed: they had never heard a similar case. They resolved to lay it before the council of Besançon. Thence it went up to the emperor and to a general council. Perhaps it lost itself on the way to Rome. The bad cause gained nothing by making a disturbance. Farel took advantage of the lull in the storm.

He preached again in private houses and on public squares. These were still his temple. When his opposers wished to drive him back he made a step in advance. One day when the people were around him, they asked, "Why should not the word of God be proclaimed in a church?" They hurried him along with them, opened the doors of the Hospital chapel, set him in the pulpit, and a large audience stood silent before him.

"As Christ was born in a manger at Bethlehem," said the preacher, in his first sermon in a church of the city, "so this hospital, this abode of the sick and the poor, is to-day become his birth-place in the town of Neufchatel." Then feeling ill at ease amid the painted and carved figures that decorated the chapel, he laid his hands on these idols and cast them down, breaking in pieces by the fall.

The civil power was now invoked by the papists. They had a right to ask its protection, but asking it they destroyed what they wished to save. The governor prayed the Bernese senate to remove Farel and his companions. But the friends of the reformer were not thus to be outdone. They also sent deputies to Berne, who asked, "Did not our young men bear arms to assist you in your reformation? Will you abandon us in ours?" The Bernese hesitated in order to decide justly between the two parties.

A dying man was to turn the scale. One of the most illustrious citizens of the Bernese republic was expiring amid the tears of his sons and his neighbours. All Berne was full of mourning for him, and in fear of the plague of which he was a victim. He was told of the two appeals from Neufchatel, and rallying his waning strength, he said, "Go and beg the senate, in my name, to ask for a general assembly of the people of Neufchatel for Sunday next. Let the vote be taken." The message of the dying noble decided the Senate. Berne sent deputies to Neufchatel, who arrived August 7, 1530. Farel thought that during the debates he had time for a new conquest, and he went into Valangin, where we will trace his steps in the next chapter.

The governor did all he could to support the priests and put down the people, but soon found himself at his wit's end. He sent to the Princess Joan, "begging her to cross the mountains to appease her people, who were in terrible trouble because of the Lutheran religion." (It was not Lutheran, however.) The princess was too much absorbed with the gayeties of the Parisian court to care for the religion of the canton.

The lines were more and more clearly drawn between the canons and the citizens. The towns-people asked the priests to give up the mass, but they refused. Then the canons were urged, by a written petition, to discuss the question with Farel. But there was the same refusal. "But, for goodness' sake, speak either for or against!" It was all of no use. They feared debate.

Sunday, October 23d, was a day long to be remembered. Farel had returned, and he was preaching in the hospital. He knew that the magistrates of the city were inclined to act with the people against the priests, and that they had talked of giving up the cathedral to the reformers. "Will you not," said he in his sermon, "honour the gospel as much as the other party does the mass? If this superstitious act is performed in the high church, shall not the gospel be preached there also?" The hearers rose at the hint. "To the church!" they cried; "to the church!" They took Farel with them, and left the hospital. They climbed the steep street of the castle. They forced their way through the array of canons, and priests, and their followers. who did all they could to resist them. Nothing could check them. Insults and shouts were in vain; they pressed onward. They opened the gates of the "Church of Our Lady," devoted to Romanism for nearly four hundred years. They entered to engage in a new struggle. The canons were there to dispute the way into the pulpit. But it was useless. The crowd was not a band of rioters; they carried a moral force with them. The gospel had a right in the cathedral, and the magistrates had so declared. They had said "that it appeared to them a very good matter to take down the altars and have preaching there." It should be done. The citizens moved on against the canons, forming a close battalion, and, in the centre, placing the reformer. At length Farel stood in the pulpit. The Reformation was victorious.

No shouts arose. All was calm and solemn in the church and at its gates. There was no wish to insult the papal party; and even the adversaries were silent. Farel delivered "one of the most effective sermons he had hitherto preached," and the people listened as for eternity. They were deeply moved; they were broken in heart; the most obstinate seemed to be converted; and from every part of the old church were heard cries,—"We will follow the evangelical religion, both we and our children, and in it we will live and die."

The zeal of the multitude was beyond control. They wished to imitate the pious King Josiah, and deal one final blow to a false religion. They asked,—"If we take away these idols from before our eyes, will it not aid us in taking them from our hearts? Once these idols broken, how many souls, now hesitating, will decide for the truth! We must save them as by fire." The latter motive decided them, and then began a scene that filled the Romanists with horror, for, according to them, it must bring down upon the city the terrible judgments of God.

In his castle, adjoining the cathedral, was the governor, de Rive, and, with anxiety, he looked upon the people while they were furnishing him with abundant materials for a letter to the Princess Joan. "These daring fellows," wrote he, "seize mattocks, hatchets and hammers, and thus march against the images of the saints." They march against the statues of certain ones who were not saints—those of the counts themselves—which the people take for idols and utterly demolish. They lay hold of the paintings, tear out the eyes in the pictures of the saints, and cut off their noses. The crucifix also is thrown down, for it has taken homage from our crucified Lord. One image yet remains, the most venerated of all: it is "Our Lady of Mercy," presented by Mary of Savoy; but it is not spared. "They have bored out the eyes of Our Lady of Mercy," writes the governor, "which the departed lady, your mother, had caused to be made." The fragments of the broken images are carried out and thrown from the top of the rock into the roaring torrent below.

All this was rude, and none can fully justify it, although it was not mere rioting and excess. The people felt that the temple must be cleansed, popery must be put down, the gospel must have its proper place, and God must be no longer robbed of his glory by graven images. They had now gone far enough; but, in the excitement they went still farther. They seized the patens, from which they emptied the "holy wafers," and then cast them into the torrent. They wished to show that they did not any longer believe that the wafers were the real body of the Lord, and they distributed them one to another and ate them as merely common food. At this sight the canons and chaplains could no longer remain quiet. A cry of horror was heard. They rushed forth, leading their infuriated party, and the dreaded struggle began in a battle of blows.

At the windows of the castle, all this time were certain dignified but wrathful and helpless spectators, the provost Oliver, and two canons; the three being members of the privy council, and other high dignitaries. They had been silent; they dared not be otherwise. But now they showed themselves to restore peace by ordering all "the supporters of the evangelical doctrine" to appear before the governor. This was like "trying to chain the whirlwind." For why should the reformed party stop? There was the authority of the magistrates on their side. They haughtily replied, "Tell the governor that in the concerns of God and of our souls he has no command over us."

The governor found that he was simply George de Rive, with no authority that weighed a feather with the people. He must yield, and save some remnant of the papal idolatry. Some images were not broken, and he had them hid away in secret chambers. The citizens allowed him to do this, saying to him, "Save your gods; preserve them under strong bars, lest perchance a robber should deprive you of the objects of your adoration."

The tumult gradually ceased, and quiet was restored. As but a comparatively small part of the citizens were actively engaged in these proceedings, the governor still believed that the majority were in favour of the Romish faith. He was anxious to have the matter tested by a vote of the parishioners. But the reformed party insisted that this step should not be taken in the absence of the Bernese deputies. They at length came, and heard both sides of the case. They proposed that the vote should be taken, when the papal party who "always took the other side," objected. Some of them rose in the council, and touching the hilt of their swords, spoke of dying "martyrs for their holy faith." The young soldiers, who had been in the Genevese war, were quite as ready for that style of arbitration as the Romanists. A little more and there would have been a battle. At last it was agreed that the votes should be taken. The cathedral was opened, and there amid the ruins of pictures and altars, the majority decided for the Reformation, and gave the last blow to popery in that city.

The mass was expelled from the churches, although it was mournfully chanted every day in the castle. It became a storehouse for various spoils, removed from the cathedral when it was thoroughly cleansed, such as relics, ornaments of the altars, much machinery of Romish worship, and even the organ. Several of the canons embraced the Reformation. Others turned their eyes to some quiet corner where they might hide the disgraces of their defeat. When the November winds were raging among the mountains a troupe of canons, priests, monks and singing-boys painfully climbed through the gorges of the Jura and took refuge in the Val de Travers, wondering if the voice of Farel should ever startle them again.

A little "miracle," such as popery often furnishes to the ignorant, occurred about this time. Two townsmen named Fauche and Sauge were going out to their vineyards. They passed by a little chapel in which the latter had set up a wooden image of St. John. The former said, "There is an image, and I shall kindle my fire with it to-morrow." So as Fauche returned he took it away and laid it down in front of his house. The next morning he put it into the fire. An awful explosion followed; the humble family were in dismay; it was a miracle caused by the anger of the saint at being burned; the priests were ready to vouch for it. The poor man made haste to return to the mass. His neighbour came to explain it, but it was in vain that Fauche protested on oath that it was only a joke. He had come at night, bored into the image (and the saint complained of no pain!) filled it with gunpowder and closed the wound. It was a very earthly thing, but Fauche would not believe one word of such reasoning. He must flee the vengeance of the saints. He took his family and settled in France. From a faith in such tricks the reformers were delivering the people by-leading them back to the real miracles of the Saviour whose words, works, and death were their only hope.

What a renovating change since the day when the people carried Farel into the cathedral! If he had been the chief mover in the scenes of October third, the governor would surely have given him a full notice in his minute letter to the princess. Yet he did not name him as taking any part in the fearful movement. Nor did Farel appear in all the business of the votes. One might have said that he was not at Neufchatel. The governor knew not of him in his report. There was something greater than Farel, the word of God. It was at work, and to its Author be the praise for the wondrous change.

Farel was held in grateful remembrance by the council and the citizens, as the chief agent in introducing the gospel. They would gladly have retained him, but he was under engagements to the Bernese authorities. He made a second visit to the Val de Ruz.

For many years an inscription was visible on one of the pillars of the cathedral. It brought to mind the memorial day, as one read,

ON OCTOBER 23d, 1530, IDOLATRY WAS OVERTHROWN AND REMOVED FROM THIS CHURCH BY THE CITIZENS.

CHAPTER XII.

MY LORDS OF BERNE.

(1530–1531.)

THERE is an old castle, built on a rock, that overlooks the town of Valangin, about a league over the mountain from Neufchatel. Here lived the counts who exercised lordship over the Val de Ruz and four other valleys, which lay among the seven mountains of the Jura chain.

In this castle dwelt Williamette de Vergy, the widow of Count Claudius, and the dowager of Valangin. She was full of reverence for the pope, and of respect for the memory of her husband, at whose burial a hundred priests had chanted high mass. Then, too, many penitent young women were married, large alms were distributed, the curate of Locle was sent to Jerusalem, as a reward for his services, and the widow herself afterward made a pilgrimage for the repose of the soul of her departed lord. That she would be a bitter foe to the reformation might be well understood. It was the one thing she hated. Her zeal for popery prompted her to much fasting and solitude. Yet her long silences and gloomy devotions were sometimes followed by merry dances in her halls, when the wife of John, the knight of Gruyere, paid her a visit, and reported his threats against Farel with exquisite satisfaction. They never dreamed that this "French Luther" had his eye upon the Val de Ruz.

Williamette and her priests, and her chamberlain, Bellegarde, who even excelled her in hating the reformation, had reason to tremble.

People from the Val de 'Ruz had come daily to Neufchatel, where they heard the doctrines of the reformers, and they carried back to their parishes certain good news, which were certain to spread far and wide. Still, they were not likely to neglect the great Romish festival on the 15th of August—that of "Our Lady of the Assumption." It was a day when the villages would swarm with people.

This was the very day that Farel selected to make a descent upon the valleys. He left Neufchatel after the affair of the placards, that the people might settle their own affairs with the Bernese deputies. With him went a young Dauphinese, a relative, (as it appears,) an ardent Christian, and a man of strong, decided character—Anthony Boyve. This family has since given several pastors to the church at Neufchatel. The two missionaries climbed the mountains through the pine forest, and then descended into the valley. They were not disposed to linger about the castle, and, shunning Valangin, as it seems, they halted at the village of Boudevilliers, and proposed to preach there.

They met some persons who had heard the "great preaching" at the capital of the canton, and all of them went into the church. On all sides the people were thronging to it, to hear the praises of "Our Lady" celebrated. The priest was preparing to chant the mass, but Farel entered the pulpit and began his form of service. While the reformer was preaching Jesus Christ and his promises, the priest and his choir were chanting the missal. It was Christianity and Romanism in open competition and contrast. The awful moment came when the wafer was to be changed into the very body of the Lord; the sacred words fell from the priest's lips over the elements. The people felt the power of their old habits and their superstition, and they deserted the preacher and gathered toward the altar. The crowd was kneeling. Rome seemed triumphant.

Suddenly, a young man, who felt indignant at seeing the mass preferred to a sermon, rushed forth, through the choir and up to the altar, and snatched the host from the hands of the priest, and cried aloud, as he turned to the people,—"This is not the God whom you should worship. He is above, in heaven, in the majesty of his Father, and not, as you believe, in the hands of a priest." This man was Anthony Boyve.

At first this daring act produced the desired effect. The mass and the chanting ceased; the crowd was silent and motionless in astonishment. Farel, who was still in the pulpit, took advantage of the calm, and preached Him "whom the heavens must receive until the times of restitution of all things." The people listened. But the priests and their party acted as if there was a sweeping fire in the town. They rushed into the towers and rang the alarm-bell with all their might. These means drew a crowd of new-comers, not so devotional as the rest. Farel and Boyve would have been slain on the spot had they not retired. "God delivered them."

In the evening they set out for home, by a narrow path that wound beneath the castle. They were stealing cautiously along, when suddenly, in a narrow pass, a shower of stones fell upon them, and about a score of priests, men, and women assailed them with clubs. The quaint old chronicler states "that the priests had not the gout either in their feet or arms; the ministers were so beaten that they nearly lost their lives." They were dragged, half-dead, nearer to the castle, to afford some satisfaction to the countess. She came down the terrace and cried,—"Drown them! drown them! throw them into the Seyon—these Lutheran dogs, who have despised the host." The priests were already dragging them towards the bridge. Never was Farel nearer death.

Just then, from behind the last rock that hides Valangin, "there appeared certain good persons of the Val de Ruz, coming from Neufchatel." They asked of the priests, probably intending to save Farel, "What are you doing?"

"Treating these heretics as they deserve. Putting them into the river."

"Put them, rather, in a place of safety, that they may answer for their proceedings. Would you deprive yourselves of the only means of finding out those who are poisoned by heresy? Make them confess who their friends are."

The priests caught the idea, and took the bruised missionaries into the chapel of the castle. Passing by an image of the virgin they said to them "kneel down before Our Lady."

"Ye ought to worship the only true God, and not a dumb lifeless image," said Farel.

But they beat the blood out of him, and for six years the stains were visible on the walls. They led them to the prison, and "let them down almost lifeless into the dungeon of the castle of Valangin." The prisoners, like Paul and Silas in the jail at Philippi, could "sing praises unto God." Bellegarde had now an opportunity to display his zeal, and he was preparing for them a cruel end. But some townsmen of Neufchatel came and demanded them. The countess dared not refuse, for Berne might show a strong hand. The senate requested her to make an inquiry and detect the outlaws; she pretended to do so "to put a good face on the matter." The canons of Valangin were ever after suspected of laying the plot in the house of the countess, where they were daily guests at her table. One account has it that, "Nevertheless the priest who beat Farel most, never failed to eat daily at the lady's table by way of recompense." This was of little moment; the great thing was that the truth had been sown in the Val de Ruz, and we shall soon see the reapers coming for the harvest.

This severe beating accounts for the gap in the previous chapter between August and October, when we had nothing to record pertaining to Farel. He was recovering from his wounds. It may have been that during this interval his letter, to a young man about to enter the ministry, was penned. "Look for labour, not for leisure. Truly a wide field lies open, but only for those who wish to feed the flock rather than to live upon it. Much reproach is to be endured. You must expect to meet with ingratitude in return for kindness, and evil for good."

Farel had now passed through the great events of October 23; he had preached in Neufchatel from a pulpit stripped of every ornament; he had visited the surrounding villages, "working at a reformation night and day." He had seen his friend Emer Beynon, who first set him up on the stone to preach in Serrière, take a decided course. This good man said one day to his parishioners, from his pulpit, "If I have been a good priest, I desire now to be, by God's grace, a better pastor." These words should go everywhere. Farel recommended to him a career of labours, fatigues and struggles in behalf of the gospel. Emer saw his parish imitate Neufchatel in giving a majority for the Reform.

There was much secret work going on among the Romanists at Neufchatel. Some persons were more zealous for popery after its downfall than they had been in the day of its power. The clergy glided into houses and said mass to a few friends darkly gathered around a temporary altar. The priest came noiselessly to baptize a child, breathed on it, made the sign of the cross on its forehead, and sprinkled it with water of Romish consecration. They hoped to build up in secret what had been overthrown openly. At length they agreed upon a counter-revolution.

A plot was laid for the vespers of Christmas. While the Christian songs were rising to heaven, the conspirators were to rush into the church, expel the heretics, overthrow the protestant pulpit and tables, restore the images, and celebrate the mass in triumph. But the plot came to light, as such schemes of darkness generally draw into them persons who will betray themselves. Berne was notified of the plan. She sent her deputies, who arrived on the very eve of the festival. "You must see to this," said they to the governor. "If the reformed are attacked we, their co-burghers, will protect them with all our power." The conspirators laid down their concealed weapons, and the Christian hymns were not disturbed. Thus ended the Neufchatel vespers.

Noble Berne! sending forth her missionaries, and not allowing a hair of their heads to be touched, if they could help it, and bringing the priests of many a village and city to the terms of the people. The bear on her shield was a terror to the Romanists. But she appeared to the friends of the gospel as a protecting shepherdess and a nurturing mother.

In the middle of winter Farel crossed the mountain and entered the church of Valangin, went into the pulpit, and began to preach just when the Countess Williamette was coming to hear the mass. She ordered his mouth to be shut, but through his lips passed a torrent of truth, carrying away the prejudices of his hearers. The aged dowager retired in haste, saying, "I do not think this is according to the old gospels; if there are any new ones that encourage it, I am quite amazed." What the priests did, this time, we do not know, but the people of Valangin were won to the truth. The affrighted lieutenant of the place ran to Berne and made complaint to the senate, but he gained nothing. Their excellencies said coolly, "Why should yon disturb the water of the river? Let it flow freely on."

On the slopes of the Jura mountains Farel wandered, preaching in the hamlets and gaining new triumphs. Curates and abbots resisted him with violence. At one place he was dragged out of the pulpit and driven away by insults and blows; at another he was wounded by a stone or a gun-shot. At St. Blaise the people, hissed on by the priests, fell upon him, and he escaped from their hands "severely beaten, spitting blood, and scarcely to be recognized." He was put into a boat, by some of his friends, and conveyed to Morat, where his wounds detained him, more wearied and restless than if he had been engaged in his apostolic labours.

The report of this violence at St. Blaise reached the reformed people in Neufchatel. They felt their blood boil. They reasoned thus—If the priests and their allies bruise the body of Christ's servant (which is truly the temple of God,) why should we spare their dead idols? They rushed to St. Blaise, entered the church, threw down the images, and broke up a vast amount of popish machinery. They went to the Abbey of Fontaine Andre, and greatly alarmed that blissful nest of quarrelsome monks by destroying their altars and images. Even granting that these were acts of an unchristian revenge, still it should be noted that these image breakers did not seek to return the wounds of Farel upon living men, but upon dead idols. Not against the priests but against popery, were their blows directed. There was no disposition to take vengeance upon a man, woman, or child, nor upon canon, monk, abbot or priest. Thus the Romanists struck at the preachers of the gospel; they persecuted even unto death. Protestants aimed at great errors and pitied the people, and proved that they were more nearly like God, who hates the sin, but spares the sinner.

One more glance at Valangin. It has generally been stated that Farel was there a third time during this period. But an old chronicler says it was "the minister of Neufchatel," and this title was never given to Farel. The minister in those days, was Anthony Marcourt, a zealous Frenchman. On a great holiday he went to Valangin, and soon had a crowd about him in the streets, listening to his words. The canons were watching from their windows, and the countess and her chamberlain from their towers. They sought how to divert the people from the preacher. They dared not use brute force because of Berne. They proposed to insult the minister, and raise a tremendous laugh in the assembly. A canon and Madame's coachman took two horses from the stables and performed a piece of vile trickery which decency will not allow us to describe. But instead of a laugh there was the most intense disgust and indignation. The schemers knew not with whom they were dealing. They overshot the mark. The infamous spectacle was scarcely over, when the multitude rushed into the church. They broke the ancient windows and the shields of the lords; they scattered the relics, tore the books, threw down the images, and turned over the altars. Then, sweeping forth like a whirlwind, they threatened the canons' houses. The dwellings were destroyed, but the canons and their pack fled wildly into the woods, and found sorrow enough for trying to raise a laugh.

Williamette de Vergy and Bellegarde, trembling behind their battlements, repented, too late, of their monstrous expedient. They saw the last offensive house sacked: they knew not what would come next. But how awful! The outraged people turn toward the castle, they ascend the hill, they draw near. Is the castle to be rifled or even demolished? Not at all, proud lady! "We come to demand justice for the outrage committed against religion and its minister," respectfully say the delegated burghers standing at the gate. They are permitted to enter, and the affrighted countess hears their case, and orders the poor wretches, who had done her bidding, to be severely punished. Still she takes the first chance to send a messenger to Berne declaring that "great insults had been offered her!" Berne hears only one side of the case, orders the reformed party to pay the damages, but insists that they shall have the free exercise of their religion. The countess must submit. James Veluzat, from France, became the first reformed pastor of Valangin. In 1531 the entire principality of Neufchatel came under the power of Francis, son of the princess Joan. He proclaimed liberty of conscience and faith in the whole canton. The sermon on the rock at Serrière had been one means of securing these great results.

And now comes another reaper into the harvest. A young Dauphinese, named Christopher Libertet Fabri, had been studying medicine at Montpelier, where he first learned the disease of his own soul and found its remedy. He still intended to go to Paris and complete his studies. Being at Lyons he met certain friends of the truth, who told him of the wonderful events in Neufchatel and the neighbouring villages. He was so interested in these reports that he changed his mind and his route; and now we find him at Morat, inquiring for the house where Farel is lodging.

Sore from the beating at St. Blaise, "shivering with cold, spitting blood," and scarcely able to speak, Farel is lying at Morat. Tenderly has he been welcomed there, and carefully is he watched by the friends who tread softly about his room. A young man wishes to see him. As he is a Dauphinese he may come. Modestly approaching the bed he introduces himself as Christopher Fabri, and says,—

"I have forsaken everything,—family, prospects and country, to fight at your side, Master William. Here I am. Do with me as seems good to you."

"I see that we have the same faith and the same Saviour," replies Farel, after being touched with the young man's lively affection and intense devotion. He looks upon Fabri as "a son whom God has sent him," and day after day talks with him. On his bed he is training a student for the ministry. He would like to keep him always at his side; but he must bid his "tenderest son" preach the more beloved Saviour.

"Go, now, my dear son in the faith," says Farel one day, "and preach the gospel at Neufchatel." Has Farel ordained him in that sick room, as he himself had been at Basle?

"O my master," answers Fabri in tears, "my sorrow is greater to-day than when I left father and mother, so delightful have been my conversations with you." He learns his duty, obeys, goes to Neufchatel and urges forward the good work.

On the Roman highway, that led from Italy to Gaul, was the ancient city of Urba, built, it was said, in the same century with Rome. The story runs that the kings of the first French race once rested near this old city, and, charmed with the valley that sloped from the foot of the Jura to Lake Neufchatel, they exclaimed,—"It is enough; we will stop here." In place of Urba grew up the town of Orbe,* which was now to talk

* The birth-place of Prof. Louis Agassiz, now of scientific renown.

of mightier personages than the old French kings, of whose wise choice they boasted, or "good Queen Bertha," who dwelt at this old town when this part of Switzerland belonged to Little Burgundy. The country is full of legends about her spinning on horseback with a distaff fastened to a saddle, which is still shown at Payerne. She was a friend to all the poor, and "the nursing mother of the nation, which she guided and fed." She had a zeal for building convents and castles, and some of the "towers of Bertha" still remain. She was anxious to impart to her people a love of industry, by setting them a good example. One day she was spinning on her palfrey as she rode through some pastures near Orbe, when she saw a young girl spinning, like herself, while watching her flock of sheep. She rode up and gave her a beautiful present, along with much praise. The next day several noble, but idle ladies came before her with their distaffs, in hopes of a reward. But she knew their vain pretensions, and told them "The peasant girl came first, and, like Jacob, carried my blessing, leaving nothing for Esau." People still talk of "the good days when Queen Bertha spun, and when she told the peasants good stories from the Bible."

In that town was a burgess, "cloth-dresser and tailor," who, one day in 1511, wrote down the name of another son—Peter Viret. The father went on fulling the cloths and associating with the best-informed burgesses, and even with some of the nobles. Peter grew up, taking no delight in his father's pursuits, nor aspiring after his official dignities. He wished for God, and took the path which the priests pointed out as the way to heaven. If alone or with his brothers, Anthony and John, he walked along the banks of the Orbe, or looked with emotion on the Jura, and caught glimpses of the Alps; then he lifted his eyes toward the Most High for help. He was ignorant, and must remain so as long as the blind were leading the blind. He resolved to be a priest. His father did not oppose, for it was counted an honour among the towns-people to have a priest among their children. He gained all that the schools of Orbe could offer him, and, when about twelve, he was sent to the University of Paris. It was the same year, (1523,) that John Calvin entered one of the same colleges. Did these two boys, who were yet to be most intimate at Geneva, meet there and begin their genial friendship? We know not. But they were alike in their love of study and their Romish style of piety. Years afterward Viret wrote of his early devotion to the church of Rome.—"I cannot deny that I went pretty deep into that Babylon."

It seems that on one of the last cautious visits which Farel made at Paris, he met the young Viret, whose modesty charmed him into an acquaintance. The young Swiss was thus led to search for the truth, and was pointed to the true path to heaven. "God took me out of error," said he, and then a decisive question was forced upon him. The time came for the tonsure, when the razor must do its part in making him a priest. He must make up his mind. He was not long about it. He refused, and was forthwith "set down as belonging to the Lutheran religion." He knew what to expect, for Beda was ferreting in all cases for heretics, and hastily quitting Paris he returned to his father's house.

The priests of Orbe set their eyes upon him. They saw that he was lonely and depressed, and they suspected that he was in a struggle between Rome and Christ. They grew uneasy about him, and told him about the fathers of the church. His foot slipped; his head was bewildered; he almost fell back again, "deep into that Babylon." But he caught the divine Word, clung to it; and, renouncing what mere men declared, he said,—"I will believe only Jesus Christ, my Saviour." He felt that he was a prisoner just released from "the citadel of idolatry."

There were two prisoners for whom he felt the tenderest affection. "Since the Lord has brought me out," said he, "I cannot forget those who are still within." His father and mother were never out of his thoughts. Between business and popery they had no thought of Christ. He prayed for them and read to them a few chapters of the gospel. They were delighted with his humble earnest life and his faith took hold of their hearts. He was, at length, able to write, in later years, "I have much reason to give thanks to God, because it hath pleased him to make use of me to bring my father and mother to the knowledge of the Son of God. . . If he had made my ministry of no other use, I should have good cause to bless him for this." He is soon to hear a most powerful voice, to see all Orbe in motion, and to be in the pulpit, astonished at himself.

The story of the castle stairs was worthy of many a late hour by the firesides of Orbe. In 1475, the Swiss took the town by storm, but the castle was to be disputed inch by inch. The invaders broke in the doors, the garrison yielded step after step, fighting, in vain bravery, on every stair, and at every chamber door. Backward and upward the defenders were driven until they took refuge in the tower. Fire completed the awful work of death. It was reserved for the missionary champion to give the townsmen other stories for their long winter evenings, and by degrees to make his advance into this strong-hold of popery, kindling the fire that would refine and purify their hearts.

A friar came to the town, about the time of Lent 1531, and noisily offered for sale the pardons of the pope. One morning he was shouting the value of his wares, with his eye on the watch, for some visitor might put to him unpleasant questions. He soon noticed a little man with a face paled by illness, and with an eye that could look through such quackery, coming near to the stall. None gave way, for none knew him. Pressing near, he raised his loud voice and asked, "Have you indulgences for a person who has killed his father and his mother?" The monk was confounded, the stranger boldly stept on the curb of the public fountain, and began to preach of the water of life as earnestly as if he were in the pulpit. The astonished people left the friar and gathered around the new orator, who was telling them how to obtain the free pardon of God, and urging them to drink freely of the fountain of life. It began to be whispered who the preacher was—William Farel, who had risen from his couch at Morat, and hearing the friar's drum, as Luther says, had come to Orbe as soon as he could venture to walk. By this first sermon, a tradesman named Christopher Hollard, and one Mark Romain, a school-master, were persuaded to accept the gospel.

There was commotion enough in the town to put Farel in his element, but wisdom dictated his departure and he left. The friar, whose name was Michael Juliani, knew not what to do, until the Sisters of St. Clair entreated him, as their dear confessor, to preach against heresy. He was delighted. He boasted that he would lead the heretics back to the faith. "Not so easy a job as you think," said certain nobles, who knew the power of Berne. The man who had authority there over magistrates was the bailiff, the lord of Diesbach, a stout Bernese in his views. What would he say?

The friar did not care; he was bent upon preaching against the Reform, and he had so published. The bells rang, a crowd filled the church, and even some of the suspected ones came.

Such an unusual audience turned the friar's head. He thought he should have such a victory as his patron Michael the archangel had over Satan. He preached up Rome, and preached down the Reformation, using the most verbose abuse and violence. Five or six friends of the gospel were there writing it all down upon little papers which they held on their knee. The sermon ended and the bailiff began. He and certain other notables begged the friar to cease from his excessive abuse, and to preach simply the doctrines of the church. But he was flattered with the idea that certain devout folks were exceedingly pleased. In their eyes Father Michael's tirades were genuine eloquence.

He was one day preaching upon "the poor in spirit," claiming that ignorance was the blessed sign of the children of God. "Sirs," said he, "the poor in spirit here referred to are the priests and friars. They have not much learning I confess, but they have what is better. They are mediators between man and God; they are worshippers of the Virgin Mary, who is the treasure-house of all graces. . . . But who are these who say they are justified by faith? Who are they who throw down the crosses on our roads and in our chapels? Enemies of Christ. Who are they who renounce their vows in order to marry? Infamous, abominable apostates before men, and before God." This last fling would not apply to Farel, for he was in single life.

Suddenly a loud noise was heard in the church, and a man was standing up in full view repeating with a loud clear voice the words, "Thou liest." The declaimer stopped, and all looked at a middle-aged man who had a brother that had believed the truth, left the priesthood, married and became a reformer at Friburg. This man was the same Christopher Hollard who had heard Farel at the public fountain, and had renounced popery. Though his protest was not the most refined, yet it came from an honest heart, which was roused, when he heard men like his brother denounced, and the word of God set at naught. His voice was soon drowned, for the men rushed from their places to fall upon him, but the women, who filled the nave, were before them. Christopher was so beset that a Romanist wrote, "If the people had been let alone, he would never have gone out of the said church, which would have been a great benefit to the poor catholics." An officer rescued him and threw him "into a dungeon to avoid a greater scandal."

The women were the champions of Romanism in Orbe, and formed their plot against the reform. But the mother of Christopher Hollard was not one of their number. She loved her son; she feared his foes. She said to herself,—"The bailiff of Berne, Diesbach, is the only man who can save my son. I will go to his castle and implore his help." Mark Romain, the school-master, went with her. The cool Bernese heard them. He was aroused, wrathy, and would show what was meant by the authority of My Lords of Berne. He came to Orbe and set officers upon the track of Michael Juliani. They searched the convents in vain. He was very quietly hidden in the house of "Frances Pugin, instructress of girls in all virtue and learning." Hearing that he was wanted, he put on a bold front, went straight to the bailiff, and saluted him with all deference. The lord of Diesbach did not feel softened by the friar's crafty courage, but, rising up, he took him by the hand, saying,—"I arrest you in the name of My Lords of Berne." Then, leading him to the prison, he "drew Hollard out of his den, and put the said friar in his place." Such was Bernese authority when the truth needed her defence.

Mark Romain was as pleased "as if he had gained a thousand crowns; and, thinking he had achieved a master-piece," was going quietly home. The mob were seeking their revenge; and, as their monk was in the castle-prison, they talked of flinging the school-master into the river. Just then, "seeing him come joyfully along," they called to him. He ran, looking on every side for an open door, and finally rushed into the church, where the women, who had wished to tear Hollard in pieces, were kneeling to Mary, "the queen of heaven." They rushed upon him; and a calm looker-on said of the affair,—"I did not think the school-master would ever get out alive." We read of those who "ceased not to beat Paul." Romain was now in his apprenticeship of perils, and he lived to become a minister of the gospel, for which he was suffering. Around the castle was another mob, enraged at seeing Hollard by the side of the bailiff, whom he was about to restore to his mother. They cried out,—"Why have you arrested Friar Michael? why released Christopher?" The cool and indomitable bailiff gave them that crushing answer,—"By the order of My Lords of Berne;" and, before their "good father" could be liberated, they must get "My Lords'" consent.

A deputation was therefore sent to the Romish Friburg to gain its interference. A committee was sent back. But Berne had a word to say. Certain Bernese gentlemen were sent to Orbe along with the Friburgers. Passing through Avenches they fell in with Farel. He had been a month among ruins older than the Cæsars, preaching to a people dead in popery. Farel joined the Bernese and returned to Orbe, where there were no ruins, and where all were alive. And while the mixed commission are doing what they can for Father Juliani and for peace, he will preach the gospel.

The services of Palm-Sunday were over; all from mass to vespers. Farel had kept quiet in-doors, but now left his inn "with presumptuous boldness." A crowd soon filled the church, and he entered the pulpit "without asking leave." Scarcely had he begun to preach when all sorts of sounds were raised, from hisses to howlings, from the cry of "dog" to that of "devil." "It was a glorious noise," says an admirer; "you really could not have heard it thunder." From rudeness they proceeded to rioting. They pulled Farel out of the pulpit, and would have beaten him, but that same dreaded bailiff strode in among them, and, taking Farel by the arm, escorted him to his lodging. Thus things went on. We give but a specimen of the rude tricks and violent efforts to prevent the reformer from preaching. The Bernese allowed the friar his liberty, after confessing his untrue assertions, provided he would preach nothing but the word of God. He left soon after for other regions. An order came from Berne, insisting that Farel should preach, unmolested.

The women's league and plot against Farel prevented him from having an audience. On the next Sunday nearly all the parish took a march out of the town, and he went into the pulpit and preached to ten persons, among whom were Peter Viret, Hollard and Romain. He left the church when the procession was returning. The clergy exulted and called him a coward, saying, openly,—"The minister who promised to refute Father Juliani cannot do it." "Indeed," said the staunch bailiff of Berne, "you have heard the monk, and now you complain that you have not heard the minister. Very good! you shall hear him. It is the will of My Lords of Berne that every father of a family shall attend his sermon, under pain of their displeasure."

They dared not disobey and the church was thronged. Farel

rose in the pulpit, with all his energies aroused by the sight of such a congregation. He exposed the errors of Father Juliani. Day after day he set forth the truth. "The penance which God demands is a change of heart and life." "The pope's pardons take away money; but they cannot take away sin." Of the confessional he said, "How many souls have been cast into hell by it! how many virgins corrupted! how many widows devoured! how many orphans ruined! how many princes poisoned! how many countries wasted! . . . O Heaven unveil these horrors! O Earth cry out! creatures of God weep; and do thou, O Lord, arise!"

Still the audiences grew less, and the bailiff had the good sense not to notice the fact. But this contempt at Orbe had its compensation in the respect that came from the neighbouring villages. Message after message came from the peasantry who urged the great preacher to visit them. He wrote to Zwingle, "Oh! how great is the harvest. No one can describe the ardour the people feel for the gospel, and the tears I shed when I see the small number of reapers." There was one young man among his hearers whom he loved with an affection only equal that which was returned. The ardent, fiery, fearless and almost rash Farel was heart to heart with the meek, timid, sensitive and always prudent Viret. In the gospel the Peters, and Johns, and Pauls, are knitted in brotherhood by more than earthly ties. Thus it became with Farel, Viret, and Calvin.

It was told through the town, now quiet through awe of My Lords of Berne, that on May 6, 1531, a son of the good burgess, clothier and tailor, a child of the place, and a favourite of all, would preach his first sermon. Perhaps few were aware that Farel had persuaded, urged and almost forced him to assume so solemn a duty. He was accused of being rather heretical, but he was so inoffensive that nobody would believe it. The young people wished to see their former playmate in the pulpit. Older ones wanted to hear what the son of their honoured burgess had to say. The day came and the church was filled, many having come from a distance. All were impatiently waiting, when at last they saw the young man of only twenty years, of small stature, pale, long and thin face, lively eyes, meek and winning expression, with his brows touched with the light of eternity. By his modesty, his eloquence, his wonderful power in handling the word of God, his persuasiveness in urging the duties of repentance and faith, his prudence in managing errors so as not to arouse bitter feelings and by his earnestness in setting forth Christ crucified for sinners, he kept the most worldly men hanging upon his lips. He was a prophet who had honour in his own country. That day was the greatest day, thus far, in his life. It placed him in the band of mighty reformers of errors and heralds of the truth.

A month had passed since Farel's return, when all at once, a report filled Orbe with astonishment. It was said, and each reporter could hardly believe it, that Madame Elizabeth, wife of Lord Arnex, was converted. She had planned the women's conspiracy against Farel, she had beaten him in the street, she had a hand in filling the church with boys (*marmaille*, brats) who laid down and pretended to be asleep until Farel began his sermon and then sprang up howling with all their lungs and leaving the preacher alone; she had suddenly become a convert to the awful heresy! They shook their heads and smiled, and felt chagrined. Nor was this all. Lord Arnex, who had pleaded for Father Juliani, given bail for him, and despised My Lords of Berne, was also converted. George Grivat, too, the best musician in the town, had gone from the choir into the pulpit. Others of note—"chief women not a few"—were among the believers in the doctrines which Farel and Viret had preached.

These disciples wished to receive the Lord's Supper. Farel was sent for and he hastened from Morat. At six in the morning of Whitsunday, he announced, to a large assembly in the church, that there would be the breaking of bread in remembrance of "the breaking of Christ's body on the cross." Eight persons came forward, Lord Arnex and his wife, Hollard and his aged mother, Cordey and his wife, William Viret the burgess, and George Grivat, afterwards pastor at Avenches. Peter Viret was doubtless absent from the town. A white cloth was laid over a bench, (for they would not use Romish tables,) and on it the sacred emblems were placed. After prayer, Farel asked, "Do you each forgive one another?"

"Yes," was the response of the little band, never before so deeply affected. Oh that Farel would forgive them!

The bread was broken and given by the hand of the minister, the wine was touched by the lips of the penitent, and the Lord crucified on Calvary was glorified in little Orbe. The only interruption was made by the priests coming in, near the close of the service, and chanting the mass as loud as they could.

But these disciples were to suffer. Hollard became too rash, and went to breaking idols with all his might. One day, when Farel was preaching, he flew at an image of the Virgin and dashed it in pieces. The church began to be cleansed, and our Romish writer "was greatly astonished at the patience of the populace." It was through fear of My Lords of Berne. But the Friburgers almost gained the day. Taking certain priests out of prison, they put in their stead fifteen of the image-breakers, and one of them was Lord Arnex. For three days they were kept on bread and water; the priests had enjoyed good "bed and board;" and then they were allowed to return home.

There may be failings in men who advocate a faultless cause; but we who may have too little zeal should be careful how we judge those who have too much. We are writing of times when the reformers had few preparatory schools for discipline, and the Romanists were not then trained into a crafty and smooth Jesuitism. Often must the whirlwind sweep through a town in advance of the "still small voice." If the preachers were sometimes rash, the papists were nearly always riotous. The one class proved what they had to declare by Scripture; the other persecuted without hearing the evidence. It is not hard to perceive which deserves *the greater amount of charity*.

CHAPTER XIII.

THE HUGUENOTS APPEAR.

(1531-1532.)

"BE prudent; do not rashly expose yourself to danger, but take good care of yourself for the Lord's future service." Thus wrote Zwingle to Farel when this suffering missionary was labouring to sound the gospel through all the country, from Berne to Basle.

"Take good care of yourself, also," was the reply, "for far greater danger threatens you than me." The warning was too late. Zwingle had fallen on the battle-field. But such words were just like Farel. He scarcely thought of himself. No reformer was more like St. Paul, in his zeal, his feebleness of body, his strength of spirit, his perils and his journeys. It is not possible for us to follow him into every town that he surprised, every pulpit where he was attacked, nor every little new church where he often brake bread with the glad disciples.

On the shore of Lake Neufchatel, at the entrance of the town of Grandson, stood the large convent of the Gray Friars. Two men came to its door one day, rang the bell, and were shown into the parlour. The superior, Friar Guy Regis, met them, and asked what they wanted. They told him they intended to see that the gospel was preached in the town, and, in passing the convent, they had said to each other that this was the place to begin. They coolly begged him, "in the name of the lords of Berne," to grant them the use of the chapel. And if he wished to know who they were, there were their commissions, bearing the names of Farel and de Glautinis, the minister of Tavannes. The friar had heard of them, and he knew all that was still going on at Orbe, and, if he could help it, the like should never occur at Grandson. It was insolent to ask what they did; he was resolute enough to repay their bold impudence. "Heretic!" said he to Farel. "Son of a Jew!" cried a listening monk. This was not a very encouraging reception. They left, and some friends put them upon another track. "Go to the priory, on the hill."

Soon they were knocking at the door of the Benedictine convent, where several monks appeared. They had a hint of the arrival of the missionaries, and with their eyes they measured them from head to foot. Farel asked permission to preach, when a loud uproar arose in the cloister. One friar came forward with a pistol hid under his frock, and thought to put an end to the "heretic who was disturbing all the churches." The sacristan pointed his pistol at Farel with one hand, and, seizing him with the other, tried to drag him into the prison. De Glautinis sprang forward, when the monk with the knife fell upon him. The friends of the preachers, waiting at the door and hearing the noise, rushed in and tore them from the stout arms of the monks. The gates were closed in scorn, and for two weeks remained shut, so great was the fear of these reformers. Farel went to Morat, but de Glautinis began to preach in the streets and private houses of the towns. Guy Regis led the whole array of the monks against him. Guy would not debate with him there; but if he would only go to some far-off city, he would prove that his preaching was mere witchcraft. After such a valiant proposal, attended with roaring abuse from the monks, the troop made their retreat behind the convent walls, where they, perhaps, talked of the terrors of the most notable year in the history of Grandson. The castle had once been defended for ten days against the assaults and artillery of the Burgundian army. Famine came, and the garrison accepted the offered pardon and surrendered. Charles the Bold received them, and vented upon them the outrages of revenge. Two days afterward his crime returned upon his own head, and, being defeated by the Swiss, he was compelled to fly for his life across the mountains, with only five followers. His splendid baggage is still among the antiquities of Geveva. Perhaps these Benedictines imagined that they had resisted Farel, and that no spiritual famine would ever cause them to yield their fortress. They may have supposed that he had fled and resolved never to appear again in their streets.

The lords of Berne heard of the treatment given their ministers, and some of them came to Grandson. Wishing to give the people the liberty of hearing the gospel without hindrance, they ordered the convent churches to be thrown open, whatever might be the will of the Benedictines. They sent for Farel, who brought Viret with him. It was but six days after his first sermon and Viret was fully in the work. The three preachers gave the friars the privilege of hearing the truth every day. The priests excited the people; the reformers were in and out of prison; Farel was struck by an officer when questioning a friar; he and Watteville, a Bernese deputy, were met in the church by two monks armed with axes; Watteville had them arrested, and after the friar ended his sermon, Farel went forward and refuted it. These two monks, within two years after, renounced popery and preached the truth which they had once opposed.

One day the preachers were holding service in the church, when a troupe of women had the masculine boldness to rush in and put an end to the preaching. The congregation, at first, tried to resist them, but it was hard to employ force against the gentler sex, especially when their will was taking such a furious way to carry a point. Farel and his companions left the women in charge of affairs until the people should prefer a change. They went into the surrounding villages and raised up majorities for the Reformation. Grandson at length gave the right vote, and John Le Compte, a young man whom Farel had known in Meaux and invited into Switzerland, became its minister. If history be silent, charity inclines us to imagine that those women received him as their good pastor, and gave their zeal to a better cause.

What Switzerland needed was religious liberty, so that priests and preachers might have a proper freedom of speech, and the people the free choice of their mode of worship. Berne had laboured for it, but papal Friburg wanted the liberty all on their own side. Little Orbe was to claim this one-sided freedom so madly that the rights of the preachers were to be declared equal to those of the priests. It was on this wise. On Christmas eve, 1531, a minister—it may have been Viret—was in the church preaching upon the coming of the Saviour into the world and into the hearts of men. Certain bigots peeped in and, seeing an attentive crowd, exclaimed, "The devil must have sent a good many there." The time for the midnight devotions of the Romanists had not come, but when the clock struck nine another crowd entered the gates to raise a riot. The gospel-party quietly retired; the priest-party set upon them in the streets, where houses were assaulted, blows given, blood shed and heads broken. The preachers were not at fault;

they were simply using the church when the priests had left it empty. Viret, with ten of the reformed, went to Berne to plead for religious liberty.

A sort of council was there held the first days of January, consisting of two hundred and thirty ministers, and many laymen. They heard Friburg the champion of popery, and Berne the staunch advocate of protestantism. "We desire," said the Bernese, "that every one should have free choice to go to the preaching or to the mass."

"And we also," said the Friburgers.

"We desire that all should live in peace, and that neither priests nor preachers should call their adversaries heretics or murderers."

"And we also," said the Friburgers.

"We do not wish to hinder the priests and preachers from amicably discussing matters of faith."

"Quite right," said the Friburgers. Thus articles for securing religious liberty were drawn, signed, and published. It is to be regretted that they were not faithfully kept, and that the Romanists, who thought discussion was folly, did not regard persecution as a crime.

We return to Farel. "Even were my father alive, I could not find time to write to him," was his frequent apology for silence. Yet he seized moments to address a noble letter to the suffering Christians of France, from whose numbers many young men were coming to labour in Switzerland. He now became interested in another body of sufferers on the slopes of the Italian Alps—the Waldenses.

For two or three years there were strange reports circulated among the infant churches which were forming between the Alps and the Jura. They heard of a wonderful people who had never been papists and had always been what they were struggling to be. These people had a simple faith, simple worship, simple form of government, and had been driven by Rome into the coldest recesses of Piedmont, and they were the most remarkable Christians ever known. But while these reports were coming over the snow-crowned mountains, other reports met them on the way. The Waldenses had rumours among them of the mighty work of God in the lands of the Rhine and the Rhone. Their preachers must go and see what Luther, and Farel, and Zwingle and their increasing hosts were doing and believing. They went on foot, and visited Germany, France, England and Switzerland, giving and receiving encouragement. They invited commissioners to their next Synod in Piedmont.

One day there came to Grandson two men, whose foreign look showed that they had come from a distance. It was in July, 1532. They wished to speak with Farel. George of Calabria, and Martin Gonin entered the room. They spoke of their people, their faith, their antiquity, and how they had not left Rome, for Rome had long ago left them. They had continued in the apostles' word and doctrine. Probably they said what some of their brethren, seated in the friendly house of Œcolampadius, had said to him. "Some people ascribe our origin to a wealthy citizen of Lyons, Peter Waldo, who saw one of his friends fall dead at a feast. Moved at the sight, and troubled in conscience, he prayed to the Lord, sold his goods and began to preach, and sent others to proclaim the gospel everywhere. But we descend from more ancient times, when Constantine was introducing the world into the church, and our fathers set themselves apart; or even from the time of the apostles." Farel was delighted with the brethren, and with joy accepted their invitation to attend their synod.

No time was to be lost,—Farel never had any to lose. He took with him Anthony Saunier, a Dauphinese, who knew popery by hard experience, having lain in prison at Paris fourten years, for daring to believe what his Redeemer taught. Certain friends had fears for their safety. Everywhere there were persecutions, and in Savoy and Dauphiny the bishops had specially "ordered a raid to be made upon the heretics." In the last days of August they passed by the caverns of Pignerol, in which the Waldenses had once their retreats and their temples; they passed La Tour, where every rock was a memorial of persecutions and martyrdoms; they went on to Angrogna. There the synod was to meet, in the parish of Martin Gonin. The people were in the fields and in the roads, ready "to be a guard to the ministers of the good law."

"That one with the red beard and riding the white horse is Farel," said John Peyret of Angrogna, the escort, to the people who gazed along the way. "The other, on the black horse, is Saunier." There was a third, "a tall man and rather lame," a Waldensian, perhaps, who had joined them. Other "foreign Christians" were gathering in this remote valley.

On the 12th of September the synod was opened "in the name of God." Farel was the leading man in favour of urging the Waldenses to renounce the papal errors that had slowly crept among them, or been forced upon them by the violence of the Romanists. The other party contended that they should compromise a little, in order to save their lives and their church. Farel gained his point with most of them. They confessed their errors and signed a covenant of faith and love.

It greatly interested Farel and Saunier to examine the old manuscripts, preserved for centuries, among which was the *Noble Lesson*, saying,—

> The Scriptures speak, and we must believe.
> Search the Scriptures from beginning to end.

And they looked at several manuscript copies of the Bible, which the Waldenses showed them with peculiar pride, saying,—"These were copied correctly by hand so long ago as to be beyond memory, and are to be seen in several families." The visitors were moved as they turned over the leaves, "marvelling at the heavenly favour accorded to so small a people."

Farel proposed to the synod that measures should be taken to have the Bible and other books translated, printed and circulated among the Waldenses, and to establish schools in all their parishes. They agreed "joyfully and with good hearts to Farel's demand." The hour came to adjourn and separate. The pastors returned to their churches, the shepherds to their flocks, the lords to their castles, and never forgot that people whose church has been "the burning bush of Christendom." Farel and Saunier shook hands with the villagers, who wept to see them go, mounted their horses and rode on, talking of teachers and translators, books and Bibles for the Waldenses. They were directing their way to an ancient city, where Cæsar had built long walls against the Helvetii, and where popery had thrown up entrenchments against the reformation. We turn now to Geneva, which God is about to make renowned for a theology that has been called "the grandest form of the grandest faith in heaven or on earth." The truth of the motto on her shield was being proved,—"After darkness I wait for light."

It was no sudden purpose, formed along the way, that led Farel to Geneva. It had long been in his mind, and before starting for Italy, he had resolved to stop there on his return. With that intent he had obtained from the Lords of Berne, certain letters of introduction to the leading Huguenots of Ge-

THE HUGUENOTS APPEAR.

neva. "I will go to them," said he, "I will speak to them, even if there is nobody that will hear me."

This plan of Farel is the beginning of the positive work of the Reformation in Geneva. But it was not the beginning of the movement against the papacy and the bishops. For years in that city, Rome had been opposed by a band of patriots who sought liberty in the state, but cared less for a new life in the church. Young Geneva had already been shaking old Rome. To understand the difficult work before Farel, it is quite important to trace the rise of the patriots, and see how they came to be called Huguenots.

There came to Geneva, in 1513, a brilliant young man, full of good-humour, making himself easily a favourite with everybody, laughing at almost everything, with wit sparkling on his pen, and Virgil and Cicero at his tongue's end. The priests admired him, the people loved him, and he was the hero of the hour. He could amuse his company, or in solitude prove himself one of the best French writers of his times. This agreeable scholar was Francis Bonivard, known in poetry as the prisoner of Chillon. "He was to play in Geneva by his liberalism, his information and his cutting satires, a part not very unlike that played by Erasmus in the great Reformation." With him there were two subjects too serious for a jest; one was the revival of letters, and the other was the love of liberty. He was born at Seyssel, and was in high favour with Charles III., Duke of Savoy, the worst of foes to Geneva. "He was educated at Turin where he became the ringleader of the wild set at the University." This, in the duke's eyes, qualified him for a work quite similar to that of Catiline when he sought to gain his treasonable plots by corrupting the youth of Rome. Charles was intent upon drawing Geneva into the snare, and annexing it to his dominions. The jovial Bonivard seemed to be just the man to prove "an excellent bait to entice the youth of the city into the nets of Savoy."

He soon met a genial companion. . Philibert Berthelier, with three centuries of noble blood in his veins, was the leader of a rising party in the city. In April, 1513, he had lamented the death of Charles de Seyssel, the bishop and prince of Geneva. This "right good person," ever mild and frank, was "for a wonder, a great champion of both ecclesiastical and secular liberty." He wished Geneva to remain with a free state and a free church. Duke Charles had sharply quarrelled with him, saying, "I made you bishop, but I will unmake you, and you shall be the poorest priest in the diocese." The bishop had just returned from a pilgrimage, and he suddenly died. It was thought that the duke made sure his threat, and poisoned him for the crime of protecting the liberties of Geneva.

When this report was on the wind there was intense excitement in the city. The gates were shut, cannon were dragged through the streets and placed on the walls, and sentries were posted everywhere. The citizens expected that the duke would seize the city, set his own bishop over them, and take the secular power in his own hands. They had good reasons for their suspicion. They gathered in groups on the streets, ready for any orator who might lift his voice.

Berthelier seized the opportunity to resist the pope and the duke, so that the one should not get the church, nor the other the state. "Let us resist the duke," said he and his associates. "Is there a people whose franchises are older than ours? We have always been free, and there is no memory of man to the contrary." "Come, you canons, choose a bishop! Elect a bishop who will defend our liberties." The man for them was at hand. They were too earthly themselves to ask for a candidate of a very heavenly spirit. Liberty, not religion, was the word on their lips. Aimé de Gingins, canon of St. Peter's, was then a firm advocate of Genevan rights. He was the best boon companion in the world, keeping open house and feasting joyously the friends of pleasure; fond of hearing his associates laugh and sing, and of rather free manners, after the custom of the church in those days. The people named him their bishop, and the canons confirmed the vote. The one thing now was to uphold their new bishop, and persuade the pope to sanction their choice. They sent men to Rome to obtain his confirmation.

The pope, Leo X., had another affair to manage. His brother Julian, the Magnificent, needed a wife. The pope had an eye upon the noble lady, Philiberta of Savoy, the sister of the duke Charles, and the aunt of Margaret, queen of Navarre. She was "a pure, simple-hearted young girl, of an elevated mind, a friend to the poor," and too good to be put up as the price of a bishopric. But so it was. With her, Charles would buy Geneva, and place over it a bishop from his own relatives.

He had a cousin, John, the son of an unmarried bishop, who was the grandson of the once married Amadeus, who was the last of the rival popes under the name of Felix V. John had no birth to boast, and was withal a puny, repulsive debauchee. "That is the man to be bishop of Geneva," thought the duke; "he is so much in my debt that he can refuse me nothing." John was ready for any bargain that would give him an office. Charles sent for him. "Cousin," said he, "I will raise you to a bishopric, if you will, in return, make over the temporal power to me." Thus John agreed to pay his debts, which the duke had "talked about pretty loudly" of late.

John went to Rome, and the pope received him with the greatest honour. "This disagreeable person had the chief place at banquet, theatre and concert." The pope kept him talking of the charms of Philiberta. "Let the duke give us his sister," said the pope, "and we will give you Geneva. You will then hand over the temporal power to the duke!" Was there not need of a Reformation?

The messengers of Geneva came to Rome, told of their choice of a bishop, but, alas! these Alpine shepherds had no beautiful princess to offer as the price of the favour they wished. "Begone," said Leo, "I know you not." The graceless John was the only one whom he would know as their bishop. The pope was thus paving the way for the overthrow of his power in Geneva, and for the Reformation.

"A fine election, indeed, his holiness has honoured us with!" said Berthelier and his compatriots. "For our bishop, he gives us a dissipated clerk; for our guide, in the paths of virtue, a dissipated bastard; for the preserver of our ancient liberties, a scoundrel ready to sell them!"

It was expected that Bonivard would take the part of the duke, the pope, and also of the disgusting John. But he took sides with the patriots. He found Berthelier to be "one of those noble natures who count glory by placing themselves at the service of the weak. No man seemed better fitted to save Geneva. . . He affected no great airs, used no big words, was fond of pleasure and the noisy talk of his companions; but there was always observable in him a seriousness of thought, great energy, a strong will, and above all a supreme contempt of life." Yet policy led him to act at first a strange part with the new bishop.

John came to his diocese and met with no violent opposition.

He must be wise in his crafty schemes, and court the leading patriots. He soon learned that there was one name on all lips; one citizen, ever cheerful, frank in heart, very popular, taking part with the young people in all their merry-making, winning them by his charming and lively manners, and gaining confidence by his willingness to render them any service in his power. "Good," said John; "here is a man I must have. If I gain him I will have nothing to fear. He must have the best charge I can bestow."

"Be cautious," whispered certain ones; "he conceals a rebellious, energetic, unyielding mind."

"Fear nothing," replied John; "he sings gayly and drinks with the young men of the town." Berthelier did this to kindle their souls at his fire. He was at last induced to accept of the castle of Peney. Bonivard said,—"Peney is the apple which the serpent gave to Eve." But Berthelier had not sold himself. The people's bishop, de Gingins, was given a large pension, and he lived in the same house which afterwards became the home of John Calvin. Bonivard was now to secure the object for which he had come to Geneva.

His uncle, John Aimè Bonivard, was the prior of St. Victor, near one of the city gates. It was a little state, and its prior a sovereign prince. The aged uncle was on his death-bed, and Francis, now one-and-twenty, sat by it. The old man grew seriously agitated. He thought of one great evil that he had done. In rashness he had once ordered four large culverins to be made at the expense of the church, in order to batter down the castle of an old friend and neighbour. None of his many other old sins gave him so fearful a pang as this. In anguish he turned to his nephew, saying,—"Francis, you know those pieces of cannon. . . They ought to be employed in God's service. I desire that immediately after my death they may be cast into bells for the church." The old prior felt relieved and died, leaving to his nephew the principality, the convent and the culverins.

On this very day Berthelier called to sympathize with his friend, and he heard the story of the four guns. "What! cast cannon into bells!" he exclaimed; "we will give you as much metal as you require to make a peal that shall ring loud enough to stun you; but the culverins ought to remain culverins."

"My uncle ordered them to be put to the service of the church."

"The church will be doubly served," retorted Berthelier. "There will be bells at St. Victor and artillery in the city." The point was gained. Berthelier laid the matter before the council, who voted all that was needed for the bells.

The duke heard of this affair, and he could not be prudent toward men whose minds would not bear provocation. He claimed the convent guns. So anxious was he to succeed in the game he was playing that he moved too rashly. His one thought was to possess Geneva. By grasping for it he was doomed to lose his principalities. The guns made a noise in the city. The council of fifty met to discuss the matter, and Berthelier was not alone in supporting the rights of the city.

A young man of twenty-five rose up and said,—"In the name of the people I oppose the surrender of this artillery to his highness; the city cannot spare them." This young citizen was Besançon Hugues, who felt that liberty was worth a war with the duke. Not yet had the sports, the music, the dances, the cup and the card caused him to forget the freedom of his country. Others of the "children of Geneva" had not been made effeminate by these soft arts. They were ready to use the culverins;

they would not give them up; and so the four guns remained in the city. But from that hour Charles shot his wrath at Berthelier, Hugues and Bonivard.

Not yet was Geneva fully given over to the duke. Perhaps these patriots hoped that they could manage the weak and unpopular John, and prevent the surrender of the temporal power. John was at Rome, urging his cousin's demand. Philiberta was about to be married, and the pope was expected to ratify the bargain as soon as she should be paid over to his brother, Julian de Medici. He did it. His bull confirmed the wedding of Geneva to Savoy, which was the real marriage intended. Charles was delighted with his triumph. He had gained what his ancestors had sought for centuries. He imagined himself the hero of his race, and told everybody,—"I am sovereign lord of Geneva in temporal matters. I obtained it from our holy father, the reigning pope."

The news went to Geneva. The whole city was in commotion. When John came, the council begged him to maintain their ancient liberties. He looked at them, but was silent. They went back thinking that the last blow was struck in the old republic. The citizens met without exchanging a word: their pale faces and downcast looks told all. One cry, however, was heard:—"Since justice is powerless we will resort to force; and, if the duke is resolved to enter Geneva, he shall pass over our bodies."

The patriot party grew. It attracted the young men with whom Berthelier had laughed and sung, and they caught his fire. The bishop, John, began to obey his masters. He laid heavy fines on the people; he deprived men of their offices; he threw good citizens into prison for imaginary offences; he carried off Claude Vandel, a distinguished lawyer of spotless character;

he pardoned a robber; and he was bent upon robbing Geneva of all her rights. The leading patriots were aroused. They prepared for the worst, if war should be necessary. Threats alarmed the Savoyards, and one night they concluded to flee. Ordering their horses they rode out by a secret gate. Nor did they go alone. The gouty bishop went with them to Turin, and in great terror crouched at the feet of his master, Charles.

"Cousin," said the duke, "in your fold there are certain *dogs* that bark very loudly and defend your sheep very stoutly; you must get rid of them."

The bishop was open to such advice, and there, in the palace of Charles the *Good*, who was cruellest of all, was plotted the death of Geneva's best citizens.

Those citizens knew what to expect. On a day when several of them met, Berthelier said, "Have done with banquets and dances; we must organize young Geneva into a defensive league."

"Yes; let us march onwards;" said Bonivard, "and God will give a good issue to our bold enterprise."

"Comrade, your hand," said Berthelier, reaching forth his own. Their hands were clasped. A cloud passed over Berthelier's face, and he said, "But know that for the liberty of Geneva, you will lose your benefice, and I shall lose my head." Bonivard could not forget this scene, and he wrote, "He told me that a hundred times." It would prove too true.

Larger meetings were held. The bell was ringing for vespers when about fifty of the patriots met around Berthelier. He told them of their history and bade them consider their destiny. The great citizen fixed on them his noble look and asked, "Do you wish to transmit to your children slavery instead of liberty?"

"No, no; but how can the liberties of the city be saved?"

"How! By being united, by forgetting our private quarrels, by opposing with one every violation of our rights. . . . If the bishop's officers lay hands on one of us, let all the rest defend him. Who touches one, touches all."

"Yes, yes, one heart, one cause! Who touches one, touches all!"

"Good, let this motto be the name of our league, but let us be faithful to the noble device."

"But what would we do," asked one among many who had their fears, "if the duke and bishop should attack the city with a strong army?"

"Fear nothing," replied Berthelier, sharply; "we have good friends; I will go to the Swiss, I will bring back forces, and then I will settle accounts with our foes."

Thus ran the tide when the bishop returned, and took pleasure in making arrests and in torturing poor Pècolat. Terrors increased in the city, the streets were deserted, only a few labourers were seen in the fields. Many citizens fled. The league of Touch one, touch all, was almost dissolved, and that at the very hour when its founder was in peril. Berthelier was threatened.

"The sword is over your head," said Bonivard. "Escape for life."

"I know it," Berthelier answered, "yes, I know that I shall die, and I do not grieve at it."

"Really, I never saw and never read of one who held life so cheap." Others joined Bonivard in urging their chief to flee. They told him of the power of his foes.

"God will miraculously take away their power," he replied.

"There happen to be here some envoys from Friburg. Depart

with them. Out of Geneva you will serve the city better than within it."

This consideration decided him. Early the next morning he put on a Friburg cloak, and when the troupe rode through the gate, the cautious guard did not suspect that the great republican was with them. The spoiler put his hand on the nest, but the bird was gone. The houses were searched for six days, but all for nothing. The bishop was raving in his castle; Berthelier was calling the Swiss to aid Geneva.

By the hearth of Councillor Marty in Friburg, sat Berthelier, sorrowful, silent and motionless. A great idea was in his mind, "Geneva must be an ally of Switzerland,"—which then included only a small part of the country now called by that name—"For that I would give my head." He began to talk with his host. "I have come poor, exiled, persecuted and a suppliant, not to save my life, but to save Geneva, and to pray Friburg to receive the Genevans into citizenship."

"Take courage," said Marty, giving his hand. "Follow me into the abbeys where the guilds are assembled. If you gain them your cause is won."

We need not follow them to hear the eloquence of Berthelier. He gained his object. The Friburgers would go and see the misfortunes of Geneva with their own eyes. They went, and talked, and dined with such men as Hugues and the Vandels. They hunted up bishop John, easing his gout in the country, and reasoned with him in a different style from that prevailing at Turin. They asked a safe-conduct for Berthelier so that he might return home. It was refused on the ground that he needed none! Nobody would harm him! "Very well," said the Friburgers, "we will collect together these grievances of the people and remedy them. We will come in such force as to take these Savoyards and then—then we will treat them as you have treated our friends." After this they rode home in great wrath.

The words of the Friburgers were repeated through the city. The league between them and the Genevans was spoken of as a mightier protection than that of the "Children of Geneva." A new German word was introduced, Eidesgenossen, the oath-bound Leaguers. The duke's party threw it in contempt at the patriots, and as it did not fit the Savoyard tongue, they put it into various shapes, Eidguenots, Eyguenots, Huguenots! Perhaps the name of Hugues helped to give it the latter form. It was a nick-name, long since made sacred by the noble character of those who bore it. It passed into France and was probably first applied to all who opposed the Papacy. At Geneva it had originally a purely political meaning, and simply meant the friends of independence. It had no religious meaning until after the Reformation.

The duke's party had no sooner started this epithet than the patriots, repaying them in their own coin, called out, "Hold your tongues, you Mamelukes. As the Mamelukes denied Christ to follow Mahomet, so you deny liberty for tyranny."

We might linger upon many a touching story of trials, banishments, tortures and executions, but space forbids. The years rolled on, the times grew worse, and Geneva found no permanent relief. After a while Bonivard was arrested, robbed of his priory, and shut up for two years in a castle. An army of the duke was in the city. Berthelier, who had returned, had reason to expect death.

Early one morning, Berthelier set out for his daily retreat, where he breathed the fresh air in a quiet meadow near the city. He was now, (1519,) about forty years of age, and so conscious of his danger that he was "always booted and ready to depart for the unknown shores of eternity." He had with him a little weasel, of which he was very fond. It was sporting in his bosom as he walked on in contempt of his enemies. An officer, who knew of these morning walks, had placed some soldiers outside the walls, while he remained within to make certain the arrest. Just as the good citizen was about to pass the gates, the troop came forward. He thought not of going back to arouse the young men of the League; he turned not from the road, but went on caressing his little favourite, and "walked straight toward the armed men, as proudly as if he were going to take them," wrote Bonivard. Thus "one of the founders of modern liberty" was arrested, and was to suffer the vengeance of his tyrant foes. He was thrust into prison, where his little weasel still played in his bosom, and at the least noise would stiffen its ears and look into the eyes of its master. He had holier means of lightening his cares; he quoted the Psalms, and perhaps, cast all his burdens on the Lord. On the wall he wrote a sentence which some think refers to the Saviour's resurrection. His foes were trying to frighten him with threats of death when he wrote, "I shall not die, but live and declare the works of the Lord." He became the martyr of liberty, but though dead, he yet spake of freedom for Geneva. "Three great movements were carried out in this city," says D'Aubigne. "The first was the conquest of independence; the second, the conquest of faith; the third, the renovation and organization of the church. Berthelier, Farel, and Calvin are the three heroes of these three epics."

This leader of the league left much work to be done. A new man came to bear his part in it. This was Baudichon de la Maison-Neuve, a man of noble family, exalted character, bold measures, welcome everywhere, and serving to clear the way for the reformation. But God was removing out of the world the bishop who was assuredly not fit to remain in power; and, unless there was deep repentance for his personal sins and shames, not fit to be taken away by death.

John lay at Pignerol, dying of diseases which charity would leave untold. At his bed-side stood Peter de la Baume, who was trying to console the bishop. The poor man had some remorse for his crimes. A crucifix was held before his eyes. His mind was upon the man whose death he had caused, and he imagined that he saw the features of Berthelier. With a wild look he asked,—"Who has done that?" Blasphemy and insult were mingled with the foam that whitened his lips. At length his heart softened a little. Giving to Peter a last look, he said,—"I wished to give the principality of Geneva to Savoy. To attain that object I have put many innocent persons to death. . . . . If you obtain this bishopric, I entreat you not to tread in my footsteps. Defend the franchises of the city." He said more, closing with the words,—"In purgatory God will pardon me." He breathed his last, and Peter rose up from his prayer the bishop of Geneva.

Worse and worse trials came. The bishop kept none of his promises. The duke entered the city with Portuguese fashions and theatrical plays. The people were expected to attend dramas, dances, games and sports in the open air, even in spite of the April rains. There were some good qualities about Peter, the bishop, and he proved the scope of his imagination, or his power to insult with flattery, when he told the Genevans of "the great love and affection which John had felt, while alive, for them and for all his good subjects," and that he "had made as holy an end as ever prelate did!"

CHAPTER XIV.

LAYMEN IN THE FIELD.

(1523–1532.)

THE Huguenots were demanding that the Genevans should be free; others, mostly laymen, were coming with a little book in their hands, to say "The truth shall make you free indeed." One class spoke in the name of humanity, the other in the name of Christianity. The two great forces were soon at work; but they did not work unitedly. Many of these political Huguenots were still Romanists. They were afraid of the Bible. Like many now in Europe, they wished to throw off the temporal power of the pope, but yet let the pope have his spiritual power. The patriot Hugues hoped for a free, but not a protestant Geneva. It was the state, not the church, that he wished to see reformed. The same mind was in Bonivard, who, like Erasmus, dealt his satires upon all parties. If these Huguenots had all been athirst for the Bible, and if they had made that the corner-stone of their liberties, there would have been less battle and a speedier victory. Farel would have found the reformation already there when he entered the city. Calvin would have had far less trouble in fulfilling his mission.

Had these patriots all been protestants, Geneva might have received her form of doctrine and polity from Wittemberg. Luther was known there in 1520. A few Huguenots had rejoiced at his resistance to the papal power. They wished to treat the bulls of the Vatican as Luther had done—burn them. His writings seem to have found their way into the city. Bonivard says in his chronicle,—"Luther had already given instruction at this time to many in Geneva and elsewhere." The duke's party heard the great monk's name and took alarm. They thought it worth while to make a splendid parade, and march out of the city with the image of St. Peter, and cry down Luther and his doctrines. The Huguenots noticed the procession of canons, priests, monks, scholars and white clerks marching beyond the walls. "All the priests have gone out," said they; "let us shut the gates and prevent them from returning." Had they done so, it would have been nothing more than a rough joke. But they lacked the courage. The idea got wind; the startled priests and monks hurried back to their nests, and had only a good fright. There was a far better way to exclude these haters of Luther, had these Huguenots been willing to learn it. They were to have the opportunity. The Bible was coming.

The deeds of men outlast their names. We know not who were the humble missionaries that came to Geneva about the year 1524; but we know what they carried. It was Lefevre's French Testament. It was borne on the waves of that missionary movement, which was started at Basle, Montbeliard and Lyons. Not in vain did the Chevalier Anemond oversee the printing of these Testaments and religious books; not in vain did the merchants, Vaugris and Du Blet, send them into those regions which swell the Rhone with their streams. The book-hawkers came to Geneva, and some of the citizens "talked with them and bought their books.".

One of the first to welcome these Bible-colporteurs was Baudichon, who read the Scriptures with astonishment, because he could find in them no Romanism, no images, no mass, no pope, no purgatory, but could find a new religion, a new authority, a new life, a new church ; and all these new things were just what the Lord and his apostles taught. Robert Vandel also read with delight, for he thought that here was the power to make Geneva a republic, independent in religion and politics. Such men saw with disgust the snares laid by the duke's party in the amusements which pretended to be in honour of Charles and the new bishop. Among other displays was a theatrical performance called "the finding of the cross." It was a lame attempt at a "mystery-play." It represented the Emperor Constantine and his mother, Helena, going to Jerusalem to find the cross, so that the precious relic might be of use to the church. Three crosses were dug up on the Calvary represented upon the stage. A miracle would decide the true one from those of the two thieves. A dead body, (so feigned,) was brought. Helena says,—

> To this corpse we will apply
> These three crosses carefully,
> And, if I be not mistaken,
> At the touch it will awaken.

The three crosses are applied and when the third one touches the corpse it is restored to life! Wonderful miracle! The Mamelukes were delighted. Charles fancied such tricks were acting like a charm. "The flies are caught by the honey," said he; "yet a few more diversions and these proud Genevans will become our slaves."

The Huguenots resolved to have a play of their own, and gained permission to honour the duke and new bishop in their own way. A great fair was drawing the people to the city, and a crowd gathered to see the Huguenot play. A bishop or two and many priests came, but Charles knew the men too well; he feared a "snake in the grass" and did not appear. The play was Le Monde Malade, the Sick World, or really the Finding of the Bible. The World was very sick, growing worse and worse, a priest comes with his wares and masses, World wants the masses very short, priest shows him some, they don't suit, priest finds that neither short nor long masses will do, a wise man proposes a new remedy—"What is it, say?"

> "A thing which no man dare gainsay,
> THE BIBLE!"

The World does not like that remedy, and proves himself a fool! Thus the play ends. The Genevans soon had more serious events to engage their minds. For two years there were banishments and martyrdoms, but the Testaments were not lost. The tyrants missed their mark by sending patriots as exiles to Berne and Basle, and other cities where the truth was preached. The Romanists were sending them to the school of the gospel.

These wanderers had woes enough, but this helped to bring about the Swiss alliance of 1526. Berne and Friburg joined hands with Geneva. The exiles returned, the duke's party began to flee "like birds of night before the first beams of day." Laymen began to talk about the gospel, and to read and think for themselves. An honest Helvetian was coming to give them a lift.

Thomas ab Hofen, a wise and sedate man, had done a good work at Berne. The alliance-business brought several deputies to Geneva, and he came along with them, greatly to Zwingle's joy. This Christian layman had no intention of reforming the city; his mission was diplomatic; but he was not one who could hide his genial light. He visited many citizens, attended the churches, met the people in their meetings, and concluded that there was much patriotism among them, but very little Christianity. The great want in Geneva was religion. At his inn he wrote to Zwingle, "The number of those who confess the gospel must be increased." There were a few Christians in the city.

The deputy of Berne was not ashamed to be an ambassador of Christ. When he could take an hour from his official duties, he conversed with the people, telling them what was going on at Berne and Zurich. Around the hearth of some Huguenot, where burned the January fire, he talked of the good gospel, and kindled a love for the liberty there is in Christ. We imagine him often at the house of Baudichon whose wife became an earnest believer. But he had a chance to learn the former fatness of the priests by looking behind the screens.

The priests honoured him at first, as one in high office. Some of them heard him often speak of religion and imagined that he belonged to their coterie. They were afraid to have a layman talk of the gospel; it looked too much like apostolic and reformation days. They sought to gain his pity by innocently telling him of the fine times they had, when presents of bread, wine, oil, game and tapers were plentiful in their houses. "But alas!" said they, with sad complaints, "the faithful bring us no more offerings, and people do not run so ardently after indulgences as they used to do." This was more pleasing news to Ab Hofen than they supposed. It might be a bad state of things for the priests, but it was good for the gospel.

The citizens became more and more attached to the genial visitor. They invited him to their homes, and their public assemblies, that he might speak of the noble things occurring at Zurich. He was cheered, and his old melancholy fits did not return so frequently. His eyes sparkled. and he felt unwearied in well doing. "I will not cease proclaiming the gospel," he wrote to Zwingle; "all my strength shall be devoted to it."

But now he finds, the darker side of his work. The Huguenots were mostly mere friends of liberty, and not of the gospel. They grew cold toward him when he spoke of certain reforms, and of that faith which saves. Those who were first to welcome him began to fall away, and scarcely saluted him in the street. The eyes of the priests flashed with jealousy and hatred, as they went about warning the people against him, lest he should ruin the city. The men were made cautious, and the women especially frightened. "All my efforts are in vain," he wrote, "there are about seven hundred clergymen in Geneva, who do their utmost to prevent the gospel from flourishing here. And yet a wide door is opened to the word of God. The priests do not preach; and as they are unable to do so, they are satisfied with saying mass in Latin. If any preachers were to come here, proclaiming Christ with boldness, the doctrine of the pope, I am sure, would be overthrown."

This simple-hearted, sensitive layman despaired of doing any good, and with a broken heart returned to Berne. He died not long after, "as a Christian ought to die." It was found after his departure, that his efforts had not been useless. Even Hugues, the leader of the Romish Huguenots, was benefited, and joined hands, for a time, with Baudichon, the leader of the gospel Huguenots. William la Mouille, the bishop's confidant, seems to have been led to the truth by the good layman of Berne.

The duke's party—the "bishopers"—were in trouble. Peter

la Baume had let the Huguenots elect their magistrates to govern the city so that he might get the temporal power in his hands. The canons must flee, and away they went, muttering, "No more canons, ere long no more bishop." Their saying was to come true, not because the duke was now against the bishop, who claimed also to be the temporal prince, but because Peter played the fool, as the robber of a young girl. One day in 1527, a report got abroad which put the whole city in commotion. "A young girl of respectable family," said the crowd, "has just been carried off by the bishop's people; we saw them dragging her to the palace." The palace gates were shut; the bishop was at dinner. The girl's mother had rushed forth, followed the robbers up to the gates, which were shut in her face, and was now pacing about the building, crying in despair. The citizens crowded in front of the palace, and were not choice of their terms in deriding the bishop.

Peter did not like to be disturbed at dinner time. He was puzzled to know what to do, and thought the best thing was to be deaf. Wine did not calm him, for he heard a furious hammering at the gates. The servants told him that the magistrates had come; he left his chair, and went to the window. There he stood, "paler than death;" the people gazed, and were profoundly silent. The magistrates made him a respectful and earnest speech. He answered, "Certainly, gentlemen, you shall have the young woman. I only had her carried off for a harper, who asked me for her in return for his services." So she was stolen to pay the wages of a musician! Guilty enough, but viler still. The gates were unbarred, the girl restored to her mother.

"No more bishop," thought the people. He might go and join the exiled canons. "Ha, you bishopers! a fine religion is that of your bishop," cried the Huguenots. On a certain night Peter took a boat, and then a horse, and made for Burgundy, where in summer he could walk "among his pinks and gillyflowers," and in winter have his "beautiful fur robes, lined with black satin," and all the year round be able to say, "I am much better supplied with good wine here than we were at Geneva." Of which wine, one who often dined with him, says, "he had sometimes more than he could carry."

"The hireling fleeth," said the people, "when he seeth the wolf coming." The wolf was the duke of Savoy, who wished to devour both hireling and sheep. But Charles was to hear that the Genevans had removed the signs of his temporal power from among them. "No more bishop," the next thing was "no more duke." Eight years before he had set up the white cross of Savoy, carved in marble, in the heart of the city. The Huguenots were grieved whenever they saw it. He had said, "I have placed my arms in the middle of the city as a mark of sovereignty. Let the people efface them if they dare!" One morning, five days after the bishop's flight, the white cross was gone. "Who did it?" asked the gathering crowd. "It has fallen into the river," but no one could see it in the clear waters. The parties began to quarrel. Bonivard at last said, "I know the culprit."—"Who? who is it?"—"St. Peter, for, as the patron of Geneva, he is unwilling that any secular prince should have any ensign of authority in the city." This event produced a great impression, and as the authors were never known, some thought it a miracle. Many said, "What the hand of God hath thrown down, let not hand of man set up again!"

Other Bernese laymen came to Geneva to continue the work of Ab Hofen. It was the Lenten season, and they said in private families, "God speaks to us of the Redeemer, and not of Lent."

"Obey the Church," said the Friburgers, "or we will break off the alliance." The Genevans thought on the subject; many of them ate meat that spring, and felt none the worse for it, however much it put the alliance in danger.

The Bernese soldiers, who had kindled their fires with the images taken from the churches, had let fall little sparks of truth, which burned and blazed in the hearts of the citizens. The Huguenots made some new signs of uneasiness; they uttered their sarcasms upon the priests in public places; they walked up and down the aisles of the churches, and talked of the needed reform. In 1530 Hugues Vandel wrote for help, and sent one letter to Farel. "The majority in the city of Geneva," he said, "would like to be evangelical, but they want to be shown the way, and no one dare preach the gospel in the churches, for fear of Friburg." Farel knew how serious was this difficulty, for stout old Berne had long been opposed by Friburg. What could be done? After much thinking Vandel suddenly gained a bright idea, and wrote to Farel and Fabri about it. His plan was this: St. Victor was a little independent state near the walls of Geneva, and Bonivard might annex it to Berne; then a Bernese bailiff would be there and "a preacher who would be our great comfort." The Huguenots could then leave the mass and go out in crowds to hear Christ preached in the church of Bonivard. The plan failed. In fact the prior of St. Victor had scarcely the control of his own possessions. He could not collect his rents, and plots were on foot to betray him and the convent to the duke. He grew sad when reduced to four crowns a month, and that a gift from the council of Geneva. By annexing the priory to the hospital of the city he hoped to gain his revenues. The duke would not permit this, for he must have the priory, as it would give him a footing close to the gates which were shut against him. Charles resolved to get rid of him.

Bonivard was in trouble about his priory, his poverty, his enemies, but above all his mother was seriously ill at the town of Seyssel in the duke's territory. He must go and see her; the duke was glad to send him a passport. He did not see the trap; he visited his mother, and left her full of anguish for his fate. She was never to see him again. He started for Lausanne, but when on the Jorat hills he was seized by ruffians and carried to the castle of Chillon, where he was to remain six long years. The duke's hand was apparent; the agent of this treachery was Bellegarde, who had slept with him the night before, and said in the morning, "I am afraid something may happen to you, I will send my servant with you." This servant led him into the ambush. Bellegarde had been the murderer of the patriot Levriere.

The brilliant existence of this Genevan Erasmus was thus suddenly ended. He was never himself again. When he came out of Chillon he was a far different man. The long caged bird had lost both voice and wing. He had not the gospel in which to rejoice like Luther in the Wartburg. He had cheated himself of these heavenly consolations by trying to keep on neutral ground and be neither a Romanist nor a gospel Huguenot. His wit, his jests and his criticisms upon everybody unfitted him for the true benefits of the Reformation. And yet we cannot but sympathize with him, when sitting in his large armchair at St. Victor, he writes, "The Huguenot leagues are not sufficient; the gospel must advance in order that popery may recede."

Again there were Bernese soldiers in the city, (October, 1530,) and they determined to have the word of God preached. They went to the cathedral and ordered the door to be opened. Some of them went into the towers and rang the bells. Their preacher went into the pulpit, read the Scriptures and delivered a sermon. Many Genevese looked on and listened, but did not fully understand. It was a new mode of worship; but, when they saw that simple prayer, singing, and the reading and explaining of God's word were the essential parts of it, they liked it better than the Roman form. From that time the reformed service was repeated daily, for weeks, and "no other bell, little or big, rang in Geneva." The priests said it was all *German*, and the people would not be the wiser for it. But copies of the Bible and tracts in French were in store. The preacher went about among the Genevans, talked with them, and, after shaking hands with them, left books in their houses whose truth would bring rest to their hearts. Some of them began to "prefer God's pardon to the pardons of the pope."

Whispers of such movements came to the ear of Farel, during the years when he was being carried into cathedrals, or was making his own perilous way into forbidden pulpits, and was settling pastors over the flocks which had been won from popery. Geneva occupied his thoughts.

In the little boat that bore him so often across the Lake Neufchatel, in his visits to the Val de Ruz, on his bed at Morat, recovering from severe bruises and the loss of blood, on his journey to the Waldenses, and still more on his return, he felt that he must preach the gospel in Geneva also. It was not enough that the Huguenots should refuse to listen to the mass, and simply walk up and down the church while the priests were chanting it. They must have the gospel. To break from error is but half a reformation; the better half is the full acceptance of the truth.

"Alas!" said he, "there is no other law at Geneva than the law of arms." The law of God must be there. The patriots had only secured a lip-revolution. The preacher must declare regeneration as the only hope for true liberty. He wished to go at once. The very fact of the strong opposition there was an attraction to his bold and quite romantic nature. But Berne had claims upon him, and noble Berne had no authority to send him into Geneva. If he liked perils, he had enough in the districts where he was already beaten for the gospel's sake. If he left those fields, Rome would regain her lost ground. He, therefore, looked about for some man who was fitted to bear the glad word to that city, of which the restless prior, Bonivard, had said, a few years before,—"God only remained; but, while Geneva slept, he kept watch for her."

We left the young Peter Toussaint at the mansion of the noble Madame Contraigues, waiting for some voice to call him into a bolder work than the Duchess Margaret was willing to have done. He went afterward to Zurich, at the call of its reformers. Here seemed to be the needed man. Farel wrote to Zwingle,— "Make haste to send him into the Lord's vineyard, for you know how well fitted he is for this work. . . It is no small matter; see that you do not neglect it. Urge Toussaint to labour strenuously, so as to redeem, by his zeal, all the time he has lost." The great doctor did all that he could to persuade the young Frenchman, who at first was inclined to go. "Enter into the house of the Lord," said the adviser; "rend the hoods in pieces, and triumph over the shavelings. You will not have much trouble, for the word of God has already put them to flight."* He did not literally mean that Toussaint should tear the friars to pieces; but the young man was afraid to see even their hoods shaking at him. He had wanted to see more courage shown at the Parisian court; he now lacked it himself when Genevan perils were before him. He shrank back and refused to take the mission with its cross.

Farel, who never shrank from any summons, was vexed. He could scarcely afterward forgive his young friend. He fell down and poured out his anguish before Heaven. "O Christ, draw up thine army according to thy good pleasure; pluck out all apathy from the hearts of those who are to give thee glory, and arouse them mightily from their slumber."

This apathy was, perhaps, charged partly upon the Bernese, who had not sent preachers to Geneva, as Farel thought was their duty. They took alarm at the threat of the Friburgers, who said,—"If Geneva is reformed there is an end to the alliance." The alliance did come to wreck; a hurricane was blowing over Geneva, for the duke of Savoy was preparing to attack the city. The Bernese gave up the cause of the Huguenots. "Alas!" wrote Farel, "the Bernese show less zeal for the glory of Christ than the Friburgers for the decrees of the pope."

One patriot heart was broken when the alliance was ended. It was that of Besançon Hugues, the duke's enemy, but the bishop's friend. He resigned his office, saying to the senate,— "I am growing old; I have many children; I wish to devote

* Eleven days before Zwingle fell in battle, (October, 1531,) Farel wrote to him,—"Many in that city feel in their hearts holy aspirations after true piety." And again, later,—"Several Genevans are meditating on the work of Christ." Such were the last good words from Farel, at Grandson, that should reach the heroic reformer of Zurich.

myself to my own affairs." He was only forty-five; but the late months had been as long years to him. His forty official missions, his dangers, his flights and exposures, his disappointments and reproaches were enough to bring gray hairs upon that head, which deserves some of our best laurels. It was God's time for him to retire. He would be in the way of the gospel movement. He was not pleased to see that the Christian Huguenots were gaining new followers every day. It was time to give space to Baudichon. His Romanism must fade before the reformation. He retired, sighing lest all liberty was lost, and in less than a year he breathed his last. Faith might have taught him that God would defeat the threatening duke of Savoy, by bringing in a mighty alliance with Heaven.

An ambassador of the heavenly alliance was coming,—a modest, learned, devout, and strong layman, who would help to prepare the way for Calvin and Farel. Farel had long known him—perhaps had seen him on the university benches, when Lefevre was awakening debates among the students—and perhaps he had a hand in bringing him into Geneva. He was not a preacher, but merely a school-master. We need to know more of him.

When Calvin was at college in Paris, he was often visited by his fellow-townsman and cousin, Peter Robert Olivetan. Calvin was then a devout Romanist, and it grieved him to find his affectionate cousin such a heretic. The grief was fully reciprocated: Robert did all he could to convert his younger relative.

"O my dear friend," said Robert, "study the Scriptures."

"I will have none of your doctrines," was the reply. "Their novelty offends me."

They parted, little satisfied with each other. Calvin knelt before the images in the chapel, and prayed to the saints for his friend. The other shut himself up in his room and prayed to Christ. The prayer to Jesus was to prevail. One day Calvin saw light breaking through the darkness that for months had gathered before him. "If I have been mistaken," said he; "if Olivetan and my other friends are right; if they have found that peace which the doctrines of the priests refuse me!" He shed tears and cried unto God. Following Olivetan's advice he studied the Scriptures—perhaps the Testament of Lefevre. It is worthy of notice that the three great Picardins—Lefevre, Olivetan and Calvin, were to have a decided influence at Geneva. It is very touching to know that the older cousin helped to lead the younger into the truth, and then, without any plan but that of God, he went to a strange city to help prepare a place for him to declare it. It was strange, too, in human eyes, that Olivetan should be led to Geneva. He was not seeking it. He had been compelled to leave Paris, and Farel had fixed upon him as a teacher for those ancient Waldenses who were holding out their hands to the modern reformers.

In the city council of Geneva there was a wealthy, enlightened and influential man, named Jean Chautemps. He needed a teacher for his sons. People spoke to him of a mild, genial man, who knew well the best society of Paris, and, "besides, a very learned man." This gentleman considered it very fortunate to have such a master for his children, and soon had in his house Robert Olivetan, who taught according to "the right mode" of Mathurin Cordier, the great preceptor of Calvin.

Was he thinking that his brilliant and powerful cousin might some time come and preach in Geneva? Perhaps; and yet he said nothing in that direction. He set bravely to work in his modest way. He held forth a shining lamp. He sometimes went with Chautemps to the churches, and was moved with grief at the errors which he saw and heard. He would return home, and, sitting with his patron, refute the opinions of the priests, and explain the word of God. The councillor became a friend of the reformation, and, amid all the strifes, upheld the growing cause. His heart was warming, and his house preparing to receive "that great missionary, Farel," about whom there were such wonderful reports in the land.

The school-master took a still wider range, and talked with the councillor's friends, and to all whom he could approach. He endeavoured to "point out *with gentleness*" to the priests the errors which they taught. Fear did not hinder him. He became so bold that Chautemps advised him to be more cautious, lest he should come to harm. Still he went on in his unassuming, but courageous way. And now the Genevans began to come to him. In small circles they sat to hear the word. Then, from private houses, he was drawn out into the open air, in front of the churches, there to touch the consciences and make the ears of his hearers tingle.

One day at a private assembly there came a few men and women, most of them known to the master of the house, and they sat down on the benches before the new teacher. Some of the intellectual men, of whom Geneva was proud, were present. After reproving their sins and their unbelief, and telling them of Christ, he said to them, "We cannot attain true holiness if the Holy Ghost, who is the reformer of hearts, be absent. By the Spirit of Jesus Christ the remains of sin in us diminish little by little. What a profound mystery! He, who was hung upon the cross, who even ascended into heaven to finish everything, comes and dwells in us, and then accomplishes the perfect work of eternal redemption." Thus taught the school-master, who was soon to rouse all Geneva.

The pope's great jubilee was coming; the people were talking about it, and some told how it originated. A witty scholar thus relates the story, "On the eve of the new year, 1300, a report spread suddenly through Rome (no one knew whence it came,) that a plenary indulgence would be granted to all who would go the next morning to St. Peter's. A great crowd of Romans and foreigners hurried there, and in the midst of the multitude was an aged man, stooping and leaning on his staff, who wished also to take a part in the festival. He was a hundred and seven years old, people said. He was led to the pope, the proud and daring Boniface VIII. The old man told him, how, a century before, an indulgence of a hundred years had been granted on account of the jubilee; he remembered it well, he said. Boniface, taking advantage of the declaration of this man, whose mind was weakened by age, declared that there should be a plenary indulgence every hundred years." As great gains were made out of the scheme, it was thought that it would pay well to have the jubilee more frequently, and it was appointed for every fifty years, then every thirty-three, and then every twenty-five. Such jubilees were held in our times in 1825 and in 1833.

The minds of the Genevans were soon in a great ferment. There was much talk and murmuring everywhere in the streets. "A fine tariff is the pope's," the bolder ones said. "Do you want an indulgence for a false oath? Pay about 29 livres. One for murder? a man's life is cheaper—only about 15 livres. It is all an invention of the devil."

"If the pope sells indulgences," said some who were beginning to have glimpses of the truth, "the gospel gives a free pardon. Since Rome advertises her pardons, let us advertise that of the Lord." They went to Olivetan, whom they had probably heard declare against these tricks to fill the treasuries of the pope. He probably was the real author of a "heavenly proclamation," which was to startle the citizens. Baudichon hurried to the printer, and had it struck off in large, bold letters. He and one Goulaz laid their plans, and while Geneva slept, as the ninth of June was dawning, they were busy in the streets. Gentle taps of the hammer fastened on a pillar in front of St. Peter's church, right over the advertisement of the pope's jubilee, a proclamation which the laziest priest would have kept awake to prevent, if he had suspected what would be seen in the morning.

The sun rises, the people awake, throw open their windows and doors, and see little groups standing here and there, staring at some new wonder. The groups become crowds. Houses are left empty, the streets are filled with readers, talkers, murmurers. Men and women, young and old, priests and friars gather in front of the placards, and read with amazement, these strange words—

GOD OUR HEAVENLY FATHER,

PROMISES

A GENERAL PARDON OF ALL HIS SINS

TO EVERY ONE WHO FEELS SINCERE REPENTANCE,

AND POSSESSES

A LIVELY FAITH IN THE DEATH AND PROMISES

OF JESUS CHRIST.

"This surely cannot be a papal indulgence," say certain Huguenots, "for money is not mentioned in it. Salvation given freely must certainly come from heaven."

"A defiance of the pope's pardon," cry the priests, in wrath that grows fiercer as they overhear the talk of the delighted readers. They insulted those whom they suspected had posted up "the general pardon of Jesus Christ." They not only used their fists, but more deadly weapons. They made a great uproar, and tried to tear down the placards. But the patriotic party, now called Lutherans by the priests, would not allow this to be done. Two parties were soon organized; those who defended the placards, and those who wanted to pull them down. One leader from each were to have a small battle.

A certain canon, Wernly of Friburg, hearing the tumult, rushed out of his house, went toward the cathedral of St. Peter, and caught sight of the placard on the pillar. He flew at it, clenched it, and tore it down, uttering a coarse oath. There he stood, a burly active fanatic, who could handle a sword as skilfully as the censer, and give a blow as readily as a blessing.

A Genevese patriot saw what was done, and walking up to the pillar calmly put another paper in the place of the one torn down. All saw that he was Goulaz, a bold spirit who could brave those whom he despised. The Friburger lost all self-control, and forgetting the placard, he rushed upon the heretic, dealing him a lusty blow. Then he drew his sword (for the canons wore swords at that time,) but Goulaz was ready to meet him with his own weapons. In the struggle, Wernly was wounded in the arm. Upon this there was a general tumult, that increased and extended through the whole city. The magistrates were scarcely able to prevent a fierce battle in the streets.

The noise of this affair soon reached Friburg, where it was said that the placards were the result of the sermons of a certain school-master, who had taught that the pardon of God was to be preferred before all the indulgences of the pope. This Romish city would not be satisfied until the council of Geneva forbade any more papers to be posted up without their permission, and ordered that "for the present the school-master should cease to preach the gospel." The priests went about visiting every family, and demanding the surrender of every New Testament.

"The priests want to rob us of the gospel of Jesus Christ," murmured the people, "and in its place give us what? Romish fables! Really it is quite enough to hear them at church." The councillors were urged to show themselves Christians. Often had Olivetan told them that there was no intention of introducing a new religion, but of returning to the old. This was easily understood. The friends of the Reformation in the council began to speak boldly for the word and the people's right to read it. It was ordered by the council that "in every parish and convent the gospel should be preached." This was the first official act in Geneva favourable to the Reformation.

The great pardon of Jesus Christ began to be understood and embraced by numbers of people. The placards announcing it mark an important epoch in the history of Geneva. From the little town of Payerne where Anthony Saunier was pastor, came to the Genevese one of the best letters ever penned. We quote one of the first and one of the last sentences. "We have heard that the glory of God is with you. . . . Be the standard bearers upon earth of the colours of our Saviour, so that by your means the holy gospel may be borne into many countries."

CHAPTER XV.

THE PREACHERS AT THE INN.

(1532.)

ON a fine October day two travellers, the one riding a white horse, and the other a black one, entered Geneva, stopped at the Tour Perce, dismounted, addressed the landlord and took up their quarters under his roof. He would never forget them, for the little slender man with a red beard and sun-burnt face was William Farel, and the other was Anthony Saunier, now on their return from the visit to the Waldenses. One of their first thoughts was to inform Robert Olivetan of their arrival.

The school-master hastened to meet them, supposing that the gospel in Geneva was to be the first and last topic of conversation. But Farel had another idea which must first be mentioned. He had fixed on this excellent Greek and Hebrew scholar to translate the Bible for the Waldenses.

"I cannot accept such a commission," said the modest teacher. "The work is difficult, and I am not qualified."

"Your excuses cannot be admitted. God gives you this call, and he has prepared you for the task."

"You could do this work much better yourself," still urged the accomplished scholar.

"God has not given me leisure," replied Farel, "He calls

me to another work. He wills me to sow the pure seed of the word in his field, and water it and make it flourish like the garden of Eden." The subject was changed to matters in the city.

Out of his pocket Farel took the letters given him at Berne for some of the chief Huguenots. They went and made several calls, talking as they went of the late affairs in the streets. The Huguenots opened the letters and found that a famous man was in town. They looked at him with gratitude to him, to Berne and to God. Certainly he should preach, not simply because Berne requested them to hear him, but because they expected that this great preacher would bring the light of heaven into their hearts. Farel left them for the night, saying that he would be happy to see them at his inn.

The great missionary had come! It was the best of news to the Huguenots. "Let us go and hear him," they said; "he is the man they call the scourge of the little priests." But there was wrath among the bigots, the friars and the nuns. They knew what to expect. Jeanne de Jussie, a literary nun, wrote thus in venting her feelings,—"A shabby little preacher, one Master William, of Dauphiny, has just arrived in the city."

To a room in the Tour Perce many of the noted citizens and councillors went the next morning to be instructed. The landlord brought in some benches and stools, and Farel took his station near a little table. On it he placed a Bible, and he drew from it the faith that he preached. He set forth before this select audience, in which were the earliest champions of modern liberty, both Romanism and the reformation. They saw the former was all wrong; the latter they wished to embrace. They rose, thanked him and left the room, saying that it seemed right to put the Bible in place of the teaching of the pope. The placards of the "great pardon" noted a first step; this preaching at the Tour Perce marked the second step toward the reformation in Geneva.

These men carried home what they had heard; they talked about it; there was a "great sensation in the city," and sister Jeanne de Jussie again journalized about "this wretched preacher, who was beginning to speak secretly at his quarters, in a room, seeking to infect the people with heresy." There was a second meeting, and still plainer preaching, "at which those who heard him took great pleasure." The priests were alarmed, and they set about alarming the women, who then were the main supporters of the papacy. The Genevan ladies begged their husbands and brothers to drive away the heretics. Some went with their husbands, angrily, to the inn, and desired the preachers to leave at once, if they did not wish to be turned out by force. But this was to Farel no storm at all; it was a mere zephyr, that he did not mind.

The council, or senate, was now in trouble. Its members were divided on the great question,—What should be done with these preachers? To keep them would rouse the wrath of the priests and their party; to expel them would greatly offend the stout old Berne. All agreed that it was fair to hear them still farther, and Farel and Saunier were led to the town-hall. As they entered the senate-chamber every eye was fixed on "that man with keen look and red beard, who was setting all the country in a blaze, from the Alps to the Jura." Before long one of the senators opened his battery upon Farel.

"It is you, then, that do nothing but disturb the world. It is your tongue that is trumpeting rebellion. You are a busybody, who have come here only to create discord. We order you to leave the city instantly." This was certainly intelligible enough, without the aid of the angry looks now turned upon Farel.

"I am not a deluder; I am not a trumpet of sedition," answered the reformer, in calm self-control. "I simply proclaim the truth. I am ready to prove out of God's word that my doctrine is true, and"—the voice grew tender with emotion,—"not only to sacrifice my ease, but to shed the last drop of my blood for it."

The senators were touched at this noble simplicity. The Huguenots were moved to defend the accused. The tone and temper of all were softened by his moderation. But Farel could defend himself. "Most honoured lords," said he, "are you not allies of Berne?" They grew solemn at the mention of that name. He placed the letters from that city before them, saying,—"They bear witness to my innocence and doctrine, and beg you to hear me preach peacefully. . . . If you condemn me unheard, you insult God, and also, as you see, my lords of Berne." The countenances of the senators changed, and they gently dismissed the preachers, simply begging them not to disturb the peace of the city by new doctrines.

Disturb such a peace as Geneva had known! It must have seemed absurd to their honours. The real disturbers were already in council under the wing of the church. At the house of the grand vicar, de Gingins, were gathered the clerical strength of the Romish party. That challenge of Farel,—"I will prove by the word of God," was a terror to them. "If we discuss," said they, "all our office is at an end." They liked not the weapons. The priests had others. They carried arms under their gowns. It was proposed to use them. Sister Jeanne de Jussie knew of the plot. The council would entrap the preachers by asking for a disputation. "Having deliberated to kill Farel and his companion," says an old manuscript, "they found the best means of getting them to come would be to invite them to a debate." The conspirators agreed that Farel was never to go alive out of the vicar-general's house; but, first of all, they must get him to enter it. The bishop's secretary, Machard, was deputed to summon the preachers and the schoolmaster to retract or to explain before the council what they had preached at the inn.

The plot was whispered. The Huguenots in the town-hall grew suspicious, and sent the two chief magistrates to go with the bishop's secretary. These three Genevans went to the Tour Perce and met the three reformers. Machard invited them to retract the doctrines they had taught.

"We affirm these doctrines in the strongest way possible," said Farel, "and again offer to die if we cannot prove them by Scripture."

"In that case," said the secretary, "come before the Episcopal council, to discuss with the priests and maintain what you have declared."

"No harm shall be done to you," added the two magistrates. "We pledge our word to it." The preachers were delighted with this opportunity of announcing the gospel, and, with Olivetan, they set out, not expecting any danger.

Already was there a suspicious-looking group in front of the Tour Perce. While the upper house of the clergy was sitting at the vicar's, the lower house had met in the streets. The armed curates and chaplains had watched the messengers going to the inn, and guessed what it meant. They gathered their followers, particularly the women and the rabble. When the three Genevans with the three reformers passed, they fell in the train. "Look at the dogs," said they, with coarse jeers and threats.

THE PREACHERS AT THE INN. 251

There was danger on every hand. In the council and in the streets men had sworn Farel's death. At the door of the vicar's house the three reformers had to wait some time, for the two magistrates went in to ask another pledge of the council that the ministers should be safe while they freely explained their doctrines. The pledge was given, and they entered and stood together before the imposing assembly, all in their sacerdotal robes. The official, de Veigy, was ordered to speak.

"William Farel," said he, "tell me who has sent you, for what reason you come here, and by what authority you speak." He knew of no authority but that of the Romish church.

"I am sent by God," replied Farel, with simplicity, "and I am come to declare his word."

"Poor wretch," groaned the priests, with a shrug of the shoulders.

"God has sent you, you say," resumed the official. "How is that? Can you show a clear sign, as Moses did before Pharaoh? If not, then show us the license of our most reverend prelate, the bishop of Geneva. Preacher never yet preached in his diocese without his leave." He paused; he scanned the decently-dressed reformer from head to foot; he feared to hear any answer from Farel, and did not intend that one should be given, and then broke forth again,—"You do not wear the robes of a clergyman. You are dressed like a soldier or a brigand. How dare you preach? A decree of the holy church forbids laymen to preach. You are a deceiver and a bad man."

Thus ran the abuse. The clergy did not give Farel time to speak. It was not for that they had called him. They were glorying in the fact that they had within their grasp the terrible heretic, of whom they had been so long talking. It was hard for them to keep their hands off him. They sat, pale with anger, and clattered their feet on the floor. At last they must speak or burst, and they all spoke at once, pouring insult on the reformer. They rose, rushed upon him, and, pulling him this way and that, they cried out,—"Come Farel, you wicked devil, what business have you to go up and down, disturbing all the world? Are you baptized? Where were you born? Where did you come from? Why do you come here? Are you the man that spread heresies at Aigle and Neufchatel, and threw the whole country into confusion?"

It was not meant that Farel should have any chance to answer these questions. The noise was so great that neither he, nor the vicar, nor the magistrates, could gain a hearing. A rattle was heard; the weapons were clattering beneath the priest's frocks. Farel remained still as he could amid all this uproar. At length the grand vicar secured order and silence. Farel seized the moment.

"My lords," said he, nobly lifting his head, "I am not a devil. I was baptized in the name of the Father, Son and Holy Ghost, and, if I journey to and fro, it is that I may preach Jesus Christ. . . . I am compelled to teach him to all who will hear me. For this cause, and for no other, I am come into this city. Having been brought before you to give an account of my faith, I am ready to do so, not only at this moment, but as many times as you please to hear me peaceably. As for the disturbances in the land, I will answer as Elijah did to King Ahab,— 'I have not troubled Israel, but thou and thy father's house.' Yes, it is you and yours who trouble the world by your traditions, your inventions and your dissolute lives."—

"He blasphemes; what further need have we of witnesses," cried out one of the raging, gnashing priests. "He is guilty of death."

"To the Rhone, to the Rhone!" shouted others. "Kill him! It is better for this rascally Lutheran to die than to let him trouble all the people."

"Speak the word of God," said Farel at these perversions of Scripture, "and not those of Caiaphas."

"Strike! strike!" cried a Savoyard, as the furious priests shouted whatever was uppermost in their minds. They divided the three reformers among them, and each was abused, spit upon and beaten; yet each was calm and patient, remembering, doubtless, the meekness of the Great Master under similar treatment. Certain of the better priests and the two magistrates were ashamed of such a scene, and tried to end it.

"It is not well done," said an abbot; "have we not pledged our word and honour to them?"

"You are wicked men," cried out William Hugues, a just, quick and energetic magistrate, who was more than disgusted with the violent party. "We brought you these men on your promise that no harm should be done to them, and you want to beat them to death before our faces. I will go and ring the great bell and convoke the general council."

The thought of a general assembly of the citizens alarmed the priests, for they might expel the authors of this disturbance and give every security for the reformers to remain. In few cities would the people side with the priests, and Neufchatel was a fearful example of the popular power. The abbot took advantage of this new lull, and asked Farel and his two friends to withdraw so that the council might deliberate. Farel left the room, shamefully insulted, and bruised.

And what does the reverend sister Jeanne de Jussie say came next? About eighty of the lower order of priests had collected about the house, "all well armed with clubs to defend the holy catholic faith, and prepared to die for it." Strange mode of defending the faith! Not much danger of dying for it when there were eighty in arms against three defenceless strangers! "They wished to put that wretch and his accomplices to a better death." Sister Jeanne knew all about the scheme.

As Farel entered a long gallery he saw a gun levelled at him, and in an instant the priming flashed, but the load was not expelled. Some say it burst in the hands of the vicar's servant who aimed it at Farel. "I am not to be shaken by a popgun," said he coldly. "Your toy does not alarm me." His friends said, "Verily, the God of mercy turned aside the blow that he might preserve Farel for more formidable struggles."

Again were the strangers summoned to the council-room. The grand-vicar said, "William Farel, leave my presence and this house, and within six hours get you gone from the city with your two companions, under pain of the stake. And know that if this sentence is not more severe you must ascribe it to our kindness and to our respect for the lords of Berne."

"You condemn me unheard," said Farel. "I demand a certificate to show at Berne that I have done my duty."

"You shall not have one," was the reply. "Leave the room, all of you, without one word more." They got out of the council of the clergy, but how were they to get away from the city? The mob must be met. They went forth into a hurricane of enmity. On a sudden there was a stir in the crowd, a falling back and parting. An armed body of men rescued them from violence, to the great grief of Sister Jeanne, who wrote of the most of the mob, that "the worthy men were not satisfied" to see the heretics depart alive, and one rushed forward at Farel with a sword "to run him through." The magistrates seized the "worthy man," and many were chagrined because the blow failed. Amid hootings, and hisses, and groans, and threats, the reformers reached the Tour Perce under guard. It grieved Farel that he must leave the generous men who had listened to him at the inn. But he intended to preach yet in Geneva.

Early the next morning a little boat lay waiting, and a few friendly citizens went to the Tour Perce to bring away the missionaries. The priest-party were there to turn their matins into murder. Some staunch Huguenots came up, brought out the two strangers, and hurried to the lake. In the boat they were carried over to an unfrequented place near to Lausanne, and after a tender parting with their friends, who had thus far attended them, they made their way to Orbe. It required faith in God to hope that Geneva would ever become a stronghold of Protestantism.

CHAPTER XVI.

FROMENT'S LITTLE SERMONS.

(1532-1533.)

AT the village of Yvonand, on the southern shore of Lake Neufchatel, dwelt a young Dauphinese named Anthony Froment. He had been more disgusted with the excesses of Rome, probably, than charmed by the riches of the Bible, and had sought peace of soul in the Reformation. He had been with Farel, helping him through some of the most perilous scenes, and was now preaching to a little flock in Yvonand.

To this village came Farel, in October, with new plans in his mind for taking Geneva. He invited several ministers to meet him in council, among whom were Olivetan, Saunier, Froment and Martin,* (probably) the Waldensian by whose parishioners he had been entertained in the "holy valley." Farel gave an account of his mission to Piedmont, and of the stormy reception he had received at Geneva. They all looked on him with wonder and gratitude to the Author of miracles. Froment could not keep his eyes off the fugitive missionary, and he pitied

* Martin Gonin seems to have spent several years in Switzerland, but in 1536, on his return from Geneva, he was seized at Grenoble, hurried through a mock trial, taken from his prison at night, and drowned in the Isere.

the Genevan patriots who seemed about to lose all they had ever gained.

"Go and try if you can find an entrance into Geneva to preach there," said Farel, fixing his keen eye on Froment. For a little the young Dauphinese was speechless with astonishment.

"Alas! father," said he, recovering himself, "how can I face the enemies from whom you are compelled to flee?"

"Begin as I began at Aigle," replied Farel, "where I was a school-master at first and taught little children, so that even the priests gave me liberty to preach. True, they soon repented, and even now I seem to hear the curate exclaiming, 'I would sooner have lost my right hand than introduced this man, for he will ruin all our business.' But it was too late; the word of God had begun its work, and the mass and images fell."

A new school-master in Geneva—an Ursinus! The plan began to appear wise and to win upon Froment. It would be an achievement to gain a position in the city that had driven out the prophets.

"You fear the men of Geneva," said Farel, who noticed that Froment was entertaining his plan. "But were you not with me when I planted the gospel at Bienne, and at Tavannes, and near that mountain (Pierre Pertuis) which Julius Cæsar tunnelled? Were you not with me when I went to Neufchatel and preached in the streets? Do you not remember that we very often received our rent, that is blows and abuse; once especially, at Valangin, where my blood remained for more than four years on the pavement of a little chapel, near which the women and priests bruised my head against the walls, so that both of us were nearly killed?"

22 *

These remembrances were not very encouraging. Some of the council sided with Farel; others thought that a man of twenty-two was too young to face the fearful storm in Geneva. Froment was not decided. Another thought was struggling for the chief place in Farel's mind.

Those Bibles and teachers for the Waldenses, must be in readiness. Again and again did Farel talk to Olivetan about the proposed version, as they met with their friends, sat together in private, or walked under the noble oaks of Yvonand. After much pressing, the scholar consented to make the translation, and a great victory was gained for the poor Christians of the valleys. They should have a good version of the Scriptures. But a journey was necessary. "Cross the Alps," said Farel, in his commanding way; "go to the Waldensian valleys, and come to an understanding with the brethren about the translation. And you, Adam, Martin, and Guido, go with him and preach to them the doctrine that will correct all their errors."

These four men set out, and had reason to use every caution lest the Duke of Savoy and his officers should seize them. They travelled by night in the last days of October. A guide led them onward, and the second day they were at Vevay where they dined and spoke of the "Bread of heaven." Then they entered Farel's old district, where his voice first proclaimed the gospel to the French Swiss. At Aigle they were welcomed, and the people gathered to hear them, happy to know that their former teacher, Ursinus, had become so great a man in the world, and happier still to hear afresh the good word of grace. Near to Bex brother Martin was attacked with severe pain. No house was open to receive him, and the walnut trees would not shelter him. What could his friends do? Some one told them of Ollen, where lived the minister Claude, preaching to a little flock that Farel had once gathered. They went, carrying the sick man, and reached the door, where Claude met them. The pastor was touched at the sight of a sick man and invited the strangers in. On a sudden the voice of a violent, pitiless, scolding woman was heard, "What's this, a sick man? If you receive him into the house, I will leave it."

The travellers saw that Claude was unfortunate in having a Xantippe for a wife. Her voice rose higher and higher; he durst not say a word; she disappeared in a passion, and he was sorely vexed and ashamed. "We will not be the cause of a divorce," said prudent Adam; "we will go away." So away they went, poor Claude not daring to harbour them. All of them were soon sick with what Adam called cholera. At last they dragged themselves to a wretched cottage, where they got a little comfort for large pay. Rest and the mountain air somewhat repaired their broken health. Other anxieties came, which they bore with good humour. "Alas," said Adam, the purser, smiling, as he held up the wallet, "our purse has been seized with such cruel pains that there is scarcely anything left of it." They met one of the monks of St. Bernard, and spoke to him of the way of life. He listened and was convinced. Said he,— "I will quit Anti-Christ."

Adam took a paper, wrote something, handed it to the monk, and said,—"Here is a letter for Master Farel; go to him, and he will tell you what you have to do." What became of the monk we know not; but the missionaries finally reached the Waldensian valleys, and began to teach and preach. Some of these Alpine shepherds went on foot a two days' journey to hear them. Poor as these Christians were, they handed over to Olivetan five hundred gold crowns, and urged him to hasten forward the work of giving them a new translation of the Bible. It was finished in 1535, and in the preface he says; "It is to Thee alone that I dedicate this precious treasure, in the name of a certain poor people, who, ever since they were enriched with it by the apostles and ambassadors of Christ, have still possessed and enjoyed the same."*

In the room of an inn at Geneva was a young man, who had felt something far more chilling than the winds of the early November. He had met the piercing coldness of the people. He had tried to talk with one and another, but they were very short with the stranger, who imagined that he could not preach with the chance of an audience. He looked about for some acquaintance, whom he could draw aside and tell his plans; but all faces were strange. He went to some of the leading Huguenots. They looked at his mean appearance rather than listened to his words; they intimated that Geneva was an important and learned city, and the accomplished Roman clergy must be opposed by a fine gentleman of a minister, or a celebrated doctor; and the little man was politely bowed out of their houses. Those who seemed willing to hear the gospel stared at him with contemptuous eyes. "Alas!" said he, "I cannot tell what to do, except to return, for I find no open door to preach the word." Yvonand would receive him again—for this was Anthony Froment. It cost the little flock there a struggle to give him up; they had wept at the parting with blessings and prayers.

* He made much use of Lefevre's version of the New Testament, but rendered certain words in terms less objectionable than those used in the Romish church. He says,—"If any one is surprised at not finding certain words in my translation, such as *pope, cardinal, archbishop, abbot, prior, monk*, he must know that I did not find them there, (in Scripture,) and for that reason I have not changed them."

He paid the landlord his bill, strapped his little bundle on his shoulders, and, without one word of adieu to the cold Huguenots, bent his steps toward the Swiss gate and—stopped. An invisible hand seemed to arrest him. A voice cried up from his conscience. A force, greater than that of man, sent him back. He took his room at the inn, sat down with his head in his hands, and asked what God wanted with him. He remembered what Farel had done at Aigle. He rebuked himself for coming there as a preacher. He will now begin in humility as a schoolmaster.

He met with a man of lowly lot, and asked him where there was a place for a school. He was led to a large hall, near the Molard, in a house on which is still seen the sign of the golden cross. With his eye he measured the room and rented it. He would have a school, if he could only get the scholars. He drew up a placard, in his best hand-writing, and posted several copies in the public places. It read thus,—"A young man, just arrived in this city, engages to teach reading and writing in French, in one month, to all who will come to him, young and old, men and women, even such as have never been to school; and if they cannot read and write within the said month, he asks nothing for his trouble. He will be found at Boytet's hall, near the Molard. Many diseases are also cured gratis."

The papers were read by the passers by, and some who had met him, said, "We have heard him speak; he talks well." To some his proposal was suspicious; others replied that it was benevolent, for "in any case he does not aim at our purses." But the priests and their followers were irritated, and exclaimed in their usual style, "He is a devil. He enchants all who go near him."

The school opened, and there was no lack of young learners.

Froment taught with clearness and simplicity. Before dismissing the children he would open his Testament, read a few verses, explain them, and then ask if any at their homes were sick. If so he gave them a few harmless remedies. The children ran home, and told everything. The mothers stopped in their work to listen, and the fathers, especially the Huguenots, made them tell it over again. Thus the children prattled about it, and the older ones were set wondering. Soon the city was quite engaged about "the school-master who spoke French so well."

The teacher was doing more than he promised; there were Arithmetic, and good manners, a thing not to be despised in Geneva, and there were those readings and talks from the Bible. The grown people must go and hear. Certain ones played off their jokes, wives held back their husbands, priests vented their feelings in coarse abuse, but still Froment found the interest increasing. There were some peeping in and slyly listening to his words. The little sermon was what most came for, and they seemed to lack ears and mouths enough to gather it all. The boys glanced on the men whom they had brought in, with a feeling of triumph, and the men came oftener and stayed longer. Many of the Huguenots began to see that true Christianity did not consist in mocking the priests and the mass, as they had so long been doing, but in knowing and loving the Saviour. "Come," they began to say to their neighbours, "come to the Golden Cross, and hear him, for he preaches very differently from the priests, and charges nothing for his trouble." Men, women, and children began to see who could get first to the hall. The poor man who had been bluffed and bowed out of their houses, had risen to high esteem among the Huguenots, and to the honour of being ridiculed by the priests. *

* "That fine preacher, Froment, who, having laid aside his apron, got

The motive which led some to the hall was not a love for the gospel, but a hatred of the priests, monks and mamelukes. Such Huguenots as Ami Perrin, Goulaz and Adda, thought that the new doctrine "which fell from the skies," might overthrow the party that opposed the liberties of the city, and they ranged themselves on the benches of the hall and supported Froment with great zeal in the city. Rome was to fare even worse. Certain more liberal priests came to hear the schoolmaster, and declared the doctrines good for all to receive. But the monks went into houses, lingered with groups on the streets, and jeered at Froment's appearance, and his doctrines. "What can that little fool know, who is hardly twenty-two?" His admirers answered, "That fool can teach you to be wise."

From the days that Paul found "the chief women not a few," to be among the first to receive the word of Christ, it has often occurred that influential women have led the advance in confessing the true faith. It was so in Geneva. For three centuries the ancestors of Paula had been styled nobles, and she had honoured John Levet with her personal merits in being an excellent wife. When the preaching of Farel reached her ear she "became very zealous for the word." She now was anxious to win her sister-in-law, Claudine, the wife of the worthy Aime Levet, to the gospel. Claudine was "an honest, devoted and wondrously superstitious woman," and more than once had shown combat when the new doctrines were broached. She lived across the Rhone.

up into his pulpit, then went to his shop where he prated (talked,) and thus gave a double sermon." Thus Calvin referred to him, when giving his dying farewell to the ministers of Geneva. Perhaps Froment had to support himself by toil as well as by teaching, at this time as well as afterwards when Calvin came to the city.

"Come, now," said Paula one day when at her house, "and hear the school-master. Those beautiful little sermons will give you delight."

"I have so great a horror of him," was the reply, "that for fear of being bewitched I will neither see nor hear him."

"He speaks like an angel."

"I look upon him as a devil."

"If you hear him you will be saved."

"And I think I shall be damned."

"Pray hear him once," and Paula in deep emotion still pleaded,—"Pray hear him once, for love of me." Claudine at last consented to go. But she would thoroughly protect herself. She gathered fresh rosemary leaves, and fixed them about her temples; she hung relics, crosses and rosaries round her neck, and saying,—"I am going to see an enchanter," she went with Paula, thinking that she would even lead back her sister into the "mother church."

In mockery Claudine sat down before the magician, who held a book in his hand. Then, mounting on a round table to be the better heard, he opened the book, read a few words, and began to apply them. Dame Claudine, not caring the least for the assembly, and wishing to make known her religion, crossed herself several times, and repeated certain prayers. Froment still unfolded the rich treasures of the little book. She began to be astonished; she looked at the minister; she was not hearing an angel, but God was speaking from that small book. Not a more attentive listener was in the hall. She asked herself,—"Can this be true, seeing that the church knows nothing about it?" Her eyes fixed on the school-master's book. It was not a missal or a breviary. It seemed to her full of life. It was indeed the word of life.

The talk was ended, and all lingered and left. She sat still, looked at the teacher, and asked,—"Is that all true? Is it proved by the gospel?"

"It is all true. It is the gospel," said he, in a pleasing voice.

"Is not the mass mentioned in it?"

"Not that I can find."

"And is the book from which you preach a genuine New Testament?"

"It is, Madame." It was probably Lefevre's version.

"Then, lend it to me," she earnestly requested. He did so, and she placed it carefully under her cloak, among her beads and relics, and went home talking with Paula, who began to hope that the finger of God had touched her soul.

Dame Claudine was in earnest. She took her room, ordered that her family should not wait meals for her, nor knock at her door, and "she remained apart for three days and three nights, without eating or drinking, but with prayers, fastings and supplications." The Testament lay open on her table before her, and she read it, kneeling and lifting her eyes to heaven for light. She had many severe struggles, but at last she heard her Lord say, through his word,—"Daughter, thy sins are forgiven thee." She discovered that "the grace of God trickled slowly into her heart," but the least drop seemed a fountain never to be exhausted. Three days she thus spent, as Paul remained three days in prayer at Damascus.

And now she must see the man who had first led her into these rich treasures. She sent for him to come to her house over the bridge. He crossed the Rhone, and was met in her home with no other language than the "tears that fell on the floor." When the tide of emotion had receded, she told him how God had opened for her the door of heaven, and so talked that the young preacher was greatly instructed. As Calvin says of Lydia,—"From this tiny shoot an excellent church was to spring."

One day she shut herself up in that room, where she had heard the call of God, and resolved to extinguish all her former glory in dress and decoration. She took "all superfluous bravery, laid aside those ornaments and trappings which had served to show her off in a vain-glorious way," and packed them up for sale. These and her most beautiful robes were sold. The money she gave to the poor, particularly to the evangelists of France, who were now exiles in Geneva. All her life the refugees were most welcome to her house. "Verily," they said, "she follows the example of Dorcas, and deserves to be kept in perpetual remembrance." She did more; she spoke meekly and frankly of the precious truth wherever she went, and presented the New Testament, which Farel was sending, to many of the Genevan ladies. Her husband had been most bitter against Froment, but he began to be softened. She gently won him to the Lord. Little meetings were held in the house of the Levets, and when Froment was not present, she read and explained the Scriptures. The modest Guerin, a cap-maker, was reading his Bible day and night, and soon he cast his lot with the labourers in the vineyard.

On New Year's day the city was to pass another crisis. The council had forbidden Froment to preach; and this made the people the more anxious to hear him. The hall was soon filled, then the stairway, then the street, and others still coming. The young preacher came, and he could not press through the crowd. What should be done? One man shouted out,—"To the Molard," and the cry became general. This was a large square, near where the Rhone pours out of the lake. Thither they went, crying,—"Preach to us the word of God." Mounting upon a little market-stall, the preacher beckoned with his hand, and there was silence. "Pray to God with me," he said, and, kneeling, the tears ran down his cheeks, while his voice rose solemnly to heaven. By that prayer, so unlike anything the people had ever heard, thousands were convinced that he sought the salvation of their souls. The text was not fortunate,— "Beware of false prophets;" but the sermon was powerful, every point being proved by the Scriptures. Various attempts were made to disturb him, until, at length, an armed band forced their way toward the stand. After much confusion Froment was carried away by his friends, and with great difficulty was saved. The school must now be given up, and preaching abandoned.

We cannot linger upon his perils—how he was almost detected in the house of Jean Chautemps and must seek another refuge, how Perrin said to him, "The law allows me to keep an honest servant unmolested in my house and I engage you," how he worked at the loom and none dare touch him, and how he began to visit cautiously at their homes, those who believed. Once he was detected crossing the bridge, and was so near to death, that his friends barely got him into the house of Dame Claudine, who must see her windows broken by the mob. At night Froment was advised to leave, and he departed for Yvonand to rest a while from the contests that make this the heroic period of his life. His work had not been in vain. Among other patriots Baudichon de la Maison-Neuve became a most zealous protestant, and his house and that of the Levets were the chief resorts for the little band of Christians.

Sometimes these believers had a great treat. A minister would be passing through Geneva; he must stop and preach in a private room, and the good news went here and there among them. "What is his name?" they would ask.

"Peter Maneri."

"Where is he staying?"

"At Aime Levet's by the bridge." And Claudine saw her rooms filled every evening while the minister stayed.

"We should have the Lord's supper," these Christians began to say one to another. It was decided, and as no minister could be obtained, they urged Guerin to preside.

"Where shall it be celebrated?" was the next question.

"At Baudichon's house," said one. "No," said the more prudent, "not anywhere in the city, for the priests and their spies will cause a new uproar."

"I have a little walled garden near the city gate," said Adda, "and there nobody can disturb us."

On an early morning in March, as it seems, these believers quietly took their seats on the rude benches, and the Lord's table was spread in this garden, reminding them of the sacred gardens where their Saviour had agonized, or had lain in the tomb. Just when Guerin sat down at the table the sun rose and, blessing the scene with his first rays, made it more imposing than the distant Alp of glittering snow. Never was this holy ordinance observed in a simpler manner. From the trembling hands of a layman, who felt that he was daring to do a sacred act with almost impious touch, they received the bread and the wine, and remembered the Crucified, praying for those who were afraid to meet with them, pledging their faith and their love, hoping for the day when there should be a reformed church in the city with a pastor who would feed the flock, and praising God for what they had already heard from his messengers now banished, and read in his word now hidden in their homes and their hearts. Thus was celebrated their first communion in Geneva.

This was not to be the end. The priests went about saying of these quiet believers, "They make so much of Christ that they deprive themselves of the church." Guerin and Olivetan (now in the city) held that the Romanists "made so much of the church that they deprived themselves of Christ." Here was the dividing line between the two parties. The honest Guerin was charged with the crime of having administered the Lord's supper in the garden, and he must leave the city. Hastily fleeing he went to Yvonand that he might be with Froment who had done so much to enlighten his mind.

The sad state of the true church led Olivetan to write of it, "I love thee; I have seen thee ill-treated, ill-dressed, torn, dishevelled, chilled, bruised, beaten, and disfigured. I have seen thee in such a piteous case, that men would sooner take thee for a poor slave than the daughter of the Great King, and the beloved of his only Son. Listen! thy friend calls thee; he would teach thee thy rights and give thee the watch-word, that thou mayest attain to perfect freedom." The little church at Geneva might have sat for this affecting picture. Yet these hidden ones "met every day in houses or gardens to pray to God, to sing psalms and Christian hymns, and to explain Holy Scripture."

CHAPTER XVII.

FAREL IN HIS ELEMENT.

(1533—1535.)

ALL seemed lost in the storm that swept through Geneva in the year 1533. We can glance at only a few other of the sad effects. There was the banishment of Olivetan, for rising upon a bench and daring to say something after a friar had been bawling like a madman in decrying the Bible, exalting the pope and abusing the people, who sought for true liberty and the new life. All that the mild translator said was,—"Master, I desire to show you honestly from the Scripture where you have erred in your discourse." It was too much for those who dreaded fair discussion. He was pushed off the bench, saved from deadly blows by Chautemps, denied a hearing by the council, and expelled from the city. There was talk that these banishments were not enough. Farel had been driven away, but after him rose up Froment. He had been expelled, but Guerin appeared in his stead. He had been cast out, but then came Olivetan. This fourth leader had been banished, and now somebody else would suddenly take his place. The whole band must be expelled or treated with worse cruelties. There were secret plots formed in the house of the grand-vicar: an armed attack, a fight on the Molard, a plan to burn out the Huguenots, and a reign of terror.

There was the restoration of the bishop-prince, Peter la

Baume, who, six years before, had carried off a young girl to his castle, and raised a tempest that bore him away into banishment. There were all his revenges upon the innocent, some of them being thrust into prison, and some put to flight. Chautemps escaped; but his wife, the delicate, accomplished, devoted and heroic Jaquema, must pay for it by suffering rough treatment in a narrow cell. Claudine saw her house again despoiled, and her husband fleeing for the mountains; and if he had not been overtaken, seized, and cast into a deep dungeon, she would have suffered in his stead. These are mere specimens of the persecution. There was almost everything to please the sister Jeanne de Jussie in making up her journal, and telling how the women met to "make war and kill the heretic wives, in order that the breed might be extirpated," and how, with their little hatchets and swords and caps full of stones, "there were full seven hundred children, from twelve to fifteen years old, firmly resolved to do good service along with their mothers." But what will she note down when Farel himself will be preaching to the nuns of St. Clair?

Yet, amid all this storm and uproar, there was a voice from my lords of Berne. Messengers went and told them all about this madness for popery, and this violence against their ministers. They were aroused, like a "bear robbed of her young." Papal Friburg should not drive out of the re-allied city the men whom protestant Berne sent there to preach the gospel. They "did not mince matters." They gave the Genevan council something to think about, and to put its members in a fearful dilemma. The council was called: there was something new; the looks of all were anxious; the premier, with an air of consternation, offered a letter from the Bernese senators. "We are surprised that in your city the faith in Jesus Christ, and those who seek it, are so greatly molested. . . . You will not suffer the word of God to be freely proclaimed, and you banish those who preach it."

What should be done? "If we yield to what Berne demands, the priests will get up fresh disturbances." It will not do to put down the priests, for Friburg insisted on their presence and power. This course, then, seemed full of danger. But was the other any safer? "If we refuse," said they, very solemnly, "Berne will break off the alliance, and the reformed will revolt." This course was dangerous. And they knew not what to do. But they murmured and set the whole city in commotion, and caused a war in their very streets. The priests had their way, one of them blustering and boasting,—"Here I am ready to enter the lists with these preachers. Let my lords of Berne send as many as they like. I will undertake to confound them all."

He should have the chance. "My lords" would send one who would be glad to meet all such debaters. They sent a deputation, and Farel along with it; but the noisy monk was gone. The stories about Farel and Viret were not of the sort to attract the superstitious. The priests said that they fed devils at their table in the shape of huge black cats, and that one hung from every beard on Farel's face, and that he had no white circle in his eyes. They declared that the preachers had brought war, pestilence, famine and discord into the city. It seems that Farel did not preach during this brief visit.

The priest-party sent for a doctor of the Sorbonne to preach the Christmas sermons. This was Guy Furbity, a man of great pomp and little discretion. He, being a Dominican, was expected to preach in the convent de Rive; but, in order to make the victory the more effective, he was led by an armed escort to the cathedral of St. Peter, some time before the Christ-

FAREL IN HIS ELEMENT. 273

mas-week. There he declaimed about the soldiers dividing our Lord's garments, and the heretics dividing the church, calling the latter by all the worst of names. One writer states that Froment and Du Moulin were present, and, after hearing the sermon, they offered to prove its fallacy by the Holy Scriptures. This caused an outcry,—"Away with them to the fire." Du Moulin was banished, and Froment was hidden in the house of a friend until he could escape.

Just before Christmas a deputation came from Berne, bringing Farel, Viret and Froment, and insisting that they should be heard, and that the friar Furbity, should be arrested for abusing their honours, their ministers and good Christians generally. The friar went so far that the senate of Geneva put him under close guard. The grand-vicar ordered French Bibles to be destroyed, and forbade any one to preach without his license. But the preachers taught in private houses, and waited for Berne to open the public doors.

"You must arrest Furbity and bring him to trial for insulting us," said the Bernese, "and he must prove from Scripture what he has declared, or recant." The Genevese hesitated. It would offend Friburg. "If you prefer Friburg to us," replied Berne, "then choose her. But what about those large sums of money which you owe us for defending your city? What about the articles of alliance? Refuse our request, and we must have a settlement. We will remove the seal from the articles, and you will look no more to us for help." The senate of Geneva could afford to give up the alliance with papal Friburg, rather than that with protestant Berne. They therefore let the Bernese summon Furbity to a discussion with Farel.

It was, no doubt, one of the gladdest days of Farel's life,

when he met this friar in an open debate. It was a delight not often afforded to the reformers. Furbity agreed to prove his points by Scripture. Many subjects were discussed through several days. The friar broke down in his undertaking, especially on the eating of no meat in Lent. "I cannot prove it from Scripture," said he, with fading pomp.

"This is keeping your promise admirably," said Farel, "that you would maintain from Scripture, before all the world, and to your latest breath, what you have been preaching."

The friar found himself mastered. He apologized to the Bernese commissioners, and hoped for the liberty of trying his eloquence in quarters where he might have less to do with the Bible. But Berne was in earnest, and too severe, no doubt. He must recant, and that in the cathedral. Then he might leave the city. Pale and trembling he went into the pulpit, and instead of recanting his errors before the people, who were already convinced of them, he began to complain of injustice and persecution! The Bernese insisted on his recantation. He refused, and thus was false to his own promises. The people became indignant. They wrongly set upon him, and almost killed him. The Bernese interfered, and put him into prison. There he was visited by Farel, Viret and Caroli. On seeing this last one, he almost fainted away, for Caroli had been his divinity tutor, and had left the Romish faith. For two hours they laboured with him, but he persisted in his errors. He was kept for two years in prison, and finally released at the intercession of Francis I. We do not justify his punishment. By Farel's triumph over him in the debates a strong turn was given to the reformation.

During the next Lent a milder monk was preaching in one of the churches. He was enjoined by the senate to publish the pure gospel, and not allude to the adoration of the Virgin Mary, prayers to the saints, purgatory, and such like subjects. He promised to obey, but did not keep his word. The Bernese deputies heard his sermons, and then asked that one of their ministers might preach, promising that he should not attack the mass, nor image worship, nor any peculiar tenet of popery. They said it was reported that their preachers kept in dark corners, met at an inn for worship, and dared not appear in the churches. But the Genevese senate feared to offend Friburg and the bishop, and the request was not granted. The people tried another plan that very day.

In a few hours the bell of the Franciscan church was ringing, and the people flocking thither almost carrying Farel. They set him up in the pulpit, and he preached without interruption. It was the first protestant sermon in a Genevan church. Every one was astonished, and the grave question was, who of the citizens had rung the bell. "It was not by our consent," said the senate. "We had no hand in it," said the Bernese envoys; "it looks like a wonderful providence." The Friburgers declared that it must not be permitted again, or they would break off their alliance. The senators asked the Bernese to send away the preachers. "Not at all," said the Bernese, who begged Farel to bear in mind the critical state of the city, and be moderate in his attacks upon the errors of the priests. In April, 1534, the Friburgers carried out their threat, tore the seal from their treaty, and left Geneva in the hands of Berne and the reformers.

It was a great victory for the protestant cause, whose weapons were those of peace and good will to men. At Whitsuntide Farel administered the Lord's supper to a large number of communicants. For a moment there was fear of a disturbance, for a priest entered the church in full dress, as if he intended to break up the services. All were breathless. He walked up to the table, threw off his robes, declared that he thus renounced popery, and wished to be received into the little band of disciples, and sat down with the communicants. The exiles began to return, and the prisoners to see hope of release. By degrees one church after another was opened to the preachers.

The Romanists began to make a new use of their old weapons. The bishop and the canons approved of a plan to surprise the city by night, expel the civil rulers, take the government in their own hands, and sweep out the new doctrines and the new church. The plot came to light, and the bishop came to grief. The pope next tried the "thunders of the Vatican," and Geneva, with her allies, was excommunicated from the church of Rome. This act raised up Huguenots in the streets and in the senate, and finally Geneva broke with the bishop-prince and with the pope.

Smaller plots were laid. A servant girl was engaged by certain priests to take off the ministers by mixing poison with their food. It happened that Farel ate nothing that day, Froment* dined elsewhere, and only Viret partook of the poisoned dish. He felt the effects of it immediately, and, although his life was saved, his health never recovered entirely

---

*Of Froment, who had done much to prepare the way for Farel in Geneva, we shall hear little more. In 1537 he became a pastor in Geneva. He was too fickle and vain to be content with that glorious part assigned to him as a missionary of the Reformation. His wife seemed to dream of a "dress reform," and, like some of later times, went about declaiming against the length of the ladies' garments, quite to the amusement of the sedate Calvin. In 1553 he gave up the ministry, became a notary, then a secretary of Bonivard, in drawing up his chronicles, and he also assumed authorship, leaving behind him some curious memoirs.

from the shock. Not long after a still more atrocious attempt was made to poison the bread and wine at the Lord's supper. These plots excited a sympathy for the reformed, and a general hatred against the priests and their party.

The preachers now resided with the Franciscans, and gained many of these monks over to the reformed faith. One of these was James Bernard, the brother of Farel's host. They often talked of the Scriptures together, and the Franciscan agreed to defend the new doctrines before an assembly of his own brethren and those of St. Bernard. Thus, to Farel's delight, a disputation was held for nearly four weeks, when all the main points between Romanists and Protestants were discussed. Caroli, of whom more anon, then showed that he was anything but a true reformer. The result was most happy. Many of the priests became obedient unto the faith, and the people were strengthened. Claudius Bernard, Farel's host, demanded that the senate make a public acknowledgement of the reformation, and declare that popery was no longer the religion of Geneva. But the senators hesitated, lest there should be a renewal of disturbances.

One day Farel was invited to preach in the Magdalen church. He went, and, as he entered, the priest left the mass and hastily retired, leaving Farel the pulpit and the audience. The vicar complained. The senate ordered Farel to confine himself to the two churches already open to him and his brethren. A few days afterward Farel appeared in another church, and for this was brought before the senate. He listened respectfully to their rebukes, and then begged to be heard. He urged "that the reformation was the work of Divine Providence, and to delay its progress was to oppose God's will; besides, almost the whole city had declared in its favour. Issue right commands if you wish the servants of God to render you willing obedience. Give

God the glory, and aid the victory of truth over error, especially when you behold some of the most zealous defenders of popery converted to the true religion." The senate did not withdraw their prohibition, and were reminded that "we must obey God rather than men." There were some Gamaliels in that senate, who would not allow any forcible measures.

Another day, August 8th, 1535, the bell of the Franciscan church was ringing, and Farel was on the way thither, when he was met by a strong body of men. They obliged him to go to the cathedral, the very throne of Romanism in the city, on whose pillar had once been nailed the "great pardon." There, in the pulpit of St. Peter's, he declared what had not rung to its roof for centuries. He was himself again, with his loud voice and his torrent of eloquence. He could not endure the images and relics that were thickly seen in all corners. No doubt he said many severe things, which excited the people against these idolatries, and when they came again in the evening in great numbers, the work of image-breaking commenced in downright earnest. Vandel, Baudichon and others led the way, and they left mourning enough for the monks. The next day they visited other churches and made rough havoc of the images.

The senate, not knowing whereunto this would grow, joined with the council of Two Hundred, and they summoned Farel to appear before them. He went with several other ministers, Franciscans and citizens. He addressed them with firmness and moderation at first, and then warming with Scripture and the greatness of his cause, he employed all his bold and masterly eloquence in defence of the faith. "We do not wish those priests, who cannot receive our doctrines, to be punished;" said he, "but we pray for their conversion. We are here to preach, not to persecute. We are ready to seal the truth with our blood. He then prayed most fervently that God would give light to the members of the council, so that they might act wisely in behalf of the people who needed salvation. All was respectful, earnest, powerful and convincing.

The councillors were touched, moved and decided. They asked the Romish clergy to come forward and state their arguments. The monks confessed their ignorance, and those higher in rank simply hurled back their contempt for Farel and their defiance of the council. It was firmly resolved to abolish popery, and to establish protestantism. In the evening of the same day, August 10, the vicar was informed of the proceedings, and that his services were no longer desired. The mass was forbidden, even in private houses. The Bible was to have its place and its power. The bishop-prince removed to the little town of Gex, and the see was declared vacant. The monasteries were suppressed, and an opportunity was given for Sister Jeanne to hear that fearful preacher, William Farel, on whom she had expended so much of her wit and her wailing.

Whether Sister Jeanne heard Farel or not, we cannot tell, but he preached to the nuns of St. Claire, and showed that Mary and Elizabeth were not shut up in convents, but were excellent mothers at their homes. They had been thrown into horrors long before, by certain women who told them, "If the heretics win the day they will certainly make you all marry, young and old, all to your perdition." And now they took to flight, furnishing Sister Jeanne a chance to employ her vivid pen in a more sorrowful way than usual. Some of them had not been outside of the convent walls for many years, and they were frightened at the most harmless objects. They spent a day in getting to St. Julien, about four miles distant. "It was a pitiful thing," she writes, "to see this holy company in such a plight, so overcome with fatigue and grief that several swooned by the way. It was rainy weather, and all were obliged to walk through the muddy roads, except four poor old women who had taken their vows more than sixteen years before. Two of these who were past sixty-six, and had never seen anything of the world, fainted away repeatedly. They could not bear the wind; and when they saw the cattle in the fields, they took the cows for bears, and the sheep for ravening wolves. They who met them were so overcome with compassion that they could not speak a word. And though our mother, the vicaress, had supplied them all with good shoes to save their feet, they could not walk in them. And so they walked from five in the morning, when they left Geneva, till near midnight, when they got to St. Julien, which is only a little league off." We should feel more pity for these nuns if they had been as simple and innocent as was generally supposed, and as they wished to be thought. It created no little surprise, after their departure, to find that there was a secret underground passage leading from their convent to the monastery of the Franciscans. From this it was suspected that they were not altogether dead to earthly vanities.

The citizens met on the 21st of May, 1535, and took an oath to support the Reformation. Geneva was rising into a protestant state, quite theocratic in its government, and powerful in its influence upon the world. Michelet, who is a moderate Roman Catholic, declares, "Europe was saved by Geneva." And who saved Geneva? So far as mere men are concerned, due credit must be given to Farel, the great missionary, and Calvin, the great theologian. Unto God they gave all the glory.

CHAPTER XVIII.

CALVIN UNITED WITH FAREL.

(1534–1538.)

LET us go back a little and see what has become of some of our French heroes, and trace the steps of others who are on the way to Geneva.

"Never tire in the middle of your journey," was the maxim of a young man who was entering the old city of Angoulême, where the Duchess Margaret was born. He walked along a street which in after years bore the name Rue de Genève, in honour of him. In this street was the mansion of Du Tillet, where he knocked and was admitted. There he had a young friend, Louis Du Tillet, to whose refuge he was invited, and he was now welcomed as John Calvin. A fierce persecution had driven Calvin from Paris, and in this retreat he found a happy home. In the large library he found books that he had never seen before, and prepared for writing the Institutes, the greatest work on theology that had ever appeared. In a vineyard near by he took recreation, and to this day it is called La Calvine. In the village of Claix he drew the notice of the people, who asked the name of that short, thin, pale young man, and they called him "the little Greek," because he was giving some persons lessons in that language.

Not far distant was Nerac, the residence of Margaret, who

was now the queen of Navarre. Calvin wished to see Lefevre before the old man was taken away, and Roussel, whom he feared was not firm enough in the faith. He set out, and at Nerac inquired for the house of Lefevre. Everybody knew the good old man, and perhaps his Testament was in many of their hands. "He is a little bit of a man," said they, "old as Herod, but lively as gunpowder." This old man, with his white hair and broken appearance, had about him a living force, meekness, gentleness, moral grandeur and heavenly brightness that charmed the young visitor. They talked, rejoiced, sympathized and wept together. Lefevre was deeply moved when he saw that Calvin was bold enough to break away from the old church and enlist "under the banner of Jesus." Gazing upon him, he said,— "Young man, you will one day be a powerful instrument in the Lord's hand. . . . God will make use of you to restore the kingdom of heaven in France. Be on your guard, and let your ardour be always tempered with charity." Thus they talked. The old man pressed the young man's hand, and they parted, never to meet again on earth.

About three years after this Lefevre died, (1537,) at Nerac, where Margaret took delight in treating him as a father. One day when near his end he burst into tears. The queen asked the reason. He replied, sorrowfully, that he could not help reproaching himself, because he had shrunk from the very cross which he had advised others to bear. While he had imparted to so many the gospel, and encouraged them in exposing their lives for its sake, it grieved him to think that he was dying in quiet, and that by flight he had deprived himself of the glory of a martyr's name.

Gerard Roussel never broke with the Romish church, although, as bishop of Oleron, he still preached the new doctrines. A

CALVIN UNITED WITH FAREL.

Roman Catholic wrote of him,—"His life was without reproach. His kennel of greyhounds was a great crowd of poor people; his horses and his train were a flock of young children instructed in letters. He had much credit with the people, upon whom he stamped by degrees a hatred and contempt for the religion of their fathers." The good man was a Protestant at heart, and he died in 1550.

Calvin left this region, gathered about him several missionaries, and they laboured in the west of France, until the wrath of the priests knew no bounds. He gained no little fame as an "arch-heretic," while his friends said,—"Would to God that we had many Calvins." But we find him and Du Tillet, with two horses and two servants, leaving France in 1534. They were robbed by one of the servants, who took their money, mounted one of the horses, and rode away as fast as he could. One horse was left, and the other servant came forward and offered them ten crowns that he had. This took them to Strasburg, where they rested and suddenly heard that a certain William Farel had made a tremendous uproar in France.

An old chronicler called 1534 the year of the placards. Certain men in Paris wished to strike a blow in behalf of rights which they dare not proclaim. They seemed oppressed into silence, and they wished to protest against errors and wrongs in a way that would arouse the public attention of all, from the king to the cottager. They sent Feret to Switzerland to learn how to do it. He consulted with Farel and his co-labourers. The scheme of the placards was proposed. Farel undertook the task. He could not write without using "his trenchant style and thundering eloquence." He wrote it, and proved himself to be what Michelet calls him, "the Bayard of the battles of God." The paper was printed in two forms, one for posting up on the walls, and the other as little tracts to be dropped in the streets. The sheets were packed, and Feret departed with "the thunderbolt forged on Farel's anvil." These were soon after distributed far and near, to be exposed in every city of the kingdom. It was long enough for a short sermon, and when it appeared men read a terrible protest against the errors of Romanism. Beda charged Margaret* with it, but she felt that it was a protest against her and her *temporizers*. Next Beda accused the king, but he cleared his hands by allowing a furious persecution to sweep the land. There were martyrs, prisoners and exiles by scores. One of the prisoners was a most eloquent preacher, named Courault, who spoke forth the gospel without reserve or disguise. He had so presented the truth to Louis Du Tillet, while he was in Paris, as to lead him out of Margaret's party of *temporizers* into that of the *Scripturists*, soon to be headed by Calvin. Aged and infirm as he was when he was brought before the king, he would not yield, and, in spite of Margaret's tears and entreaties, he was sent back to the convent. Did Margaret have a hand on the keys? Whether or not, he in some way escaped, and, though nearly blind, he took the road to Basle. We shall meet him again in Geneva.

Farel was represented at Paris by one of the martyrs, and it will not be a mere episode to tell the story of the converted friar, Le Croix. While a Dominican at his convent in Paris, he was startled in mind by the teaching of Cop and young Calvin. He longed for the gospel, dared not hear it in the

---

*After this affair the queen of Navarre was less openly favourable to the Protestants. She, however, took an unceasing interest in their cause, and wished Calvin to demand of her any aid that she could render. In her later years she fell into a sort of mysticism in her struggles for a purer inward faith and devotion. She died in 1549.

capital, and resolved to go to a country where it was freely preached. The eyes of Duprat were on the watch, but he escaped and went to Neufchatel and Geneva, leaving his cowl in the convent and his monkish name in the air. He was thenceforth Alexander Canus. Heartily was he welcomed by Farel and Froment, who carefully taught him the glad tidings which they preached. He was converted—completely transformed. He must proclaim the Sun of Righteousness, point to the cross, preach the Kingdom. One thought absorbed all others, "O my Saviour! thou hast given thy life for me; I desire to give mine for thee."

But he could not declare the truth in Geneva. The priests controlled the magistrates, and the magistrates wrote him a heretic and condemned him to death. They, however, lifted the sentence "for fear of the king of France," and he was simply turned out of the city. On the high-way beyond the walls he stopped and preached to the people who followed him. All were charmed by his powerful eloquence. "Nobody could stop him," says Froment, "so strongly did his zeal impel him to win people to the Lord."

He went with Froment to Berne, and there asked himself and heaven where he should go and preach. To Switzerland? It had already able men. To France? Prisons and death awaited him there. But France needed preachers; he might, perhaps, do something for the gospel. He crossed the border, and went into the region of Macon, where Margaret's chaplain, Michael D'Aranda, had preached nearly ten years before. He raised his voice among the simple and warm-hearted people, who were exposed to the wildest fanaticism. Wandering along the streams he entered the cottages, talked unto the peasants and planted the truth on the plains of Bresse.

Certain pious goldsmiths in Lyons heard rumours of his wonderful work. They probably remembered that a certain William Farel had filled Dauphiny with his doctrine ten years before, and that Peter Sebville was not allowed to preach the Lenten Sermons in their city. They were ready to run risks and to make sacrifices for their faith, and they sent for Alexander to visit them. He went and entered their shops, talked of the new doctrines, and found several "poor men of Lyons" rich in faith. The conversation was pleasant, but he was not satisfied. He must teach more openly. He preached from house to house, then drew the people into larger assemblies. The good word grew. Opposition sprang up like tares to choke its growth. He exclaimed, "Oh that Lyons were a free city like Geneva."

Those who wished to hear the truth became more thirsty every day. They went to him and listened to his messages; they dragged him to their homes; they gave him more work than he could do. He asked Farel to send him help, but none came. The persecution was thought to be so fierce at Lyons that nobody dared face it. He worked on alone, in by-streets or in upper rooms. The priests and their pack were always on the watch ready to seize him. But as soon as his sermon was ended, his friends surrounded him, carried him away and hid him in safe retreats. But he could not remain silent. Wistfully putting out his head and looking round the house to see that no spy was near, he sallied forth, went to the other end of the city, and there preached with all his energy. Scarcely was his sermon finished when he was again taken and hid in some new retreat where he could not be found. "The evangelist was everywhere and nowhere." When the priests were looking for him in the southern suburbs, he was preaching on the northern heights that overlook the city. Thus he was the invisible preacher, a mystery to the people, a marvel to the police.

He did still more: he visited the prisons. One day he heard that two men, well known in Geneva, had come to Lyons on business; the Genevan priests had informed against them as heretical Huguenots, and the bishop had thrown them into a dungeon. They were the energetic Baudichon de la Maison-Neuve and his friend Cologny. Alexander asked to see them; the gates opened; the strange preacher, who had baffled the police, was inside the Episcopal prison. He was in jeopardy every moment. Had any of the agents, who were searching for his track, recognized him, the gates would never have opened to him again, and his sudden disappearance would have been another of those mysteries which Rome has ever been skilful in preparing. He felt no fears. He spoke to the two Genevans "a word in season;" he went to other prisoners with the heavenly consolations, and left the cells, no man laying hands on him.

The priests found out what a chance they had missed, but it was too late. He was off, they knew not where. They were "near bursting with vexation," and lamented with one another, saying,—"There is a Lutheran, who preaches and disturbs the people, collecting assemblies here and there in the city, whom we must catch, for he will spoil all the world, as everybody is running after him; and yet we cannot find him or know who he is." More diligently did they watch and search; but all was useless. Never had a preacher in such strange ways escaped so many snares. They began to say that the unknown man must be possessed of strange powers, by which he passed about invisible.

Easter came — the time when the reformers in Lyons were to boldly raise their banner. The goldsmiths were no longer content with secret meetings; they had made every preparation for a large assembly; the place was settled; they talked of little else, and notice was quietly given from house to house. The day brought the people, and the converted Dominican preached to a large audience. Whether in a church, or hall, or in the open air, the chronicle does not say. He moved and swayed his hearers, and "it might have been said that Christ rose again that Easter morn in Lyons, where he had been so long in the sepulchre." Spies were present; knowing glances were cast; the preacher was no longer invisible; the detectives saw him, heard him, studied his features, took note of his heresies, and hurried to report them to their superiors.

The gladness of many a heart found vent in many an humble dwelling. The cautious believers had a taste of the good word. They wanted a perpetual feast. They requested him to preach again on the morrow. He was ready, and he spoke to a larger audience than before. Eyes were fixed, ears attent, hearts open, and souls rejoicing. But the police were there, charged to seize the mysterious preacher. After a touching sermon his friends surrounded him to take him safely away. But the officers laid hands on him and took him to prison. He was tried and condemned to death. This cruel sentence caused many to mourn. They urged him to appeal. He did appeal; but the result was he was transferred to Paris. They remembered that Paul had once appealed to Cæsar, and thus he won over a great nation at Rome. Why might not Alexander do the same at Paris? He was led away by a captain and his company, who knew not the nature of the preacher's offence.

The captain was a worthy man. He rode beside Alexander,

and they soon were in conversation. The officer asked him why he was arrested. The cause was told. The captain was astonished; he became still more interested in the story of the mysterious preacher; new truths entered his mind, and he wished himself like the pious prisoner. "The captain was converted," says Froment, "while taking him to Paris." Alexander did not stop at this. He spoke to the guards, one by one, and several of them were won over to the gospel. They halted for the night at an inn, and there he found means to address a few good words to the servants and the heads of the household. This was repeated at every stopping-place, and he was happier in receiving the attentions of the villagers to the things he told them, than ever was prince in having suppers and ovations at the towns through which he passed. It was often whispered abroad that a strange captive was at the inn, and the people came to hear him. Now and then they brought the priest or the orator of the village to dispute with him; but he soon silenced them with arguments, and went on touching the hearts of his hearers. No mob could be raised, for a captain was in the crowd. Many left the inn, saying,—"Really, we never saw a man answer his adversaries better by Holy Scripture." Thus Alexander, the captive, marched on as a conqueror, waited upon by increasing crowds. "Wonderful thing!" remarks Froment; "he was more useful at the inns and on the road than he had ever been before."

The Easter of 1534 had passed in Paris—a very happy one for Roussel and Courault, who were set at liberty; but a wretched one for Beda and his pack, who were thrust into prison in place of the preachers. All this was done by the king, in answer to Margaret's entreaties. All Paris had enough to talk about, along with the rumours from Lyons concerning an invisible preacher, who kept the police in perplexity. But a change was suddenly given to the conversation. One day a man loaded with chains entered the capital. He was escorted by archers, who treated him with the greatest respect, even when leading him to the great prison. It was Alexander. The Dominicans remembered him as the friar, Le Croix, and they made the most noise. If Beda was taken from their party, they said, one should be taken from the other party to match him; and Francis I. let matters take their course. Alexander was brought before the court. "Name your accomplices," said the judges. He had none to name. The order was declared,—"Give him the boot."

The reader will remember William Budœus, the illustrious scholar. He was at the trial; he saw the awful tortures applied until a limb was crushed. He heard the groan and the prayer, "O God! there is neither pity nor mercy in these men! May I find both in thee!"

"Keep on," said the chief of torture.

"Is there no Gamaliel here to moderate these cruelties?" asked the victim, as he turned on Budœus a mild look of supplication. The scholar had been astonished at the patience of the sufferer.

"It is enough;" said the man of weighty words. "He has been tortured too much: you ought to be satisfied."

The inhuman work ceased. The poor man was lifted up a cripple, and carried to his dungeon. Not long after, amid great display, the sentence was pronounced, "Alexander Canus, of Evreux, in Normandy, you are condemned to be burnt alive." A flash of joy lit up his face.

"Truly, he is more joyful than ever before," said the spectators. The priests then came forward. They feared lest Alexander should preach the gospel even at that very hour.

"If you utter a word," said they, "you will have your tongue cut out;" a practice that began about this time. They shaved his head and took off his clerical dress; meanwhile he was silent, only smiling at some of their absurdities. They brought the rough robe to put it on him.

"O God!" he exclaimed, "is there any greater honour than to receive this day the livery which thy Son received in the house of Herod?"

He was put into a mean dust-cart, and as it jolted on, he stood up, leaned toward the people, and "scattered the seed of the gospel with both hands." The hearers were moved, some with rage, some with pity; the Dominicans, in the cart with him, pulled his gown and in every way annoyed him, but he would not be checked.

"Either recant, or hold your tongue," said they.

"I will not renounce Jesus Christ," he replied, turning round to them with a withering look. "Depart from me, ye deceivers of the people."

The ruling passion for preaching was strong in death. Alexander saw some lords and ladies in the crowd, along with his friends, the monks and common people, and he asked permission to speak a few words to them. A dignitary, unusually gracious, gave his consent. Then with a holy enthusiasm, Alexander confessed himself a believer in Christ. "Proceed," said he to the executioners. They bound him to the pile, but above the roar of the flames his voice of faith was heard, saying, "O Saviour, receive my spirit. My Redeemer! O my Redeemer!" At last all was still—the people wept—the executioners said one to another, "What a strange criminal!"

"If this man is not saved, who will be?" whispered the monks, no doubt remembering their good brother friar, Le Croix.

"A great wrong has been done to that man," said many who were beating their breasts and starting home. "It is wonderful how these people suffer themselves to be burnt in defence of their faith."

Burnt in defence of the gospel! Truly this was the only real defence it had in France when but a few months before this monk had left the capital to be taught of William Farel, to preach and found a church in Lyons, to talk of the good tidings along every road and in all company, and to return a martyr, and leave the world a lesson from his short but glorious career.

But if the faith be defended by the death of one champion, it is to be fortified by the life of another. It was Calvin's duty to escape, for the Lord had need of his active energies.

In the summer of 1536 a young preacher came to the house of Viret in Geneva, intending to stop there for only a night. He had been in Italy and was on the way to Basle where he had spent some time as an exile from France. Some one— Du Tillet* or Caroli—discovered him, and went and brought Farel to see him. He was already in high repute as the author of the Institutes of the Christian Religion, and Farel met, for the first time, John Calvin, from the country of his noble friends, Lefevre and Olivetan. Farel thought what Beza afterwards said, "God conducted him hither," and was resolved to secure his services in that city. He at once presented the case to the guest of Viret.

"I cannot bind myself to any one church," says Calvin, "but I would endeavour to be useful to all. I have my plan for study

---

* This gentle and genial man was about two years in Geneva. He thought it too perilous for him to remain a Protestant, and going back to France, returned to the Romish Church. He still was a friend to Calvin, and offered him kindly aid in the days of the Reformer's distress.

before me, and I am not one of those who can afford to be always giving without receiving."

"Now," said Farel, with that manner and voice which filled thousands with awe, "I declare to you, in the name of the Almighty God—to you who only put forth your studies as a pretence—that if you will not help us to carry on this work of God, the curse of God will rest upon you, for you will be seeking your own honour rather than that of Christ."

The conscience of the young traveller was so touched that he never forgot it. Toward the close of his life he said, "As I was kept in Geneva, not properly by an express exhortation or request, but rather by the terrible threatenings of William Farel, which were as if God had seized me by his awful hand from heaven, so was I compelled, through the terror thus inspired, to give up the plan of my journey, but yet without pledging myself, for I was conscious of my timidity and weakness, to undertake any definite office." He is first noticed in the archives of Geneva as *iste Gallus*, "that Gaul," but in the spirit of modern appreciation Montesquieu says, "The Genevese ought to observe the day of his arrival in their city as a festival."

In the highest part of the city, where once stood a temple to Apollo, visitors still enter the old cathedral of St. Peter, dating back to the sixth century, and gaze on the same little pulpit in which Calvin preached his powerful sermons. We suppose that he there stood when his first sermon in Geneva created such an enthusiasm that the people could scarcely restrain their delight. They followed him to his lodgings, and he was obliged to promise that he would preach the next day, so that their friends might hear him. Farel was overjoyed; for if he were thus eclipsed, there would be all the more light in that dark city, which was waiting for it. Calvin, soon after his arrival, was elected preacher and professor of theology. He at first declined the former office, but was so urged that he accepted it the next year. His first labours were almost gratuitous, but none the less cheerfully rendered.

With no little joy to Farel it was arranged to have a debate at Lausanne, where he had made several attempts to gain a footing for the truth. Viret had succeeded and gathered a small church. The priests agreed to the discussion. All the Romish clergy were urged to come. And some of them, who knew not so much of the Bible as even the ten commandments attended. The elders of the chuch and the citizens were invited. The bishop protested; but the lords of Berne had a will of their own in such matters. On their way thither the Protestant ministers narrowly escaped the hands of some assassins, who had been planted on the road to murder them. Farel, who took the leading part, drew up ten propositions relating to the true faith, the true church, and the true ordinances of worship. Several days were spent in the discussions; and if the cathedral ever had more priests in it—for there were many—it certainly never before had so many Protestants. After one of Calvin's arguments against transubstantiation, a Franciscan, named Tandi, arose before the whole assembly, confessed that he was overcome by the power of the truth, and declared that henceforth he would live according to the gospel of Christ. Viret spoke more than Calvin, and Farel more than all. In closing the debates he said,— "We do not thirst for blood, like those who laid in wait to destroy us on our way hither. So far from seeking to punish them, we interceded on their behalf, and our only wish is that they may receive complete forgiveness." The result was favourable to the Protestant cause. Several of the principal persons on the papal side went home convinced of their errors, and became advocates for the reformation. The Bernese divided the canton into seven districts, and appointed ministers in them all.

At Geneva Farel still pushed on his schemes. With the help of Calvin he drew up a brief confession of faith and certain rules of discipline. It was not easy to break up the old customs of the people, and many of Farel's new measures were not to their taste. They were lively and fond of excitement, and had been used to an almost unbounded license. In clear weather they loved music and dancing in the open air. On rainy days they had their cups and cards at the wine-shops. Among all their holidays Sunday was quite as gay as any, when masquerades and other mummeries were their delight. But, as all this was connected with the baser forms of profligacy, Farel attempted to suppress these amusements. The silver tones of the convent bells, which had been baptized in order to give their sounds a power over bad weather, ghosts and Satan, were to be heard no more. The bells were to be cast into canon for the defence of the city, thus changing their carols into thunders of war. Gambling, swearing, slandering, dancing, the singing of idle songs in the streets, Sabbath-breaking, and absence from church without good reasons were forbidden. The people must be at home by nine o'clock in the evening. The senate passed these laws, and they were proclaimed with a trumpet.

To the confession of faith was added Calvin's catechism, and it was ordered to be printed and read at St. Peter's every Sunday, until the people should understand it. It was adopted, so that Calvin wrote,—"We easily succeeded in obtaining that the citizens should be summoned by tens, and swear to adopt the confession, which was done with much satisfaction." Those who would not adopt it lost their rights as citizens. On a solemn day, July 20th, 1537, the people took the oath, for the third time, to support the reformation.

Murmurings began to be heard; then louder opposition; and a party grew up which held their meetings, and wore fresh flowers as a badge. The lines were drawn, and the contentions became bitter. What they complained of most was the determination of Farel not to use the stone fonts for baptism, nor unleavened bread in the Lord's supper, nor to observe the festivals of Christmas, New Year, Annunciation and Ascension. Berne was consulted and decided against Farel. The Genevan senate followed in the same decision, and the Bernese began to have more and noisier friends than ever before in that city. This party now made use of the awful name of my lords of Berne, in order to threaten and insult the ministers whom Berne had such trouble in keeping in Geneva. Troops of them went about parading the streets by night, insulting the ministers at their homes, and threatening to throw them into the Rhone. Berne had preserved the stone fonts, the unleavened bread, and the four festivals, and they would hold fast to them, for they were not able to see the principle which Farel thought was involved in them. He regarded them as relics of popery, and feared these relics would lead back the people into the old reality. Calvin took his side, although he declared,—"Little will be said about ceremonies before the judgment-seat of God." Councils and synods failed to restore peace. A plot was suspected against the preachers.

The aged, blind and eloquent Courault, whom the Queen Margaret had tenderly cherished as his sight was failing, and whom the placards at Paris had sent into exile, was now at Geneva. He preached with much fire against the decision of

Berne, and handled Genevan politics in too rough a way to gain his point. He was forbidden to preach, but he again entered the pulpit. He was then cast into prison, and for some time his best friends could not procure his release.

A bold step was taken by Farel and Calvin. They refused to administer the Lord's Supper with unleavened bread in a city that would not allow any proper church discipline. Easter Sunday was coming, and the Sacrament was expected on that day. The council urged them to administer it; they refused, and were forbidden to enter the pulpit. They, however, went at the time and each preached twice, Calvin at St. Peter's, and Farel at St. Gervais, without any communion. A great principle was now coming to light, that of not allowing the state to rule the church in matters of religion. But a great disturbance arose in the city. Some took the sword, but the reformers employed the weapons of Scripture. No blood was shed, and what was gained by Farel and Calvin could not be seen for a few years. They first must suffer for their principles.

The next morning the senate met and passed sentence of banishment on Calvin and Farel. In three days they must leave the city. They were informed of the act, and said, "Let it be so; it is better to serve God than man." Courault was released and permitted to go with them. He went to Thonon where Christopher Fabri was preaching, and he was welcomed as a father in this excellent pastor's house. Of the style of hospitality which he enjoyed, Calvin can tell us in a letter to Fabri, written after a journey through the cantons. He says, "I could never get your wife to treat us in a plain homely way. She repeatedly requested me to ask for whatever I chose as if it were my own. She entertained us too sumptuously. We felt just as much at home as if you had been there." The good hostess was surely none the less kind to the aged refugee. But he could not rest even there. He must preach the faith so long unknown to him while a monk, and he was afterwards settled at Orbe, where the zealous, blind, and lovely old man gained many friends, and in a few months they wept when they laid him in the grave.*

The lords of Berne had not dreamed that they were causing such a result as this. A violent man named Peter Konzen, a Bernese minister residing at Geneva, had a prominent hand in the mischief, for he had misrepresented all parties. In a few weeks Farel and Calvin appeared before the senate of Berne. The Bernese wished to undo what had been done under excitement. After many discussions and several messages to the Genevese senate, they resolved to send back the ministers, along with Viret, whose milder methods might restore order. Two senators went with them, but the ministers lately exiled, met with a cold refusal near the gates of Geneva. One of them thus describes it: "We were about a mile from the city when a messenger, in great haste, met us and stated that we were forbidden to enter. The (Bernese) messengers held us back or we should otherwise have tranquilly pursued our journey. But this saved our lives, for we afterwards learned that an ambush

* There was a strong suspicion that Courault had been poisoned. Calvin, in a letter to Farel (Oct. 24, 1538,) says, "I am so bowed down by the death of Courault that I can set no limit to my anguish. None of my usual employments is sufficient to keep my mind from perpetually reverting to the subject. . . . My mind is chiefly burdened with that iniquitous deed, which, if my suspicions are well grounded, I must, whether I will or not, bring to light." He laments that "where there are so few good ministers, the church should be thus deprived of one of its best."

had been formed outside the city, and that close to the very gates, twenty gladiators, known banditti, were lying in wait for us."

The Bernese ambassadors and Viret went on and entered the city. They appeared before the Genevan senate. They asked that the exiles might be admitted, their apology heard, and their sentence expunged. They pleaded the very eminent services of Farel to whom his opposers were greatly indebted for their present liberty. They said that Calvin and Farel would now baptize at the fonts, use the unleavened bread and allow the festivals to be prudently observed. Viret put forth all his eloquence, and the senators and citizens were moved. But it was all in vain. New charges were founded upon mere trifles and quibbles, and the senate, in a stormy assembly, renewed the decree of banishment.

Bound in heart as brothers, Farel and Calvin took their way toward the cities on the Rhine, where a protestant could find refuge when no other place would receive him. "Wet with the rain and almost dead with weariness," they entered Basle.* Bucer sent word to Calvin to come to Strasburg, but as Farel was not invited, he chose to remain with this Boanerges whom he loved with all tenderness. The gentle sunbeam was wedded to the lightning by the power of that

---

*"We have, at length, reached Basle, but well soaked with the rain and completely spent and worn out. Nor was our journey free from perils, for, in truth, one of us was almost carried away by the swollen currents; but we have experienced more tender usage from the impetuous river than from our fellow-men; for since, contrary to all right and reason, they had decided that we should travel on foot, that also has been complied with through the mercy of the Lord in preserving us. *Calvin's Letters, No.* xx., *May* 1538.

grace which unites the most diverse natures. It is a proof that Farel was not all fury and self-will, when he drew so closely to him such gentle men as Lefevre, Œcolampadius, Viret and Calvin.

CHAPTER XIX.

PEACE TO THE STORMS.

(1538–1549.)

THERE lived in Basle one of the best of men, named Symon Grynæus, a school-fellow of Melancthon, who said that he had "a mildness of temper that was never put out, and an almost excessive bashfulness." Beza compared him "to the splendour of the sun, that overpowers the light of the stars." The papists of Spires knew his worth, for they thought it policy to attack him with such violence in 1529 that he barely escaped. He was invited to Basle to take the place of Erasmus as a professor. When Calvin was there in 1534 he met this good man and was captivated by his gentleness. They became most affectionate friends, and often shut themselves up in their room for study. To his house Calvin went as a very damp and chilly exile from Geneva, and there he found a cheerful fire, a sympathetic heart, and a home where he remained for many months.

In the house of Oporinus, the printer, Farel was lodged, waiting for Providence to open some new door to him. Toussaint wished him and Calvin to return to Lausanne, and there labour. But in a few weeks there came a very unexpected call. Two councillors and two ministers of Neufchatel came to see him. They said their people had heard of Farel's sufferings, and their old attachment to him had revived in such strength that they must have him among them. They could not forget how he had preached on the stone in Serrière, in their streets, and in the cathedral on the hill. They had first heard from his lips the word of God, and his weighty voice seemed yet ringing in their ears. They had prayed fervently for God to send them a chief minister, and all wanted Farel. Besides, Viret and Fabri were urgent in pressing the call upon him, and so, too, were the neighbouring churches.

At first he hesitated, for the desire to be with Calvin and to engage in study was strong. Then the church at Neufchatel was sadly in want of discipline. He might have the late experience at Geneva all over again, and be exiled in less than a year. But duty began to impress his mind; conscience lifted her voice; his soul caught the old fire, and he was himself again,—bold, fearless, ready to sacrifice himself, intensely anxious to preach, and possessing an "ambition for God's glory without bounds." His mind was made up, and at once he set out for his parish.

Soon after his arrival mournful tidings followed him. His sister had followed him to Basle, and there she saw her son die of the plague. Calvin wrote thus, in a letter to "Farel, the faithful preacher at Neufchatel, my beloved brother. Your nephew, last Sabbath-day, fell sick here of the plague. His companion and the goldsmith, who bore witness to the gospel at Lyons, immediately sent to me. As I had taken something to cure my headache I could not visit him myself. . . . Grynæus visited him frequently. I did so as soon as my health allowed it. When our T., (Du Tailly,) saw that I did not fear the danger he insisted on sharing it with me. We spent a long time with him yesterday. When the signs of approaching death were evident, I imparted spiritual rather than bodily comfort. His mind seemed to wander; but he still had sufficient consciousness to call me back to his chamber, and to entreat me earnestly to pray for him. He had heard me speak much of the usefulness of prayer. Early this morning, about four o'clock, he departed to the Lord."*

There were many difficulties at Neufchatel. The ablest ministers had been sent by the Bernese lords into other cantons, and some of the old priests were in the churches, consuming the revenues and corrupting the people by their bad example. The reigning prince also had laid his hand upon the revenues of most of the churches, and it was a serious question how to support pastors in the different parishes. The neglect of pastoral attentions to the sick, the poor, the ignorant and the young was

* In this same letter there is an unobtrusive proof of the straits of poverty through which Farel and his relatives had to pass. "Concerning the wearing apparel and other movables of your nephew, thus you have it:— The son-in-law of the old woman, (the nephew's nurse,) affirms that all his clothes, which, however, were not many, were left to him, but with no appearance of truth, since he could not have done so except in the intervals of delirium. He has a sword and a shirt with Wolf. I know for certain that he had no money when he fell ill. His landlord, Wolf, thinks that the story about the legacy of the clothes is a pure fable."

There were some debts incurred by the sickness and burial of this nephew, and the generous Farel seems not to have been able to easily pay them. He could not pay Oporin for his seven weeks' board when he left Basle. Calvin was to settle the matter, and, after receiving some money on Farel's account, he wrote to him,—"I yet owe you one gold crown and a half, which I will pay as soon as possible. Here, unless I would be a burden to the brethren, I must live at my own expense. . . . My outlay on account of your nephew I have received, except about ten shillings, which Claude, (probably a deacon of the French church of Strasburg,) was about to send me. I mention that lest you may think that I had received nothing."—*Calvin's Letters, No. xvi.*, October, 1558.

disheartening. The governor had lately adopted the reform, but he still disliked Farel. This was probably George de Rive, whom we well remember.

There was also much to cheer his heart when he recalled the day that he first crossed the lake in his little boat. Fabri had gone into the parish of Boudry and given the papists a chance to repeat their tricks of ringing bells and shouting to drown his voice while preaching, and then fall upon and nearly kill him after the sermon was ended. But the parish finally had decided for the reformation. The young minister proved that he not only admired Farel, but took him for his model.

The shepherds and hunters of Locle often came to a little oratory, about which there was a legend which was truer, in their view, than the gospel. St. Hubert was once riding through these mountains on a hunt, when a bear met him and killed his horse. But, nothing daunted, he mounted the bear and rode safely home, to the amazement of everybody. Hubert was the hunter's patron saint, and a celebrated lover of the chase had built this oratory. The prayers offered there were probably few, and certainly very superstitious. A greater hunter was coming to Locle. John de Bely was on the way at the time of a fair, when Madame Williamette, of Valangin, had him seized and brought into the castle. She forced him to debate for two hours with her priest. "Put him in prison," she exclaimed; but the good-natured priest interceded and he was released. Bely found a friend in this worthy vicar, who took him by the arm, led him to the parsonage, refreshed him with bread and wine, and sent him on rejoicing. The people said that "the mountain bears were beginning to be tamed."

One day the people of Brenets, far up in the Jura mountains, resolved to take the images out of their church, so that they might worship God in spirit and in truth. They removed them and prepared to break them in pieces and throw them into the river as had been done at Neufchatel. They looked up and saw two fine oxen coming, driven by some villagers from a little town in France, just over the border.

"We offer you these oxen," said the villagers, "in exchange for your pictures and images."

"Pray take them," said the people of Brenets. The idols were gathered up by one party, and the oxen driven away by the other, and an old chronicler says that "each thought they had made a fine exchange." In such ways the gospel was working in the canton of Neufchatel. "With the exception of one village, the evangelical faith was established throughout the whole principality, without the aid of the prince and the lords, and indeed in spite of them. A hand mightier than theirs was breaking the bonds, removing the obstacles, and emancipating souls. The Reformation triumphed; and after God, it was Farel's work." He had sown bountifully a few years before, and now he has returned to reap in the same fields. History dwells less upon the peaceful progress of his work than upon the disturbances raised by the foes of the truth.

There was one man who made himself such a thorn in the sides of Farel and his co-labourers that, on their account, he should be mentioned. This was Peter Caroli, whom Farel had known in Paris as a dissolute doctor of the Sorbonne. A few of the adjectives applied to him by historians, are these, vain, fickle, frivolous, insinuating, servile, quarrelsome, hypocritical, ambitious, dangerous, insufferable, seeking to push himself forward, and unworthy of notice had he not had the honour to excite trouble among the reformers.

In this shrewd and crafty man Beda had found his match, after he assailed the priests. Had he been a thorough reformer he might have been burned, but he was too trifling a character to be worthy of death. It was said that two such men as Caroli would have wearied out the activity of Beda himself, but he was not content with provoking the Romanists. He left Paris in fear, and, for safety, took refuge with those who favoured the gospel.

For a while he was with Lefevre and Roussel; and Margaret, who gave him the parish of Alençon, could make nothing of him, for there he persecuted the Protestants. Changing again, he put on the face of a mild reformer, and was driven out of France. He wandered about for a time, and at length appeared in Geneva.

There he fawned on Farel and Viret, but would not subscribe to their confession of faith, lest he should not seem to be above these brethren. He sought to be the chief director in the protestant council, and gave all the annoyance possible when Anthony Saunier was chosen. At one time Farel detected him in pocketing a collection for the poor. There were rumours that he still led a very disorderly life. He professed to be very penitent and to reform. In 1536 he went to Neufchatel, preached there, and married into a respectable family. By dint of entreaty he got the Bernese to appoint him chief minister at Lausanne, where his age and doctor's degree gave him the precedence over the tried and meritorious Viret. His ambition rose, and he soon went to Berne, asking to be appointed the overseer of the whole clergy of the district. The Bernese saw his pride, sharply rebuked him, and ordered him to pay deference to Viret. This mortified him exceedingly, and he began to meditate schemes of revenge against Viret and Farel.

PEACE TO THE STORMS. 307

After long endurance of his insults, slanders, and half-popish sermons, Viret brought him before the lords of Berne at Lausanne. Farel had shown the utmost solicitude for his welfare and hoped yet to see him a truly converted man, all to no purpose. Viret also had dealt gently with him although he suspected him of bad conduct.

He was found guilty by the council and required to make a confession to those whom he had injured. But to avoid this he left the country in great haste and secrecy. He stopped at a little town on his way and there wrote an abusive letter against the ministers who had shown all the gentleness that they could. He wandered about, found Calvin at Strasburg and reconciled himself to the evangelical party, and just when they hoped he might become a firm and consistent protestant, he went to a cardinal Tournon in France, forsook the reformation, embraced popery again, was recommended to the pope, and boasted that he had won a victory over the gospel preachers. The pope restored him to the Romish church, released him from his wife (whom he did not call by so tender and sacred a name,) and Caroli became again a priest. He honoured Farel by calling him the chief of all heretics.

To the great surprise of Farel it was reported that Caroli had appeared at Neufchatel. He had not found that a second return to his "mother church" had secured him the preferment which he wished. He desired to return to the church which he had so vilified at Rome, and was even willing that "the chief of all heretics" should receive him. Farel passed over all the slanders and abuse that had been flung at him, and believing that the power of God could yet convert even a Caroli, hastened to visit him. The great waverer showed some signs of repentance when Farel, Viret, and their friends met him. They plainly brought to his remembrance all the evil that he had done, and he begged their forgiveness, hoping that his past errors might be for ever buried. They gave him the right hand of fellowship, and promised to do what they could in his behalf. They were not agreed as to his restoration to the church and the university. Some thought that he was a worthless individual, on whom all forbearance and kindness would be lost. Farel, who had most reason to be severe with him, was most anxious to see this wandering sheep brought back into the fold.

The senate of Berne had a matter to settle with him, for he had left the country despising their orders and slandering their honours to the pope. They cared nothing for the pope, but they had a high self-respect. They had him arrested, and tried. Again Farel interposed as a peace-maker, but the senate condemned him and let him off with a fine and a lecture. There was a general distrust of him among the reformed churches, and he was advised, by Farel, to go to Basle and there remain until he could gain the esteem and confidence of those whom he had offended. Those who charge the Genevan reformers with severity amounting to persecution, may well study this case, and learn how much they are mistaken.*

* "I entreat you my dear brother, when I expostulate with you, chide you, get warm with you, accuse you, that you may take it all the same as if you were dealing with yourself. Concerning Caroli, the Lord will give counsel, in whose case, if there had been anything sinful on our part, the Lord can correct it. Our friends also acknowledge that they were more lenient than they ought to have been. . . . If he shall return, let us take care that our gentle treatment of him may not prove hurtful to you. . . . I am already aware that he thinks better of you than rashly to entertain any accusation." Thus Calvin wrote to his "much longed for brother" Farel, 1540.

Peter Toussaint was preaching at Montbeliard, the first parish in which Farel had laboured. To his surprise, Caroli came there to get an appointment from the Duke of Wurtemberg. Toussaint found that he was the same man that he had long been, and dismissed him. At Valangin he went next, and the wonder is that he did not enter the service of Madame Williamette. Farel still aided him, insisting upon his thorough repentance. Then he went to Strasburg to see what he could do with Calvin, who asked advice of Farel, and was answered that Caroli should be helped in making a living, but not placed over a church until he gave evidence of his conversion. Thence he went to Metz where he wrote a "vapouring letter" to Calvin, asking for a parish. The reply was that neither he nor Farel had any churches at their command, and even if they had, he could not have it until he should prove himself worthy of the trust. When we meet him again he will have made another shift for bread, reputation and power.

It is not strange that Farel was sick after these contacts with this ambitious waverer, but we should barely notice his illness did it not bring to light the esteem and friendship of Calvin, who felt that his life was almost bound up with that of his friend. After his recovery Calvin wrote to him; "While I reflect how much of the greatest importance may depend on the little man, it is not possible for me not to be, in a more than ordinary degree, anxious about your life. Wherefore from the time that the report of your illness was brought hither [Strasburg,] I have not enjoyed one pleasant moment until I heard you had recovered. On that account, I experienced the like joy from hearing, by the messenger, good news of your health, as he enjoys who is delivered from a long continued sickness."

The life of Farel may appear much tamer while he passes

several years as a minister in one place, than while he was imperilling his life by his journeys and his contests as a missionary. But it may have been equally useful. By his correspondence he still held a great influence over the whole region where his voice had been heard. In his charge he was greatly annoyed by the opposition to his discipline. It grieved him to give the bread, at a communion, to those who showed no evidence of conversion, and who thought that their high rank entitled them to share in all the privileges of the church and yet neglect the practice of their duties. He had put down the useless holidays, and to a good degree had broken up the dances and the idleness and the drunkenness of the people, but those who wished such pleasures and sins were restless and quite ready for a riot. They wanted Farel to leave them, and sought for some occasion to exhibit their feelings and their strength.

There was a lady of high rank in the town who had for several years lived on bad terms with her husband, a man of integrity, separated from him, set a bad example to her children, brought suspicion upon her own character, and given very general offence. Yet she claimed her place at the sacramental table. Farel tried to bring her back to her duty, by serious but gentle remonstrances. After several such attempts, with no success, he gave his opinion of such conduct publicly, but mentioned no names. At this she ceased to go to church. The congregation and senate would do nothing, and he at length declared that the authorities were shamefully negligent, and that such a pest ought not to be endured in the church as a member of it. The sermon was not politic; it arrayed against him all the young and old who had before felt stung by his rebukes. No efforts were spared to raise a general commotion. The whole town was divided in two parties; the one intent upon retaining their pastor, and the other upon dismissing him. His opponents at last gained a majority for his leaving within two months. The greater part of the senate and the better class of the people were on his side, but the governor and some others of rank so excited the common people that the vote against him was obtained.

It was a day of trouble to the minister. The first friend who came to console him was John Calvin, who was on the way to Geneva,* and who turned aside to use his good offices for his brother. He pleaded with the people, and thence went to Berne to engage their help in behalf of the preacher and the endangered church. All efforts seemed in vain, until a mysterious Providence secured a reconciliation of the parties. The plague began to rage in the town. The courage of Farel rose with the dangers of his situation. He acted the part of a pastor who had never been disowned by any of the people. He visited the sick every day, relieved the poor, and sought to win his enemies by kindness. They could not but respect him for all this, and the bitterest opposers began to be the warmest friends. A day of humiliation and prayer was appointed. Every one partook of the sacrament. The preachers warned the people and urged them to unity and peace. The example of their devoted but injured pastor softened their hearts, and they wished to retain him among them. Some weeks after this he was re-elected for life, and by degrees every trace of the disturbance was gone, and complete harmony was established.

* " Having heard at Soleure that there was some trouble in this church, I have been constrained, in brotherly love, to go out of my way to see whether I could do anything to remedy it."
Calvin to the Lords of Geneva, dated Neufchatel, September 7, 1541.

Calvin spent some time with his friends, and we must now see how this exile came to be on the way to Geneva.

The faction, which had expelled him and Farel, enjoyed their triumph by trying to undo almost all that had been gained. The old manners were restored, and carried to such an extreme as to create disgust. From liberty the people passed to licentiousness. Every social tie was broken; order gave way to discord, tumult and deeds of violence. The reading of the Bible was totally forbidden to the women, and very much restricted among all others. The teachers were removed from the schools that Farel had established; the preachers were set aside for mere hirelings, and the fanatics seemed to rule the day. But a re-action followed. The people saw that masquerades, balls, blasphemies and indecencies must be checked. They began to wish for the return of the banished ministers. Many prayed for it. The subject of calling back Calvin was openly discussed; the senate held meetings; and, at last, on the first of May, 1541, the act of banishment was revoked. To show their sincerity, the people intimated that the amusements and dissipations, which the reformers had once tried to put down, should be abated.

But it was not so easy to persuade those whom they had expelled to return to Geneva. Farel was now settled, and Neufchatel refused to give him up. Calvin did not wish to go unless his vigorous friend could join him in the difficult work, and, besides, Strasburg was not willing to part with him, for he was now a pastor in that city. From all sides went letters urging Calvin to accept the call, but Farel and Viret had the chief influence in securing the end. With great reluctance he went. The troubles at Neufchatel detained him, as we have seen, on the way, and prevented Farel from attending him.

There was reason for Calvin to expect a hearty reception.

James Bernard* had written and told him how the weeping people had prayed, and how, the next day, the great council met and said, with one voice,—"Calvin, that righteous and learned man, it is he whom we would have as the minister of the Lord;" and with much warmth Bernard continued,—"Come, therefore, thou worthy father in Christ; thou art ours; God has given thee to us; all sigh for thee; thou wilt see how pleasant thine arrival will be to all." On the thirteenth of September, 1541, this promise was fulfilled. A herald met him; the gates were crowded, the city full of joy, and the senate soon entreated him never to leave Geneva.

We left the Chevalier Esch at Metz, and we cannot learn what became of him, except that persecution drove him to Strasburg. The agents of Beda had waged a merciless war† upon the believers in that free and imperial city; but they had not entirely suppressed the desire which many of the people felt for the gospel. At length the times seemed to favour new efforts. Some of the Dominicans began to preach sounder doctrines and a purer life. In 1542 Casper de Huy was elected to fill the highest office of the city, that of sheriff, (*echevin*,) or mayor. He and his brother permitted the Protestants to meet in their

---

* Bernard had been induced to vote for the expulsion of Calvin and Farel from Geneva, but he was penitent for it, and was ever afterward the friend and helper of Calvin.

† There were other sources of trouble. "At Metz, when everything was opposed to pure religion, when the senate was sworn to its destruction, and when the priesthood had joined them with all their fury, then has arisen the plague of the Anabaptists to create a fresh scandal. Two were cast headlong into the Moselle, a third was punished by banishment with the brand of infamy. . . . I fear that this pestilential doctrine is widely spread among the simple sort in that city."—*Calvin to Farel*, 1538.

private houses for worship, and also on their estates, where multitudes assembled to hear it. Nothing seemed wanting to the organization of a regular church but an efficient minister. One had been invited, but he lacked the courage to brave all the dangers of the post and even death itself. Proposals were made to Farel, who saw that quiet and prosperity were restored at Neufchatel, and he might leave it for a time. The new field had charms for one so bold and zealous, whose element was to reform, to hazard everything for the gospel, and to do the work of a pioneer. Several of his friends disapproved of the step, but he was urged to go by Calvin, who thought no one so well qualified as this experienced and dauntless missionary.

Early in December, 1542, Farel went to Metz, and he was urged to preach on the next Sabbath. In the church-yard of the Dominicans a pulpit had been raised, and he mounted it to preach his first sermon in that city. The number of hearers was very great. During his sermon two of the monks came and ordered him to be silent. He gave no heed to their command. They called their friends and began to ring all the bells, but his voice of thunder rose above all the din. The next day more than three thousand persons came to hear him. That he should preach and baptize without any Romish ceremonies excited great attention among the people and high wrath among the friars. The pulpit was ordered to be pulled down, and various threats were made. The sheriff, de Huy, and his friends saw that in so large an assembly a little flame might become a vast fire, and they persuaded Farel to postpone his preaching until there was more assurance of the public safety.

The news of his arrival had reached the ears of the council, and Farel was summoned before that body.

"By whose orders are you here?" they asked.

"By the order of Jesus Christ, and at the request of some of his members."

"Name those who invited you," said they, glancing at one another, as if certain of them were held under suspicion. He refused to give any names. He then addressed them and withdrew, leaving them to consider what they should do with him. Soon after a man of his size and appearance was seen riding out of the gates. It was reported that Farel had been sent away by his friends, who were alarmed for his safety. He was, however, concealed among the Protestants.*

The fearful plague fell upon the city. Many who felt that they must be abandoned by men and die in loneliness, without pastor or priest, found a plain, bold man urging his way to their couches. There he told them of Christ's death, free pardon and holy heaven; there he carried such consolation for the dying as they never had heard before, and even into houses that would otherwise have been shut against him he found a welcome. Full scope was thus given to his fearless activity, and many recognized Farel, the preacher who had declared the good tidings in the church-yard. In the meantime he sent word to the neighbouring cantons, which had united in the Protestant league of Smalcalde, to send deputies to Metz, and receive into their union the Protestants of that city. The senators would not allow the deputies to enter the gates, and they imposed a fine upon any one who should visit Farel. They secured a mandate from the emperor forbidding him to preach, and declaring that all the citizens should remain Roman Catholics until the next

---

* Calvin, from the time that he went to Metz, felt great anxiety about his safety. In his letters he writes of waiting anxiously "until we know that he has escaped in safety from the jaws of death," and "praying the Lord to restore him to us as soon as possible."

general council. The emperor's mandate was posted up in the streets and pulled down by the children.

In this state of affairs Farel retired to the neighbouring town of Gorze, under the protection of Count William, of Furstenberg. At his court Walter Farel was engaged in an honourable service. Another brother, Claudius, came from Strasburg to visit the preacher. At Gorze he preached in the parish church and in the abbey chapel. A monk was one day descanting on the glories of Mary, when Farel called his statements in question. The women in the audience attacked him, and handled him so roughly that he came near losing his life. He was obliged to keep his room for several days, but, with this exception, he preached with growing success. At Easter many came from Metz to hear him and to celebrate the Lord's supper.

This enraged the Romanists in Metz, and they formed a conspiracy against Farel and his hearers. The renegade Caroli seems to have been at the head of the plot. He persuaded the duke of Guise to send a body of soldiers to Gorze, and there fall upon the congregation. About three hundred persons had just celebrated the Lord's supper on one Sabbath, when suddenly a trumpet was heard, and a troop of armed men fell upon this helpless and unsuspecting company. A son of the duke led the band, and it is said that Francis I. sanctioned the plot. Some were slaughtered and others drowned; Farel was wounded, and with great difficulty he and Count William escaped into the castle. It was some time before the friends of the preacher knew what had become of him. The count had him and many other wounded sent on litters to Strasburg.

Caroli was now preparing for the great master stroke which, as he hoped, would bring him honour and office. Having failed to murder Farel he attempted to crush him. The clergy and council of Metz so favoured him that he had the insolence to send Farel a pompous and noisy challenge to a dispute. And, to gain the more glory, the dispute should not be held in Metz, but before the pope or the council of Trent, or in some of the great universities. It was to be held at the risk of each life: the one who should be defeated was to be put to death. In order to effect this Caroli would become a prisoner at Metz, and Farel might place himself in the hands of the French king. Caroli sent this absurd challenge to the great powers in the Romish church, so that they might know what a champion was about to appear.

Farel replied, asking him who had commissioned him to hold such a debate, and suggesting that it would not be so expensive to have it in Metz as in some distant city. "If you have not sufficient influence to have a debate appointed in your own city, how can you secure one in a place where you are unknown?" The ridiculous proposal was thoroughly exposed. Farel employed his pen, in replying to various slanders set on foot by Caroli. In one letter to him he says, "If I am rightly informed, you have publicly declared that I am the greatest heretic that the world has ever seen. Might it please the Lord that I could in truth say, you are the most faithful and pious servant of God that ever appeared! . . . I beseech you to retrace your steps, and to employ the good gifts, which God has bestowed upon you, for his glory. I am ready to hold a friendly conference with you, at Metz, and endeavour to restore harmony among the people."

This man had circulated such reports about the Genevan ministers, that they thought it wisest to have a public disputation with him, and thus assert, defend and prove their doctrines. It might open the eyes of the people of Metz, and put the reformation there on a good footing. They cared very little for the aspersions of Caroli, and had no fears for their own personal characters, but they wished to see the truth established among its enemies. The Genevese sent Calvin to Strasburg for the purpose of securing the debate. He and Farel begged the senate to give them a safe-guard to Metz, and a request to the senate there to grant them an audience. But it was all fruitless. Caroli was the last man who wished to meet them in a discussion. His pretensions brought him a fall; his haughty spirit was a token of his utter ruin. The papists must have laughed at his absurd challenge. He never came again in contact with the admirable men whom he had abused. He surrendered himself to his weaknesses, or rather his strong vices, and, at last, one might have seen, in a hospital at Rome, a poor, disappointed, wretched and forsaken victim of excess, dying in disgrace. It was the last of Peter Caroli, who is a first-class specimen of several men with whom the reformers had to contend. He could never justly complain that Farel and his brethren had treated him with severity.

Farel had been absent from his parish about a year, when he returned to Neufchatel. His recent sufferings in the Lord's service brought him new esteem from all who were able to appreciate his merits. But there were also fresh troubles. His colleague, Chaponneau, seemed disposed to act over again the part of Caroli. By degrees Farel won him to the right path. The church became more settled under a better organization. Elders and deacons were appointed, and there was a firm but kindly discipline. The children were carefully taught the Bible and the catechism, and the plan of a Sabbath-school appears to have existed. The form of church government was Presbyterian, and its principles were derived, not from the Waldenses, but from the apostles.

CHAPTER XX.

FAREL'S NEIGHBOURLY VISITS.

(1549—1558.)

NOT long after Farel's return from Metz, he paid a visit to Geneva. His garments were a proof of the persecutions he had endured, as well as of his poverty, or his disregard of dress. The senate had given Calvin a new suit when he returned to the city, and now a similar one was voted to Farel. He seemed to suspect that it was meant to buy him off from speaking his mind, or he felt that he did not deserve it; and when he appeared before that dignified body he admonished them to lead good lives, maintain justice and revere the word of God. He respectfully declined the present. He also refused to accept their invitation to reside in Geneva. The suit was put in Calvin's keeping. Some time after Calvin wrote to Farel, "The suit is at my house, until some one be found to take it. Your refusing it was all very well; but you may now very properly accept of it." It seems that he laid aside his scruples, accepted the present, and allowed his personal appearance to be improved by dressing in the style of Geneva.

It was still a favourite plan of Calvin to have Farel in Geneva as a co-labourer, feeling that he would be most useful in that city which owed so much to his missionary efforts. In 1545, this proposal was again laid before him. Berne was willing, but he would not consent to go unless a minister could be found to take his place at Neufchatel. Toussaint was invited, but refused to leave Montbeliard. After the death of Chaponneau, who on his death-bed and in tears ordered all his writings against Calvin to be burned and bequeathed him a copy of Augustine's works, there was some difficulty in choosing a colleague for Farel. Some wished Anthony Marcourt, but Christopher Fabri was chosen, and Farel was delighted to have this devoted and zealous young friend to take from his weary shoulders many of the heavy burdens.

In a few months Calvin and Viret made another effort to draw Farel into their nearer fellowship. A new professor of divinity was to be appointed at Lausanne, to share the labours with Viret. No one appeared more suitable. He was congenial with Viret; he was no mean scholar in the Bible languages; he was a good expositor of the Scriptures, and the system which he had introduced at Geneva was proof that he was an excellent theologian. Calvin noticed that as his years increased he became more gentle and cultivated in his manners. If any one could fire the students with a love for preaching and for missionary toils, Farel was the man.

But the chief opponent to this arrangement was the senate of Berne. The senators admitted the very arduous and eminent labours of their great missionary, and rendered thanks to him for establishing the gospel in their districts and canton; but they were not willing to have so bold and uncompromising a man in the seminary at Lausanne. They, too, were offended because Farel had not formed the church at Geneva on the model of that at Berne. Very likely, also, they were afraid that Calvin, Farel and Viret would form a triumvirate of which they might be jealous, and Geneva might rise far superior to Berne as a powerful republic. Thus the new chair of theology was not filled by Farel. It was occupied a few years afterwards by Beza. The old tutor of Calvin, Mathurin Cordier, was now head master of the school at Neufchatel. He was taken from that place to teach at Lausanne. The Bernese senate advised the senate of Neufchatel to pay attention to their schools, as a wise means "for promoting the glory of God, and instructing the young in the Divine word and in propriety of conduct. Certain tyrants, who undertake to suppress and extirpate the gospel, know of no better way than the abolition of the Latin schools."

Most heartily did Farel enter into these views. He saw that darkness would again overspread the church, unless the young men were carefully educated in science and the Holy Scriptures. He sought out young men who might be qualified for the ministry, and urged the senate to educate them, if need be, at the public expense.

The persecutions in France put the lives of two of his brothers in danger—Walter and Daniel. They were already in prison. In company with Viret he went to Berne and Basle to gain their release. They were at length set at liberty. The next year these ministers made another visit in behalf of the Waldenses, many of whom were fleeing to Geneva and other Swiss cities for refuge from relentless persecutions.

Men were constantly coming into Farel's parish who proved to be disturbers of the peace. This caused him great trouble and sorrow. His friends advised him to be patient in his spirit and moderate in his censures. One day he exclaimed,—"I am already advanced in years, and have not vigour enough to urge those under my care who need a continual spur. In the church courts I am a novice, and stand alone. I am honoured with the title of father, it is true; but my sons have little respect for my authority." In writing to a neighbouring minister, he said,—"I conjure you to admonish me faithfully of what you see amiss, and remember me in your prayers. Thus you will profit me and the church, also, far more than by your commentaries, which proceed from an excessive attachment." Those who caused most trouble were the sect called "Libertines," who were free-thinkers, free-lovers, free-livers and mischief-makers in every possible way. They gave still greater trouble at Geneva, where some of the patriots were led into their absurdities.

Calvin was greatly annoyed by this sect, and his life was not free from danger. It was reported afar off quite frequently that he had been killed. The great council did not support him. In a letter to Viret he wrote,—"Wickedness hath now reached such a pitch here that I hardly hope the church can be upheld much longer, at least by my ministry." And, again,—"If I ever needed your assistance, it is now more than ever necessary." To Farel he wrote,—"I wish you could cheer me again by coming hither." These friends came, and saw Calvin arraigned by his enemies before the senate of the republic. He was charged with having shown too little respect for the magistrates of the city in not letting them rule over the church. The worst sentence they could find in his letters was,—"Our people, under pretence of Christ, want to rule without him." They thought this was a deadly arrow shot at them. Farel pleaded for his friend, with all his warmth and powerful eloquence, on two or three occasions. He said that the senate had not enough respect for the character and merits of Calvin, who had no equal in learning; that they should not be so nice about what he had said of them, as he freely reproved even the greatest men, such as Luther and Melancthon; and that they should not credit what a pack of useless men, who were the pillars at taverns, whispered about the man that was saving Geneva from Anti-Christ. The senators took the reprof most kindly, and ceased to be reprovers. They thanked Farel by a vote for what he had said, and there the affair rested for a time.

So interwoven is the life of Farel with that of his more distinguished friend, that we are tempted to enlarge upon the biography of Calvin. In their letters, their visits, their requests for each other's advice, and their books, there are proofs of their warmest and most firm friendship. Calvin submitted many of his manuscripts to Farel and Viret, and dedicated some of his volumes to them, that the world might know how sacred were the bands that bound them together and how harmonious they were in all their labours. On one occasion Farel was so cast down by the troubles of his friend, that he could find no rest. He took up Calvin's new work on the Council of Trent, and was so cheered that he spent the whole night in reading it.

In 1553 Calvin made a visit to Neufchatel, for his friend Farel seemed to be lying at the point of death. The physician had said that there was little hope of his recovery. A celebrated French jurist, Charles Du Moulin, had just come, anxious for a personal acquaintance with so distinguished a champion of the reformation. It was an honour paid to him just when all human honours were fading to nothing. Farel made his will. It was mainly a setting forth of his gratitude to God, his faith, his doctrines, his confession and his hope that his last words might confirm those who had received the truth from his lips. He bequeathed his little property to his brothers Walter and Claudius (to whom he had left his paternal inheritance when he left Dauphiny,) and exhorted them to remain steadfast in the faith which they had before accepted through his agency. A fourth part of his books he left for the ministers in his district, and the rest to his brother Walter and to his nephew, Caspar Carmel, the minister who afterwards preached on the estates of a brother of the Admiral Coligny, and became pastor of the reformed church in Paris. A third part of what was left of money and furniture was to be given to the poor, thus retaining sufficient to pay all his debts. Calvin wrote his name as the first witness. Gladly would Farel have departed to his Lord, but the Master had another design. Calvin prayed for his sick brother, and the Lord restored him to health. *

The world will be old before a certain class of men will cease to charge John Calvin with the burning of Servetus. The truth about this painful case will, probably, not be fully examined until the millennium; the misrepresentations have already had a long day and a wide circulation. We cannot fully enter into the subject in these pages. If Calvin has been blamed, Farel has been reproached for cherishing a more bitter spirit toward Servetus.

After a long course of heresies, blasphemies and profanations; after years of disturbance which he caused among the churches, and after various attempts to correct his errors and reform the man, this Spaniard, Servetus, was arraigned before the council of Geneva. Calvin was not the instigator, nor the plaintiff, nor the judge. Servetus was not condemned for heresy, nor for his

---

* After his recovery Calvin apologizes for the shortness of his visit, saying, "I was desirous of escaping the remainder óf the grief incident to your premature death. . . . Since I have buried you before the time, may the Lord grant that the church may see you my survivor. My own private comfort is joined with the public good of the faithful in this prayer; for my warfare will be the shorter, and I shall not be subjected to the pain of lamenting your death." The old hero must have been touched by such evidences of Calvin's tender love and high regard.

falsehoods, nor for his opposition to the Genevese ministers. It was for blasphemy, a crime punished by death under the law of Moses, and regarded as worthy of such rigour by almost all men in his own times. For many years after him the blasphemer was put to death. The blasphemies of Servetus are too awful to be written.

The Libertines and all the enemies of the truth and of the church took the part of Servetus, and this put Calvin in such a position that he seemed to be severe against him, when his motive was to defend the gospel, the church and the honour of Jehovah. The accused was not at all in Calvin's hands. This great reformer had never such absolute power in Geneva as his enemies represent, and he had almost the least power when Servetus was on trial. His influence just before this, was at so low an ebb that he was tempted to leave the city. The senate was against him; the ruling party was composed of his enemies, and among them were the Libertines, who rejoiced at the prospect of being able soon to overthrow him. They deprived the clergy of all share in the management of the state.

It is true that Calvin laid his complaints against Servetus before the senate, and, although its members were mostly utterly opposed to Calvin, they took up the charges and brought the man to trial. Dr. Henry, who has most thoroughly sifted the case, says,—"Calvin had no intention to expose Servetus to capital punishment. He only wished to render him harmless, to make him recant his blasphemy, and so preserve Christianity from injury." And, further, "We find that it was his blasphemy, his rash jesting with holy things—the insult with which he had treated the majesty of God, that weighed heaviest upon, (against,) him. The judges passed over everything else." The law of that day punished blasphemy with the sword. The majority of the judges decided that Servetus should die by fire. So little had Calvin to do in this matter that he wrote,—"What will become of the man I know not: as far as I can understand sentence will be pronounced to-morrow and executed the day after." He again wrote to Farel,—"I think he will be condemned to die; but I wish that what is horrible in the punishment may be spared him." And, again, after the sentence had been fixed, he wrote, urging Farel to come to Geneva, and saying,—"We have endeavoured to change the mode of execution, but without avail." Farel was soon in the city, to learn what we have not space here to write. It was Calvin's wish that this excellent man should attend the condemned to the place of execution, so that in his last hours he might have the ministries of truth and kindness from one whom he had not reviled.

Early on the morning of October 27, 1553, Farel went to the prison. He inspired confidence in Servetus, who could not have desired a better companion on the terrible journey to the Champel, where he must die. Farel was intent upon leading his soul to the true faith, and he began to remind him of his errors, and their only remedy in the love of God. He urged him to acknowledge Christ as the Eternal Son of God, a fact that Servetus had strongly and blasphemously denied. After this attempt was proved to be in vain, he told him that if he would die as a Christian he should forgive all men, and be reconciled to Calvin, whom he had grossly abused. Servetus consented. Calvin was sent for, and he came. One of the council asked Servetus why he wished Calvin to come. He replied,—"To ask his forgiveness."

"I readily answered," wrote Calvin, "and it was strictly the truth that I had never sought to resent any personal affront received from him. I also tenderly reminded him that, sixteen years before, I had diligently sought, at the hourly peril of my life, to win him to the Lord; that it was not my fault that all pious people had not extended to him the hand of friendship, and that this would have been the case had he but shown some degree of judgment; that, although he had taken to flight, I had still continued to correspond peaceably with him; that, in a word, no duty of kindness had been neglected on my part, till, embittered by my free and candid warnings, he had resigned himself not merely to a feeling of anger, but to absolute wrath against me. Turning, however, from that which concerned myself, I prayed him to implore the forgiveness of God, whom he had so awfully blasphemed. . . . . . ." But Servetus answered nothing, and Calvin left him.

The council assembled and waited for the unhappy man to retract; but he renewed his assertions of innocence. Farel had a tender heart toward him, and implored the council to soften the punishment: but the members were so horrified at the wickedness of Servetus that they would not change the sentence.

A hill outside the city still bears the name of Champel, and thither Servetus was led, preceded by a throng of people. He saw the stake prepared for him, and he threw himself upon the earth, where he seemed to be praying in silence. Farel turned to the multitude, and, believing that Satan had such blasphemers in his power, he said,—"You see what power Satan has when he once gets possession of us! This man is learned above most others, and, perhaps, believed that he was acting right: but now the devil hath him. Beware, lest this same thing happen to yourselves."

Farel still urged him to acknowledge his errors, to speak to the people and publicly retract his blasphemies; to pray to Jesus, not only as the Son of the Eternal God, but as the Eternal Son of God, and thus he might still touch the hearts of the council, and be spared the worst horrors which he dreaded. But it was all in vain. At Farel's request he did at last ask the people to pray for him. When Farel told him that if he had a wife or child, and desired to make his will, there was a notary present, he made no answer. During the terrible scene that followed he cried continually to God for mercy; but he would not address Christ as the Eternal Son of God. Among his last words were these, in which he still persevered in one of his doctrines,— "Jesus, thou Son of the Eternal God, have mercy upon me." He would not say "thou Eternal Son of God."

We are very far from justifying these proceedings. But let it be remembered that in his day the Romanists were burning men for what they called heresy; that the law, public opinion, the Bernese senate and most of the reformers of the Rhine countries were against Servetus because of his blasphemies; and that after a fair trial, he was sentenced, chiefly by the enemies of Calvin, to a far worse death than the Genevan ministers had expected. Farel returned home soon after the execution.

The enmity of the rising party in Geneva increased against Calvin. The council wished to compel him to administer the Sacrament to Berthelier, one of the senators who had been excommunicated. He would not yield. This was but a test in regard to many other matters between the state and the church. The design was to get some hold upon him and drive him from the city. Plots were laid against him during the trial of Servetus, whose punishment would have been the same had Calvin been expelled. He had made up his mind to leave the city unless some sudden change appeared in his favour.

Farel heard of this resolution and hastened to Geneva, in order to lift his powerful voice again in support of his friend. He did not think what a storm he was about to bring down upon his own head, or if he did, he was willing to sacrifice himself for the sake of Calvin and the church. He entered the pulpit and preached a powerful sermon to a multitude that had rushed to hear him. He was carried away by the spirit of his own mighty eloquence, and was too unsparing of his rebukes upon the Libertine-faction. He, probably, held up their leader, Perrin, in the light of truth rather than of tenderness, and made severe reflections upon the senate for opposing the church. He closed his sermon, entered the streets, and went home as abruptly as he had come.

The noise of the sermon rose loudly through the city. The opposers of the church declared that it was an insult to the state. They constrained the senate to give them a letter to the senate of Neufchatel, demanding that Farel should be sent back to be tried for an offence which they regarded as no less than capital.* Calvin thought that Farel could defend himself, and advised him to come to Geneva, rather than wait for the senate of Neufchatel to take up the charge.

The old man, therefore, set out, on foot, in the roughest of weather, and found Geneva in a great excitement over him.

* "When our brother Farel, to whom, as you well know, our people owe everything, was lately here, and admonished them, as he was well entitled to do, they burst out into such a rage against him as not to scruple at capitally indicting him. They demanded of the people of Neufchatel that they should deliver up *the father of their liberty, yea, the father of this church.* Farel came, before he entered the city, the officer of the council delivered an official intimation at my house, that he was not to enter the pulpit."— *Calvin to the Zurich ministers.*

He had seen it so before, and was fearless. The senate sent word to Calvin that he should not allow Farel to preach, for they knew his ruling passion and his power. He was in great peril. Berthelier tried to form the workmen in the mint into a gang that should go to the senate hall and raise a disturbance. Some think that from them arose the cry to fling the staunch old preacher into the Rhone; a cry that was not new to the ear of Farel. Others gave another version of the matter, and both may be true. The senators were making out the charge against him, when the hostile party in the hall cried out, "Throw him into the Rhone." But Farel had friends.

A young man boldly stepped forward and warned Perrin, the would-be-Cæsar of Geneva, to take care that the "Father of the city" suffered no harm. Other young men came forward to the defence of their former teacher and spiritual father. Perhaps they had been eager lads in Froment's school at the sign of the golden cross. They formed a guard about the fearless old man. Friends came in still greater numbers and among them Calvin, Viret and other ministers, who felt that justice demanded a loud protest in behalf of the accused. The citizens left their homes and shops to defend their ministers, and the factious party began to understand that all the strength of the city was not on their side.

The Genevese preachers made their voices heard in the senate hall. They set forth the evil designs and plots against Farel. The accusers became alarmed and dared not proceed to violent measures. Farel was permitted to speak. He contended, in a long and animated speech, that his adversaries could not have heard his sermon, for they had altogether mistaken his meaning, and that nothing was farther from his thoughts than to insult a city toward which, as all men knew, he cherished the kindest feelings. They began to perceive that they had acted hastily, on mere rumours, and in a bad temper. The fiery eye, the loud voice, the persuasive address and the earnest self-defence of the old man, had a powerful effect upon the senators and the crowd which had pushed into the hall. Many who had been most active against· him were moved and melted. The majority now declared that he had only acted as a faithful preacher in his reproofs and admonitions, and that he was a true servant of the gospel and their spiritual father. Upon this the senate ordered that every one should give him his hand, and that a feast should be held in token of the general reconciliation. That Farel should be honoured with a feast in Geneva must have even exceeded his surprise, and the warm grasp of his hand must have put the most unmusical heart-strings in good tune for harmony at the banquet. Perrin, the leading senator, was obliged to declare, with trembling, that Farel's sermon was quite right, and that every one must live by the word of God. The Libertines, who had raised all this tumult, plainly discovered that the mass of the people overpowered them, and Perrin humbled himself before Farel, declaring that he was under obligations to him as his former friend, and should ever regard him as his father and pastor. How sincere all these demonstrations were, and how the feast passed off, we are not able to state, but Farel was at last dismissed with a request that he would retain the Genevese in his affectionate remembrance and prayers. He returned home, cheered by the friendly termination of this noisy affair.

This, however, was not quite the last of it. An unworthy pastor, Peter, of Cressier, took advantage of these events to abuse Farel as "a savage man, a perverter of the truth, and possessed of two devils." He had, we believe, never before been charged with having more than one. The slanders caused no slight trouble in Neufchatel. Farel brought the accuser to public trial, when he was convicted of slander, and ordered to beg pardon of the injured old pastor, the governor and the citizens. Not often did Farel thus pursue false reports. He was inured to personal insults, and wisely left calumnies to refute themselves, or perish on their wearisome rounds.

Thousands of exiles were taking refuge in the countries whose streams fed the Rhine and the Rhone. The young king of England, Edward VI., died, and the "bloody Mary" reigned in his stead. Great numbers of them left the shores of England, among whom were John Fox, the author of the "Book of Martyrs," several bishops of renown, and John Knox, for whom Scotland was waiting, that his mighty voice might shake her castles and her mountains. From France and Piedmont also the persecuted were coming — poor, weary, shelterless, and cast upon the mercy of God and of the Protestants, who had mercy upon them. It is hard to resist the temptation of describing the welcome which they received in the villages and cities where Farel was spoken of as the father of the feeble churches that had been gathered through his missionary labours. He ever took the most tender interest in these exiles.

After taking up a collection in Neufchatel for the exiles of Locarne, he wrote to them,—"O ye happy ones! to whom it is given to prefer the gospel to every temporal blessing. It is delightful to the friends of Christ to hear how fathers are willing to forsake their sons on account of the word of God; how sons love Christ more than parents, brothers or tenderly beloved sisters, and young women cannot be restrained from choosing the gospel. What heart is so hard as not to be softened at the holy sight! It would be almost incredible if the stony and cruel-hearted persecutors, who thirst after such sacred blood, should not at last be brought to change their hatred into love and their violence into tenderness."

In Geneva the enemies of the truth were bold in their threats and their violence against Calvin. The senate opposed him, and the Libertines sought his life. For a time he could not walk the streets without being insulted. Once, on his return from the church, he was attacked on the bridge of the Rhone. He told them that the bridge was wide enough for them all, and when his coolness abashed the ruffians they turned upon a French exile, chased him into a shop and wounded him, crying out,— "Death to the foreigners." By day and by night such assaults were occurring. But at length Calvin gained his point, not by arbitrary power, but by his preaching, his persuasions, his calmness and his trust in God. He declared to the senate,—"I would rather die a hundred times than claim for myself an authority which belongs to the whole church—that is the right to establish rules of discipline." And yet this is the man whom his opposers to this day hold up as "the pope of Geneva."

The spirit of Calvin prevailed at last, and the church of Geneva was permitted to guide her own affairs. And when the system of church government, introduced there by Farel and perfected by Calvin, was put into fair operation, its excellency was proved beyond any doubt. John Knox was so charmed with it that he wrote to his friend, John Locke,—"I always wished in my heart, nor could I ever cease to wish that it might please God to bring me to this place, where I can say, without fear or shame, the best Christian school exists since the time of the apostles. I allow that Christ is truly preached in other places also; but in no other have I seen the reformation so well wrought out, both morally and religiously, as in Geneva." Let Farel, "to whom our people owe everything," as Calvin declared, have the honour due to him, while unto God be all the glory.

Most heartily did Farel render thanks to the Lord for the flourishing state of the church at Geneva, after passing through so many relapses and perils. In a letter he wrote,—"I was lately in Geneva, and such was the pleasure I felt that I could scarcely tear myself away. Not that I wished to be the teacher of a church so large and so eager for the word, but only to hear and learn as the meanest of the people. Very different is my feeling from that of the man who said that he would rather be first in the mountains than second at Rome. I would rather be the last in Geneva than the first anywhere else. If the Lord and the love to the flock entrusted to my care did not forbid, nothing should keep me from ending my days with that people, to whom I have always been united in spirit." Nor were the Genevese forgetful of his labours, sufferings and love for them. When, as an aged father, he visited them, they strove together for the favour of showing him hospitality, and the senate proposed that a special sum be given him in order to detain him in their city, so that it might never be said that Geneva had treated him with ingratitude. But he was not willing to retire upon such honours and such generosity.

Amid these stirring events Farel had an unexpected call from that very France out of which he had been barred in his younger days. Even Paris was now open to him. A reformed church had grown up in that city where the voices of Lefevre and Farel had once been heard and hushed. A child had something to do with its organization. When the disciples were few, they met in the house of the Seigneur de la Ferrière "to offer their prayers in common and read the Holy Scriptures." This gentleman had a son that he wished to have baptized by a reformed minister. He made the proposal to the church in his house and begged them to choose a minister. They chose John de Launay, who organized the church in Paris, destined to be renowned for the number of its devoted pastors and its triumphant martyrs.

In 1557 this church asked for a new minister. Farel must have felt it hard to deny the call. The perils of the capital were inviting him. But Switzerland could not spare him. Nor could Fabri leave Neufchatel. Gasper Carmel obtained the dangerous honour, and he went to the city where his uncle (by marriage) had first found that light which had been borne by him into Switzerland, and was now to be carried back by his relative, whom he regarded as his own son in the faith. Thus Farel was at last represented in the heart of France, an instance of the power of a delayed but yet widely extended personal influence. The great stream had run eastward and flooded the Swiss valleys with truth; but the clouds rising from those valleys were carried back westward to drop refreshing rain upon the spiritual desert that Farel had once been obliged to leave.

The church and the school of theology at Lausanne preferred the doctrines and government of Geneva to all those of Berne. This greatly offended the Bernese senate. The strife waxed warm, until finally Viret and the professors left the city; more than a thousand people went with them to Geneva, where they were most kindly received. Viret became one of the pastors there for two years, when he was called into France. Beza became the colleague of Calvin, and the rector of the new academy. Thus the losses of Lausanne were the gain of Geneva. The noble Bonivard, some years after his release from the Chillon prison, gave his whole fortune to aid the schools of Geneva.

CHAPTER XXI.

OLD LIFE WITH NEW LOVE.

(1558—1564.)

THE Waldenses in "the holy valley," where Farel had once been so happily entertained, were threatened with utter extermination. They sought aid from their true and tried friends in Geneva and Neufchatel. Farel and Beza set out upon a visit in their behalf. The journey would give them an opportunity to plead the cause of the churches in which the French language was used, for they were not yet fully recognized by the German churches. They afterwards were called by the term, the Reformed Church. John Budœus, son of the William Budœus whom we saw at Paris, reviving the ancient learning, also travelled on this latter mission at a later day. *

The assistance, rendered to the Waldenses by the churches from Berne to Basle, was greater than Farel expected. The cantons united in sending an embassy to the court of France, in order to stay the persecution. The king, Henry II., at least made some fair promises, leaving his officers to break them as

---

* As William Budœus (Bude) ordered in his will that his body should be buried without ceremony, some have inferred that he died in the Reformed faith. In 1549 his widow and children went to Geneva, where his descendants are still found.

they chose. Farel paid a visit to Montbeliard, and he was pained to find that his friend Toussaint had lost much of his brotherly love. Certain men, who had favoured Servetus, had gained an influence over this excellent pastor, and his heart had grown cold toward the Swiss ministers. Farel clung with a father's heart to the first fruits of his pastoral toils in that city, and he could not do less than persuade Toussaint to renounce the views which had poisoned his heart. He had counted on him once as a colleague, and still, probably, as a successor.

War brought Toussaint and his church into peril. He was obliged to escape to Switzerland where the Count of Montbeliard was also a refugee. Some years after he was restored to his parish, where he probably ended his labours with his life.

A new field soon was opened to Farel where his zeal might meet with some of the old romance of missionary labour. When Philip, the Roman bishop of Basle died, an appeal came to the Swiss ministers for some one to carry the gospel into that diocese. There were signs that it would meet with a favourable reception. But no one had the courage or the liberty to go. Farel had now the time and the spirit to undertake the work. He went to St. Leonard, collected the people, preached, and was gladly heard. He remained but a short time, and on his departure many hundreds gathered about him to bid him farewell.

Then taking with him Emer Beynon, who had helped him on the stone to preach his first sermon in the canton of Neufchatel, he went to Pruntrut, where all kindness was shown to the bearers of the good tidings. The mayor and town-clerk supped with them at the inn. The next day they appeared before the council. The deep interest shown to Farel's address made him as eloquent as in his best days. The councillors were pleased with the offer to have the gospel preached there, but preferred to wait a little for a more convenient season. Meanwhile the new bishop had a word to say, and sent for certain of the council. He inquired and learned the object of this visit, and summoned Farel and Beynon before him. The bishop set forth a councillor named Wandelin, to express his sentiments.

"Farel, you came here formerly to sow your tares," said the bishop's mouth-piece, "and, having been sent away by the late bishop, have refrained hitherto from repeating the attempt. We may reasonably be astonished at your daring to appear here again; but you are now advised, in a friendly way, to retire before any mischief befall you."

"I am here, by the authority of my Lord, to preach Christ and him crucified," Farel replied, "and to call this sowing tares is a grievous sin against the Saviour, and contrary to the Holy Scriptures. Besides, I have preached freely at places in this diocese, without ever being sent away, and I have taught doctrines which are the surest means of uniting people and princes, flocks and pastors, namely, obedience to Christ and to his word. If my doctrines can be proved to be false, I am ready to submit to any punishment."

"I approve of your principles," said Wandelin, perhaps speaking for himself rather than the bishop; "but I must be excused from putting them in practice. Wherever you have preached you have abolished the mass, and Berne has not allowed it to be restored. It will be so here if you gain a foot-hold, which we will do our best to prevent."

Farel bade the council a respectful farewell, and, entering the streets, he saw multitudes, whom the news of his arrival had brought from all quarters to hear him. But he had now the moderation of old age, and he took a friendly leave of them, planning some other mode of taking the town.

The report of Farel's visit reached the ears of the arch-bishop of Besançon, who forthwith sent a grand-vicar and a monk to Pruntrut, and they set themselves to work to counteract any impression that the preachers had made simply by their presence in the town. What impression, then, would their preaching make! Of course the grand-vicar was ready to dispute with the ministers against their "false, impious and scandalous doctrines," and he ordered a courier to be sent to him, if the heretics should dare to come again. He then took his way whence he came, no doubt thinking that he had inspired sufficient terror to make all things safe for a season.

The people of Neufchatel heard of this movement, and sent Soral, the pastor at Boudry, with letters to the council of Pruntrut. He reached there on St. George's day, when the mayor and his deputy were absent. Some of the citizens were lounging about their doors, and courteously invited him to be their guest. He had not been long in the place when the parish priest came to him, and, with more rage than religion, accused him of sowing tares, and called him a deceiver, a teacher of error, and uttered very brave threats. A nobleman also reviled him, beat him with a club, and almost killed him.

Farel now felt that he was really invited to make a second attempt. Taking with him Beynon and Soral, he set out to hold the disputation proposed by the grand-vicar. On the way they were roughly assailed by some priests, and it was in vain that they called for the man who boasted of his readiness to meet them in debate. He had the prudence not to appear. Again they returned to their homes. These attempts created a great sensation through all Burgundy. The arch-bishop was unusually gracious to the people of Pruntrut. He granted them indulgences and released them from fasting. One would suppose that fasting would have been enjoined on them as a preventive of heresy. Still the people showed a partiality for Farel and the reformed doctrines. During Lent a special effort was made to confirm the people in the Romish faith by sending a doctor of the Sorbonne to exhaust his eloquence in reviling Farel, Calvin and Viret as the most awful heretics.

Farel tried to bring this monk and doctor to trial. He went to Berne on a busy holiday, and stood shivering and gazed at by the citizens for an hour at the door of a senator, and at last was coolly received. The senate took steps to have the monk arraigned for slandering the preachers, but nothing further was done. When Calvin was urged to push the matter, he replied to Farel,—"It would be a strange thing were I to require justice against a monk at a distance, when I am daily reviled as a heretic before the gates of Geneva!"

"What a young man I still am," said Calvin, at the age of forty-four. Farel must have felt quite as young even at the age of sixty-nine, for he then filled all the country with surprise at one of his so-called indiscretions. Faith and love are constantly renewing old age. He, who had so long remained in single life, at last gave way to a tender sentiment. He had advised the preachers to marry, lest they should be exposed to the common charges brought against the priests, but none supposed that he would illustrate his precept by his own example. He had knitted no such ties, lest they should be broken by his violent death. But the old man thought that he now needed a gentle comforter, and the right one was well known to him.

Madame Torel, a widow, had fled with her daughter, Mary,

OLD LIFE WITH NEW LOVE.

a few years before, from Rouen, in order to escape persecution. She kept house for Farel in Neufchatel, where the daughter had ceased to be regarded as very young. His choice fell upon the daughter; and, after his hand was pledged, he wrote to Calvin, as the latter had done to him when he was about to be married to the worthy Idelette de Bures. "I am dumb with astonishment," wrote Calvin, and then proceeded to give him all needed advice. The affair became more public in the parish than Farel expected. It was very strange, the people thought, for they had looked forward to his funeral rather than to the festivities of a wedding. They had become so accustomed to look upon the venerable missionary, daring all the dangers of the field, single-handed, that they quite forgot his bold, eccentric and romantic nature; nor did they fathom the depths of tenderness that lay in solemn silence within his heart. The banns were thrice published, and, committing his betrothed to the care of a French refugee, he set out upon a visit to the churches. His object was to bring the Lutherans in closer union with the reformed, and to gain help for Pruntrut. He returned and was married the 20th of December.

These solemn men had their wit as well as their wisdom; if not we should fail to understand their lively and cheerful natures. Calvin wrote at once to the clergy and elders of Neufchatel, pleasantly asking them to pardon this little escapade in their aged pastor, on the score of thirty-six years of faithful service. A son was born to Farel, six years afterwards, but he did not long survive his father.

But these new ties could not keep Farel at home, and he left the fireside for the field. He was soon at Strasburg, engaging assistance for the Protestants of Metz, to whom he had given many anxious thoughts. His efforts promised to be successful in securing to them freedom of public worship. Then he was travelling again on behalf of the Waldenses. On his return he found letters from France, urging him to send back the exiled preachers to the hundreds of churches that had lately abolished the mass, and were longing for faithful pastors. The whole of France seemed on the point of becoming Protestant. As a specimen of these letters we quote from one written by Beaulieu then, (1561,) at Geneva.

"I cannot tell you how much grace God is bestowing upon our church, (in France.) There are men here from various places, as from Lyons, Nismes, Gap, Orleans and Poitiers, anxious to obtain new labourers for these portions of the new harvest. From Tournon especially was the application made, and that in obedience to the urgent wish of the bishop. There are five hundred parishes in these parts which have discontinued the mass, but are still without ministers. The poor people are famishing, but there is no one to give them the bread of heaven. It is extraordinary how many hearers there are of Calvin's lectures; I believe there are more than a thousand daily. Viret is labouring for Nismes. I have heard men say that if from four to six thousand preachers were sent forth places would be found for them." The Admiral Coligny was appointed by Catharine of France to number these churches, and he reported two thousand one hundred and fifty. A glorious church was rising in France, to be almost drowned in the blood of the saints massacred on St. Bartholemew's day.

A special invitation came to Farel from Gap, his native district. Fabri went to Vienne, and he set out with a brother preacher for Dauphiny. Often had he lamented that he must live an exile from his native land, and with what emotions did he now look onward to the home of his fathers, after an absence of forty years! His relatives were not the only attraction, although that had its power. His father was dead, and so also must have been his mother. His brothers had been won to the gospel: three of them were exiles for their religion; one other, John, was as bold an expounder of the truth as himself; and a nephew, Carmel, had been preaching in Paris, where a large reformed church was gathering. His brother-in-law, the noble Honorat Riquetti, has lately been found to be "one of the ancestors of Mirabeau," the talented and terrible Mirabeau of the French revolution, whose family name was Riquetti. D'Aubigne says,—"There are certainly few names we might be more surprised at seeing brought together than those of Farel and Mirabeau; and yet between these two Frenchmen there were at least two points of contact—the power of their eloquence and the boldness of their reforms."

Farel arrived at Gap in November, and was received with joy and veneration, as the man whom God had honoured in leading thousands from darkness to light. Multitudes thronged to hear his first sermon, so that the church could not hold them, and he was heard with profound and uninterrupted attention. The councillors had requested the bishop's vicar to prevent any disturbance, and he kept his word. As Farel did not wish to be reproached for acting secretly, he went on the same Sunday to the vice-mayor, along with the king's advocate and the chief senator. He was told that all such meetings were forbidden under pain of death, and was asked by whose authority he had come. He held up the commission of his Lord, and said that since that edict had been published such meetings had been held at Lyons and other places, and that certain ministers had preached before the king. The vice-mayor requested him to refrain from preaching until the governor and the parliament of Grenoble had been duly informed of his intentions. Farel exhorted him to listen to the gospel, which must condemn those who opposed it, and would save all who embraced it. He was honourably conducted back to his inn, and on that evening baptized a child.

The next evening all public meetings and the use of the churches were forbidden to the reformed party. But one meeting was held on the following morning. As Farel was coming out of church, a servant of the vice-mayor handed him the order in trembling haste. In the afternoon the friends met for prayer, and resolved to continue steadfast in the faith for which so many had been martyrs. They demanded of the vice-mayor a written statement of his proceedings, in order to make an appeal to the king and his cabinet.

From a dusty corner some one has lately drawn an old copy of the "annals of the Capuchins" of Gap. These friars gave no little space to the visit of the aged reformer, and their story is tinged with the colour of their strong prejudices. It runs, that Farel, already an old man, wishing to preach in his native province, before God summoned him from the world, went and took up his quarters in a corn-mill at the gates of his native town—they do not mean Fareau but Gap—and then he "dogmatized" the peasants from a French Bible which he explained "in his own fashion." Ere long he began to preach in the very heart of the town in the chapel of St. Columba. The magistrate forbade his preaching, and the parliament of Grenoble wished "to have him burnt." Farel refused to obey, and upon this the vice-mayor, a zealous catholic, along with several policemen, went to the chapel where Farel was preaching. The door was shut; they knocked but nobody answered; they broke in and found a considerable throng; no one turned his head; all were listening greedily to the preacher's words. The officers

OLD LIFE WITH NEW LOVE. 345

went straight to the pulpit; Farel was seized, and with "the crime" (the Bible) in his hands, he was led through the crowd and shut up in prison. But the followers of the new doctrine were already to be found among every class of people—in the workman's garret, in the tradesman's shop, in the noble's castle, and sometimes even in the bishop's palace. During the night the reformers, either by force or by strategem, took the brave old man out of the prison, carried him to the walls, and let him down, by a basket, into the fields. "Accomplices" were waiting for him, and he escaped with their help.

By another version, however, we are told that the old preacher felt his youth renewed, when he saw a harvest, upon his native soil, all ripe for the reapers. He made no personal attack upon the priests, who were more anxious to get their tythes and tribute than to preach. He persuaded his hearers to give up festivals, holidays, masses, indulgences and the like. It grieved him to leave a field where there were so many encouragements. He entreated Calvin to send a preacher to take charge of the growing congregation, until he could find a suitable minister or return himself; for he could not now remain, as duty called him to his own post. He met the friends of the good cause at Grenoble, where many still remembered Sebville, and he addressed them in the house of a merchant, leaving a deep impression. His companion, Pichou, remained behind to preach in that town.

Not long after his return home Farel had cheering news from the much persecuted church at Gap, for the brethren kept their pledges of faithfulness. Fabri and Viret were labouring in that region with great success. The plague broke out fearfully at Lyons, and extended to other places, but they took advantage of it to let the gospel win its way by its consolations. They were allowed to visit the houses of Romanists and point the sick to the Saviour. Fabri wrote, "Neither life, nor wife, nor children are so dear to me as my Lord Jesus and his church."

While Farel was absent, Neufchatel was favoured with a visit from the duchess of Longueville—whether the same Joanna who had so long been trifling at the court of Francis I., we cannot say, but it seems that she was the one, and that she was greatly changed. Her son was with her. The ministers counselled with her in settling several church questions. A synod was held, and the custom of letting the churches choose their pastors was confirmed. Much was done to promote better discipline and to found schools in destitute parishes. She corresponded with Calvin, and he praises her courage and steadfastness in the faith. In France her house had been a refuge for the persecuted.

She visited Landeron, a town in her canton. The papal party had only one vote in their majority over the reformed party. The duchess wished to have Protestant service performed, the next morning after her arrival, by a preacher who attended her and the young duke. The people were assured that no allusion would be made to popery, nor any one be compelled to attend, as the service was for her and her retinue. It was intimated that she, being the ruler of the land, had a right to the free exercise of her religion, especially as she gave her subjects the same liberty. But all this was in vain. The authorities were the first to take up arms, and, with covered heads, they rudely threatened to throw the preacher from the pulpit. She again urged that their sovereign should not be thus prevented from hearing the gospel, which they need not hear unless they chose; but her condescension availed nothing. The alarm-bell was rung, the inhabitants armed themselves, surrounded the chapel, and compelled the duchess to put a stop to the preaching. Farel, on his return, was greatly annoyed by this outrage; but he thought the priests more to blame than the people.

CHAPTER XXII.

THE CALL TO GLORY.

(1564–1565.)

JOHN CALVIN was dying near the age of fifty-five, and the dear old man of seventy-five was very anxious about him. Farel wrote thus to one of his friends,—"I have not yet heard any certain report of the departure of our brother, Calvin, so dear and so necessary to us; but the current rumours and the state in which I left him afflict me greatly. Oh that I could be put in his place, and that he might be long spared to serve the churches of our Lord, who, blessed be his name, caused me to meet with him when I little expected it, and retained him, against his own purpose, at Geneva, to employ him there in his service, and ordered other things in a most wonderful manner, and, strange to say, by my instrumentality, for I pressed him to undertake affairs harder than death. And sometimes he besought me, in the name of God, to have pity on him, and to let him serve God ardently in the way in which he had always been employed. But, seeing that what I demanded was according to God's will, he did violence to his own will, and has accomplished more and more rapidly than any one else, and has even surpassed himself. How glorious a course he has run! God grant that we may run as he has, according to the grace given unto us!"

It seems Farel heard more definitely that his friend was still alive, and expressed his intention to visit him. Calvin knew what an effort this would cost the aged pastor, and thus wrote to him,—"Farewell, my best and truest brother. Since it is the Lord's will that you should survive me in this world, never forget our friendship, which, so far as it has been useful to the church of God, will bear fruit for us in heaven. Pray do not weary yourself by coming hither on my account. My breath is weak, and I expect that every moment will be the last. I am contented that I live and die in Christ, who is the reward of the people, both in life and in death. To you and the brethren, still once more, farewell."

This letter could not stay the feet of the good old man. He went to Geneva with the feeling,—"Oh that I might die for him!" He wept, prayed, spent his last night and took his last leave of him, whom he ever regarded too great for him to call a son, and the next day returned home. Not many days after Calvin had fallen asleep in Christ,—May 27, 1564. It is not probable that Farel stood with the multitude who followed him to his burial, when the republic was laying in the grave one of its wisest counsellors, the city one of its truest guardians, the church its chief pastor, the academy its highest teacher, and many of the people their faithful comforter. One may now stand in the very pulpit of St. Peter's, from which his commanding voice was heard; but we seek in vain for any monument to his memory. There is a doubt about the very place where his body was laid, although later hands have set upon a small level grass-plot a little square stone, about a foot high, and having cut on its top the letters J. C. It was his wish to be buried without pomp, without a monument. His name is upon an enduring system of doctrine and polity in the Christian church, and upon the civilization of the past three

30

centuries, which have recognized him as one of the great fathers of civil and religious liberty.

The close and undisturbed friendship of Calvin, Farel and Viret has been the pleasing theme of all writers, who have sought to do justice to their excellence. The first two seemed unfitted by nature for such a holy brotherhood, for each was firm and stern in his opinions, strong in his will, bold in his temper and mighty in his power to rule. The wonder is that they did not wish to rule over each other. But neither was jealous nor envious; neither wished to exalt himself, nor to prevent the other from having an influence for the good of the church and the glory of God. Both gave their thoughts, their time and their energies to the work of that Master, in whose service they were brothers. An unlimited confidence bound them together. Calvin was the great thinker, Farel the great worker of the Reformed church. By nature Calvin was weak for battle, cautious and reserved, but conflict made him strong. Farel was bold enough from birth, always in advance, venturing where others would hardly dare to go, fearless of consequences, and often checking the first good movements by his very bravery, but often conquering by making himself a terror to his adversaries. Conflict subdued him, and while Calvin admired his inexpressible activity and courage, it pleased him to see his "best and truest brother" becoming more gentle and tender in his ways. It might be said of each of them, as of a celebrated crusader, "He was a lamb in his own affairs, but a lion in the cause of God."

Calvin dedicated his Commentary on the Epistle to Titus to Farel and Viret, in these touching words, "As the condition of my charge resembles that which St. Paul committed to Titus, it seemed to me that it was you, above all others, to whom I

THE CALL TO GLORY. 351

ought to dedicate this, my labour. It will, at least, afford those of our own times, and, perhaps, even those who come after us, some indication of our friendship and holy communion. There never have been, I think, two friends, who lived together in such friendship, in the common intercourse of the world, as we have in our ministry. I have exercised the office of a pastor here with you two, and with such entire freedom from any appearance of envy that you and I appeared but as one."

The subject is worthy of D'Aubigne's enthusiasm, and when writing of the different work of the scholar and of the missionary, he says "Calvin was the great doctor of the sixteenth century, and Farel the great evangelist; the latter is one of the most remarkable figures in the Reformation." "Farel had the riches of nature, of art and of grace. His life was a series of battles and victories. Every time he went forth, it was conquering and to conquer."

The scholar of the Swiss reform is now dead; the missionary must gird himself, old as he is, for another march and another triumph. His burning zeal must have vent, and he cannot rest at home. If he cannot go into the heart of that France whose invitation just missed him, when he first entered among the Alps, he will cross the border and try to see the glorious gospel established in Metz before he dies. This city has given him the good chevalier Esch, and Toussaint, who has reaped what he had sown at Montbeliard, besides giving him many honourable scars to signalize his courage, and touch the hearts of those among whom he has sought aid for its suffering protestants.

The ministers consented to his plan, and the senate of Neufchatel commissioned one of their number to attend him, lest their very aged father should fall into danger. There was extraordinary joy on his arrival in the city. On that very day he preached with such energy and power that the church took fresh courage. But it was too much for him; the light was cast at the expense of the lamp. He sank down upon his couch after his return from the pulpit, and with difficulty was carried back to Neufchatel. His room became his church, and he was visited by people of all ranks. He exhorted them to obey the laws of the state and of the church, and to hold fast their profession of faith. Like an apostle he counselled them; like a brother he shared in their sympathies, and like a father he comforted them. All were astonished at his love and zeal in coming to them when so feeble, and at his patience and resignation. "See," said they to one another, "this man is the very same that he has always been! We never knew him depressed, even when our hearts were failing us for fear. When we were ready to give up everything in despair, he was full of hope, and he cheered us by his Christian heroism!"

He lingered a few weeks, proved to all, who came in tears to his bedside, the power of the Lord to give life to the dying, and gently fell asleep in Christ. He died, September 13th, 1565, in the seventy-sixth year of his age, about fifteen months after Calvin's departure. He was buried in a church-yard of Neufchatel, where he had seen most marvellous changes since the day that he had boldly preached in the streets. The churches of the whole canton lamented his death. The ministers felt that his merits should be known to posterity, and, at once, proposed to collect materials for his biography.

Who should be his successor at Neufchatel? Viret was chosen, but he declined, for he was engaged in France, probably then at Lyons. A school of theology was rising in Navarre, where the

THE CALL TO GLORY. 353

influence of Margaret, the queen, had so favoured protestantism that it had been a refuge and a stronghold. Viret was called thither and died two years before the massacre of St. Bartholomew's day crushed the glorious church in France and filled all Christendom with horror.

The next choice fell upon Christopher Fabri, long before sent into the field by Farel from his couch at Morat. Farel had been so earnest for labourers in the great harvest that he had sometimes put forward young and untried men, who proved unworthy of the trust, but in this brother he was not disappointed. He testified that, during the thirty-one years Fabri had assisted him at Morat, Orbe, Grandson, Thun and Geneva, and during the three different periods in which they were colleagues at Neufchatel, no grievous misunderstanding had ever arisen between them.

He also was loved by Calvin, who had first heard of him in a strange way. When Calvin was at Basle, before he dreamed of ever living in Geneva, a total stranger one day called. He came to deliver a message from a medical student of Montpelier, who had lately entered the ministry, and had been reading a new book of Calvin's, that was having a wide popularity. "Fabri has desired me to inform you," said the unknown, "that he does not entirely approve of certain passages in your book on the *Immortality of the Soul.*"* Brave message, certainly, furnishing a hope that, if the young Fabri should be on the right side, he might prove a courageous reformer. With touching humility Calvin afterwards replied,—"Far from being offended

---

* This was Calvin's first theological work, published in 1534. The title was unfortunately changed to that of *Psychopannychia*, or the sleep of the soul. He showed from Scripture that the soul knows no sleep between death and the judgment.

30 *

at your opinion, I have been much delighted with your simplicity and candour. My temper is not so crabbed as *to refuse to others the liberty I enjoy myself.* You must know, then, that I have almost entirely re-written my book."

Few of the many young men, whom the illustrious missionary was the means of putting into the ministry, had so much of his independence as Fabri. As he had been free with Calvin's book in his younger days, he probably had, in older years, been frank with Farel's opinions. Once this caused a slight difference between the two pastors at Neufchatel. It was shortly after Farel's severe illness in 1553, and after Fabri had taken to himself a new wife. What the misunderstanding was, we know not, but a letter of Calvin shows so much of the spirit of the two pastors and the writer, that we hope it will secure a fresh reading. Calvin writes thus to Farel about his colleague,—

. . . . . "As you are well aware that there are many things which we must endure, because it is not in our power to correct them, I need not spend many words in exhorting you to show yourself gentle and moderate in a contest which is evidently not embittered by personal hostility, if, indeed, that should be called a contest in which your colleague differs from you, without any malevolent feeling or desire to breed disturbances. In what points I think him defective, as you yourself are my best authority on that subject, I shall for the moment forbear to mention; but one thing we know, that the man is pious and zealous in the discharge of his duty. Add to that, he loves you, is anxious to have your approbation, and both considers and respects you as a parent. Now, if he sometimes carries himself rather more forwardly than he ought, the chief cause seems to me to be this: he fancies that you are too rigid and morose, and so he aims at a certain popularity which may smooth down

offences. Thus the good man, while he is consulting your tranquillity and guarding against ill-will, which he believes neither of you can stand against, forgets the firmness and dignity which should belong to a minister of Christ; and, while he imposes on you the necessity of resisting him, he furnishes the gainsayers with arms to assail your common (mutual) ministry. I see how vexatious and provoking a proceeding this is, nor am I ignorant how much blame his fault deserves. But your own prudence and love of fair-dealing will suggest to you that you ought to number up the good qualities which counterbalance his defects.
. . . . You bore with Chaponneau, not only a man of no mark, but one who seemed born for kindling strife. . . . With how much greater reason, then, should you strive to foster peace with a man who both desires to faithfully serve the Lord along with you, and abhors all rancorous dissensions! If you bear in mind how few tolerably good ministers we have in the present day, you will be on your guard how you slight a man who is both honest and diligent, endowed, moreover, with other most estimable gifts. Let him only feel that you love him, and I answer for it, you will find him tolerably docile."

This balm healed the wound, and at death Farel could look back on the past and declare that no misunderstanding had ever arisen between them, so completely was this affair forgotten. In this Farel proved how worthy he was of the titles so often found in Calvin's letters, such as "my sound-hearted brother," "my very honest friend," "my excellent and upright brother," "my guide and counsellor."

The new pastor, Fabri, could join with the people of his charge in holding sacred the memory of their much-loved father, and in carrying forward their enterprises after the plans which he had adopted. Elisha was content to follow in the steps of the ascended Elijah. When the ministers met for deliberation, years afterwards, it was often said of certain measures proposed,—"So it was in our Father Farel's time;" or, "So Father Farel would have ordered it."

The church at Neufchatel was very zealous for the doctrines which Farel had taught them, and they also insisted that they were more indebted to him than to the government. When the Helvetic confession appeared, and a French edition was published at Geneva, the ministers of Neufchatel were notified that their church, that planted by Farel, had been overlooked. They had not been asked to sign it. They translated the slight to mean that they were not considered sound in doctrine. Therefore they wrote to the clergy of Zurich, assuring them that they still held to the doctrines avowed by them in Farel's time. And, if it was supposed that they could not adopt the confession with the consent of their government, they have this to say,—"When our forefathers, by the grace of God, received the gospel, it was done without the consent and even the disapprobation of the government. For in religious matters we have so much liberty that no one can exercise any arbitrary power over us. If our departed friend, Farel, had done nothing without such consent, he would never have established the reformation among us." Not only does this show their respect for the devoted missionary, but also the religious liberty he had introduced among them by his example and his doctrines. He had broken the chains of mental bondage, and, with Calvin, had brought freedom of religious opinion and worship.

This Swiss Elijah was not simply a powerful preacher; he was a man mighty in prayer, and when he must face opposition he laid firmly hold of the promises of God. He felt that they were meant for him. In his letters and writings he often

THE CALL TO GLORY. 357

breaks forth into thanksgivings, prayers and intercessions. His element was fellowship with God. At the "altars of Baal," he lifted up his commanding voice to heaven, and help came from on high. His fervent prayers carried away his hearers. When from the pulpit he earnestly implored the divine power, Christ came down and touched the hearts of the hearers; the Holy Dove came brooding upon the assembly and stilling the tumult of the people. When they were in rage against him, he could pray them into silence. In his preface to the Psalms, Calvin paid a hearty tribute to the eloquence of his friend, and to "those thunders of the word by which he had been enchained at Geneva." In a letter, cautioning him against the length of his sermons, he refers also to the fervency of prayer, and says, "You are mistaken if you expect from all an ardour equal to your own."

Having fulfilled those words of our Lord—"I am not come to send peace on earth but a sword"—he placed over the sword in his family arms, the motto, "What would I, but that it were kindled?" Farel had wielded the sword of the Spirit, and brought down fire from heaven, and of all the reformers he was the one who most appeared in "the spirit and power of Elias."

THE END.